# Losing Your Job—
# Reclaiming Your Soul

# Losing Your Job— Reclaiming Your Soul

## Stories of Resilience, Renewal, and Hope

Mary Lynn Pulley

*Foreword by Terrence E. Deal*

Jossey-Bass Publishers • San Francisco

Substantial discounts on bulk quantities of Jossey-Bass books are available to corporations, professional associations, and other organizations. For details and discount information, contact the special sales department at Jossey-Bass Inc., Publishers (415) 433–1740; Fax (800) 605–2665.

For sales outside the United States, please contact your local Simon & Schuster International Office.

Jossey-Bass Web address: http://www.josseybass.com

 Manufactured in the United States of America on Lyons Falls Turin Book. This paper is acid-free and 100 percent totally chlorine-free.

**Library of Congress Cataloging-in-Publication Data**

Pulley, Mary Lynn.
    Losing your job—reclaiming your soul / Mary Lynn Pulley.
    p. cm.—— (The Jossey-Bass business & management series)
    Includes index.
    ISBN 0-7879-0937-8 (acid-free paper)
    1. Unemployed—Psychology. 2. Unemployment—Psychological aspects—
    Case studies.
    I. Title. II. Series.
    HD5708.P85 1997
    650.1'086'941–dc21
                                                       97-4700
                                                        CIP

FIRST EDITION
*HB Printing* 10 9 8 7 6 5 4 3 2 1

The Jossey-Bass
Business & Management Series

# Contents

# Foreword

"Knock-knock."

"Who's there?"

"Not you anymore."

This short dialogue between a boss and an employee comes from the comic strip *Dilbert*. In an uncanny way, it captures the essence of corporate America in the 1980s and early 1990s. Whatever the label—downsizing, rightsizing, restructuring—thousands of American workers learned—often abruptly—that their services were no longer needed. While economic realities justified the layoffs, the personal costs were enormous. Both those terminated and those who survived were psychologically wounded. As a result, many of the envisioned savings of employing a smaller labor force never materialized. And many individuals who were let go struggled to piece together shattered lives.

This is where Mary Lynn Pulley's work offers a distinctive ray of hope. Her contribution is unique in several ways. First, she has been there herself and knows what it feels like to be let go. While a graduate student at Vanderbilt's Peabody College, Mary Lynn took a course I taught—Symbolism in Organizations. As the final assignment, each person was required to write a journal reflecting on how the course's theories related to life experiences. Mary Lynn's contribution was a masterpiece of integrating ideas with her personal story. Unlike many graduate students, she found her voice and was speaking from both her head and her heart. Second, she has done her homework. Her inquiry has both a solid intellectual foundation and a well-thought-out empirical approach. She reviewed relevant literature and interviewed others who experienced layoffs. She wanted to find out why some people survive the experience and move on while others are unable to pull their lives back together. She gave people an opportunity to tell their stories.

She highlights their accounts with relevant concepts and ideas. Third, her work is accessible and practical. It offers people who have been downsized a transition pathway. Even more, it gives executives and human relations experts an insight into other people's lives so that companies can make necessary layoffs as humane as possible.

Mary Lynn's work speaks for itself. But I would like to underscore the important contribution it makes to the literature. For so long, American managers have been captive of two facets of organizations—rational and psychological. Political realities are shunned because of a widespread belief that all politics are inherently negative. Even more damaging, we too often forget that people have spiritual needs. Churches, synagogues, families, sororities, and clubs are not the only places people search for meaning. As other institutions falter or fall, many Americans find their faith in the workplace. For some, there is no other option.

Downsizing, rightsizing, or whatever we choose to call it often undercuts people's existential pillars. Spirits are dashed, hearts are broken, souls are wounded. What separates the survivors from the victims seems to be a conscious or unconscious realization that the real issue is not psychological, it is spiritual. In the depths of despair, victims wallow in fear, sadness, and depression. Survivors follow the traditional path of the hero or heroine. They embark on an inner journey of self-discovery. They confront their demons and use wounds as an eye to deeper revelations. The pain leads them toward their spiritual core. Once they have found it, what once appeared as a disaster now seems an opportunity to reembrace life and explore new possibilities. The lessons to be learned from reading this book are life's lessons. Mary Lynn Pulley, through her experiences, reflections, and courage, has given us all a great gift. Enjoy these stories and her remarkable ability to weave individual tales together in an interpretive group narrative.

*March 1997*                                          TERRENCE E. DEAL
*Nashville, Tennessee*

# Acknowledgments

Though writing a book is in many ways a solitary endeavor, it is not a solo effort. This process has brought me in touch with some wonderful people and led to many conversations that clarified and deepened my understanding. I particularly want to thank Wendy Hamilton Hoelscher, at the Center for Creative Leadership, for her ongoing enthusiasm and encouragement, and Carolyn McManus for her insightful reading and editorial help. Others who read early drafts and provided useful editorial comments include Jane Graham, Claudia Skelton, Barbara Lucey, Deborah Kondis, Greg Toy, Kelley Reid, and Sharon Hazzard. Betsy Collard, at the Career Action Center, reviewed the manuscript with great acuity and furthered my own thinking. Members of the faculty at Vanderbilt University who influenced and supported this work include Pat Arnold, Terry Deal, Neal Nadler, and Roland Rust. Other friends and colleagues who supported both me and my work through conversation are Cheryl Lison, Bonita Barger, Rocky Sasser, Juliane Engel, Syd Shera, and Corinn Bohn. I am grateful to David Noer for encouraging me to publish my research. Bob Burnside and Martin Wilcox, both at the Center for Creative Leadership, have also been real allies. I want to thank my editor, Larry Alexander, for believing in this book and providing motivation along the way. I also want to thank Carrie Castillón, Judith Hibbard, and Kathy Dalle-Molle for their follow-through and attention to detail. I am grateful to Dick Runyeon, Russell Lockhart, and Joel and Michelle Levey for the ways they have taught me to listen to my heart. Finally, I want to thank my family and especially my parents for providing a stable and loving home base.

# The Author

MARY LYNN PULLEY is a principal of the Linkages Group, a workplace consulting firm. She is also an adjunct instructor for the Center for Creative Leadership. Mary Lynn served for eight years as president of MyoData Systems, an international publishing and consulting company, and has since been an organizational change and management consultant to a wide variety of companies, including Boeing, J.C. Bradford, Vanderbilt University Medical Center, the Port of Seattle, TCI Communications, and many others. The author of numerous professional articles, Pulley has taught classes in organizational behavior and small group behavior at Vanderbilt University, and has served as director of values education at the College of Wooster. She has a doctorate in human and organizational development from Vanderbilt University and a master's degree in counseling psychology from the University of North Carolina at Chapel Hill.

If you are interested in the ideas in this book, you may contact http://www.linkages.com on the Internet.

*This book is dedicated to the people who shared their stories with me. Without them this story would not have been written.*

# Losing Your Job— Reclaiming Your Soul

# Introduction

"Is there life after Digital?" A former manager told me that this was the question being asked during Digital Equipment Corporation's downsizing of about fifty thousand people. It was meant to be a joke. But we know that much truth is spoken in jest. Losing your job often feels like a life-or-death question. For people who have never experienced it, it is a question that reveals the depth of their unknowing.

I am writing this book for those of you who are asking new questions about work and what it means to your life. For many of you, these questions are rising out of your personal experience with organizational downsizing or restructuring. Perhaps you have lost your job, or are concerned that you might. Or perhaps you are working harder and harder, while feeling emptier and emptier. You realize that there is a growing disjunction between who you are and what you do. All of this is fueled by the widespread anxiety about jobs and the realization that job security, as we understood it, is gone.

If you are looking for techniques for finding a job, this book is not for you. But if you are wondering how to be resilient in today's and tomorrow's work environment, then this book will be helpful. If you are curious about how others have found new sources of meaning and security through job loss, then read on. This book is about the deeper issues of job loss and job insecurity. It is about questions of personal identity, meaning, and purpose. Through the stories of professional people who involuntarily lost their job and bounced back—feeling better off than they were before—it provides insight and hope.

This book does not debate the pros and cons of organizational downsizing and restructuring. We are in the midst of it, and the clock is not going to turn back. While I was writing these pages, the

*New York Times* announced that forty-three million jobs had disappeared since 1979, and that nearly twenty million of them were lost since 1990.[1] By the time this book is published, these figures will be outdated. The article was part of a week-long series on job loss and downsizing, and a note at the end of the series estimated that 15,962 workers lost their jobs during the week that this series ran.[2] If you think that you or someone near you will not be touched by these changes, you'd better think again.

This book tells how people are restructuring their lives in ways that are more fulfilling and meaningful. The people I interviewed were doing well with the way things used to be. They were successful professionals, many of whom spent years working their way up a corporate hierarchy. They explain how the structure of their lives collapsed, along with its comfort and security, and how they picked up the pieces and put them back together in a different way. Unlike Humpty Dumpty, who was left shattered and waiting while all the king's horses and men failed to put things back together again, these people put their own lives back together with some enduring changes. For some, the experience of losing their job brought about personal transformation.

Occasionally when I begin to explain my research findings, I am accused of being Pollyannaish. I am not attempting to tell the entire story of downsizing with all its many complex implications. I realize that most people who lose their jobs do not have a transformative experience. Many never recover economically. They can't reflect on the experience because all their time and energy goes into making ends meet. Some never recover emotionally. They realize how easily the carpet can be pulled out from under them and they walk on eggshells for the rest of their days. Some feel so humiliated and betrayed that they never move beyond cynicism and bitterness. The news media have focused most of their attention on this point of view.

Several years ago, an article in the *New York Times* called "The Humbling of the Harvard Man" caught my attention. This article pointed out that by the thirty-fifth class reunion of the Harvard class of 1958, an estimated 25 percent of this all-male class had lost their jobs.[3] This is an experience that these privileged men never expected to encounter in their lifetime! What interested me most was how various members of the class responded to the reversal.

One man, a former corporate vice president, sent out thirteen thousand resumes, received almost no response, and was bitter and angry at the time of the interview. Another man had lost his job as an executive at Honeywell. Just prior to losing his job, he had decided to return to school and get his master's degree in classical civilization—something he had always been interested in exploring. At the time of the interview he was cataloguing ancient Greek coins at the Harvard museum and sounded reasonably content. I wondered, what makes the difference? In this case it did not seem to be an issue of social class, opportunities, intelligence, or past performance. Why was one man locked into a pattern of behavior that was not working, while the other was able to adapt?

The difference has to do with resilience. Resilience is generally associated with the ability to bounce back from adversity. Nearly two hundred years ago, a physician named Pinel wrote about the psychiatric risks associated with adverse circumstances. His first question to patients was, "Have you suffered vexation, grief, or reversal of fortune?" Today there is no standard definition of resilience, but the word implies elasticity or buoyancy. George Vaillant, a Harvard psychiatrist who has spent years studying adult development, uses a metaphor from nature to describe it: "Resilience reflects that which characterizes a twig with a fresh, green, living core: when stepped on, such a twig bends and yet springs back."[4] Definitions of resilience suggest strength through flexibility. Through yielding, or bending, resilient people have an inner life-force that allows them to spring back and carry on. It is a multidimensional concept like intelligence or athletic ability, and therefore it cannot be easily isolated and resilient people cannot be easily put into a slot.

I set out to explore why some people who lose their job are more resilient than others. My assumption is that resilience will be an essential quality as we move into the future, whether working within an organization or outside one. In my research I made no attempt to find an objective cross-section of people. Instead I sought out people who were doing well. The only objective criteria I used were to look for people who had lost their job at least six months earlier, had worked in their chosen professions for at least five years, and were at least thirty years old. I also wanted people who had to work—in other words, who could not retire or fall back on their spouse's income for sole support. For the most part I interviewed people who had involuntarily lost their jobs, because the lack of choice in the decision is often a bigger blow and a bigger hurdle to overcome. But in the course of my research I also spoke with a few people who chose to leave their jobs because they were in untenable job situations.

I contacted outplacement firms, career counselors, and career support groups and asked for names of people they knew who seemed to have learned from their job loss and transition experience and who felt better off than they were before. Notice that I paid no attention to whether or not my participants had found another job. My hunch is that people can lose one job and find another quickly, while nothing really changes except that they are running more scared in a faster treadmill than before. I was more interested in people who learned from the job loss experience and changed their perspective as a result.

Abraham Maslow is known for his research on basic human needs and his studies of people whom he called self-actualized. These are people who are extremely healthy and have a superior capacity for love, individuality, and self-fulfillment. Maslow did not research the average person. Instead he referred to the use of "growing tip" statistics. He explained that in biology, the growing tip is where all the action takes place, where all the chromosomes are dividing, and where all the growth processes are most vivid and active. This involves pulling out the best specimens rather than sampling the population as a whole. This is what I attempted to do with my research.

This exploration is important because right now the ground is shifting beneath our feet. At worst, people are feeling wrenched apart by the changes that are taking place in the world of work. At best, many are feeling uncertain and insecure. Recently a friend told me that she has three sons—one in academia, one in government, and one in business. Though each son has a track record of good performance, each also lies awake at night wondering if or when he will lose his job. We are in new, uncharted territory. This is why we must pay attention to our scouts, those people who are slightly ahead of us and already figuring out how to navigate successfully in the new world.

This book is about their stories. My role might be likened to a collector and interpreter. I gathered stories, sorted and examined them, and decided which ones to keep and how to fit them together. Through the course of these interviews I became increasingly aware that the stories were affecting me—both as I listened and later, as they resonated in my mind. I thought about my own unfolding journey and my own fears and anxieties and found that the stories I heard provided me with insight and encouragement. They were comforting, and they gave me courage to face my own uncertainties.

I realized that I was hearing a larger story, a story that needs to be told. Though each person's experience is different, there are common threads. Many are asking questions such as What's the point? Why am I here? Who am I to serve? Job loss is an experience that brings many of us face to face with these questions of meaning. It also may bring us face to face with our despair. Our tendency is to want quick answers and prescriptive fixes. Wouldn't it be nice if we could get all this settled in a weekend or a week-long workshop? But these are questions that don't have instantaneous answers, because they are questions that come from our soul. If they are not answered on a soul level, the answers seem hollow and empty and they fail to infuse us with energy, motion, or spirit. I realized that the real question is How do we find soul-full guidance? I think we do so through stories.

When stories are deeply personal, they touch larger themes that are universal. They lead us back to ourselves by triggering recollections of our own experiences and possibly changing our interpretations of these experiences. At the same time, our experiences will shape what we hear in the stories. This dialogue between our own and others' stories can bring new learning and meaning into our lives: "Stories set the inner life into motion, and this is particularly important where the inner life is frightened, wedged, or cornered. Story greases the hoists and pulleys, it causes adrenaline to surge, shows us the way out, down, or up, and for our trouble, cuts for us fine wide doors in previously blank walls, openings that . . . lead us back to our own real lives."[5]

Stories provide our learning and our inspiration. Roger Schank, who started the Institute for the Learning Sciences at

Northwestern University, has spent over twenty years working with the creation of intelligent machines. He is exploring how to teach computers to tell meaningful stories.[6] Keep in mind how far we have come. The first computer, built in 1944, took up more space than an eighteen-wheeler's tractor trailer, weighed more than seventeen Chevrolet Camaros, and could execute up to 5,000 basic arithmetic operations per second.[7] The Pentium microprocessor is built on a piece of silicon about the size of a dime, weighs less than a packet of sugar, and can execute up to 270,000,000 instructions per second. But computers can't tell stories. Computers can solve problems with clear-cut answers faster than any human being. Yet when it comes to problems for which there are no clear solutions—the kinds of issues we face in everyday life—computers are still at a loss. Schank has a great deal of understanding about how the human mind works. He views intelligence as the ability to tell the right story at the right time to shed new light on a situation. Can we get a machine to do this?

Perhaps indigenous people know something that we don't know. Jean Houston tells of asking an aboriginal woman how people differ from animals. The woman looked astonished at such a question and replied, "Why, we're the ones who can tell stories about all the others!"[8] Stories are basic to our humanity. We are our stories. They literally organize our memory and determine our behavior. Stories also feed our imagination and in doing so, they form the fabric of our soul.

This book is about job loss and resilience, but its intent is to teach through the use of stories. In the first section I will address what happens when old stories such as our notion of job security or the American Dream die, and how we must infuse these cultural myths with new life. The second section draws from the stories of professionals who involuntarily lost their job and bounced back, feeling better off than they were before. It begins with two in-depth stories that illustrate many common themes that emerged in my research. The remaining chapters in this section explain how these resilient people felt and what they did after losing their job. The third section shows how responses to job loss varied and I discuss why some people experienced transformative change as a result of losing their job. In the fourth section I will address the lessons learned about how we can be more resilient now and into the future.

Throughout I will also draw from old stories and mythology to create a linkage between personal stories and larger themes. Often when we think of the word *myth,* we think of stories or beliefs that are not true. Myths are stories that may not be literally true, but symbolically they teach us great truths. This is why they have flourished throughout all cultures at all times. They place us on a strand of an ancient web and remind us that our lives are deeper, broader, and bigger than we might realize. Myths speak a symbolic language and make use of metaphor. A *metaphor* presents a way of seeing something as if it is something else, such as "the moon is an ivory saber," or "the marketplace is a jungle." Metaphors serve as a lens to highlight certain features or make a particular point. By combining both personal stories from individuals with these big stories that use symbolic language, I hope to offer you clues to questions that don't have simple answers.

So I would like to lead you into this book with a story. This is a parable that I came across in *Breakfast at the Victory,* by James Carse:

> One morning the teacher announced to his disciples that they would walk to the top of the mountain. The disciples were surprised because even those who had been with him for years thought the teacher was oblivious to the mountain whose crest looked serenely down on their town. By midday it became apparent that the teacher had lost direction. Moreover, no provision had been made for food. There was increasing grumbling but he continued walking, sometimes through underbrush and sometimes across faces of crumbling rock. When they reached the summit in the late afternoon, they found other wanderers already there who had strolled up a well-worn path. The disciples complained to the teacher. He said only, "These others have climbed a different mountain."[9]

On one level this is a parable about the idea that the more difficult the journey, the greater the potential for transformation. But it is also a story about the role of the teacher. The teacher did not prevent his disciples from getting lost. All he did was change the way they viewed their journey. I hope this book does the same for you. If you are on the brink of a transition, or in the midst of one, I hope this book sheds new light on your experience. While you read, I would like you to think about your own story. As a culture we are in the midst of a huge and tumultuous transition. We need new stories that will bring meaning and imagination to our experience. I believe that you will be able to learn from these stories and realize that you are not alone. And I also have a request. If you find these stories are helpful, please pass them along.

# Part One

# The Death of Job Security

## Chapter One

# Tidal Waves

*The tides of change that move society on to new solutions
or catastrophes run deeper than the swirling events of the
day. In relation to these great tidal movements, the trends
we observe in our lifetimes are surface currents and the
crisis of the morning newspaper the merest whitecaps.*
—JOHN GARDNER[1]

I was on a ship. We'd been warned of a storm but I never expected
this! First I felt heat. It was coming from down below. Intuitively I
knew that the ship was on fire. The heat from the fire intensified
but I moved in slow motion, like a movie that's slowed to increase
the suspense. I was vaguely aware of other people on the ship moving around—they seemed afraid but they were not in total chaos or
panic. I became intrigued with watching bubbles forming in the
paint along the ship's railing. First they were tiny and then they
grew large and soft like a bad case of poison ivy. I knew that I had
to abandon ship, I knew I had to jump. I also knew that I was an
excellent swimmer and would probably be all right. My guess was
that we were not too far from shore. But something was slowing me
down. The heat grew worse and I realized that I could not wait any
longer so I jumped into the water. The water was cold and choppy
but the swells were certainly not stormlike. Again I reassured myself
that my swimming skills are strong. But I wondered, how deep is
the water and how far am I from shore?

This dream was relayed to me by someone who lost his job. We
talked on his first day home. He is a successful entrepreneur and
former CEO. Three years earlier, he'd sold his company to create

11

a merger with another company and stayed on to run the new, larger business. The business did not go as well as hoped and now it was downsizing. The terms of his departure were mutually acceptable. A few of his long-term employees left with him and they hoped to start a new company of their own. This is a man with a strong track record of success, a financial cushion, and a following. Yet even in this case, he told me that his first day of being at home and not at work felt like jumping into the waters of Puget Sound. He knows he has the skills that will contribute to his buoyancy. He also has a large mortgage and two daughters in college. So the questions of his dream echo in his mind: How deep is the water and how far is the shore?

We all might ask this question. It is relevant to all of us because we are in the midst of one of the three transforming changes in human history. Futurist Alvin Toffler calls this the Third Wave.[2] It is the shift from a manufacturing society to an information, or knowledge-based, society. The implications involve a sea change in how we think about work.

Job loss caused by organizational downsizing and restructuring is the fallout of this transition. Even when we don't have personal experience, the headlines scream in our face: "On the Battlefields of Business, Millions of Casualties"; "Corporate Killers"; "The End of the Job." However, most of us don't need to read these headlines because we have been personally touched by the fallout. A recent poll shows that since 1980, three-quarters of American adults have been affected by job loss, either personally or within their family, and one in ten says that a lost job has precipitated a major crisis at home.[3] Within the country, this growing tide is swelling into a tidal wave that threatens to engulf us with anxiety and insecurity. An electrical engineer who lost his job after working for nearly thirty years with Xerox said, "Losing my job was the most shocking experience I've ever had in my life. I almost think it's worse than the death of a loved one, because at least we learn about death as we grow up. No one in my age group ever learned about being laid off."[4]

Yet in his book *JobShift*, William Bridges reminds us that jobs as we know them are relatively young.[5] We did not organize work by dividing it into jobs until the Industrial Revolution. To put things in perspective, if we imagine all human evolution charted on a twelve–hour clock, the industrial age would represent no more than the last five minutes.

The First Wave of revolutionary social change occurred with the agricultural revolution around 10,000 B.C., when hunters and gatherers began cultivating the earth and domesticating animals. Mobile bands of people became settled village communities. The invention of the plow increased the productivity of the land a thousandfold. Now that there was some surplus of food, members of the communities could take on diversified roles, specializing as artisans, merchants, and priests. The family was the basic unit of production. This is how all civilization was organized until industrialization, which began in northwest Europe between the sixteenth and eighteenth centuries.

Moving from farms into factories was not an easy transition for most people. It led to a division of labor and a way of working that was completely different from what people were used to when the agrarian family was the unit of production, consumption, socialization, and decision making. In America in the late 18th century, nine out of ten people lived off the land. In 1785, Noah Webster wrote, "In countries thinly inhabited, or where people live principally by agriculture, as in America, every man is in some measure an artist—he makes a variety of utensils, rough indeed, but such as will answer his purpose—he is a husbandsman in summer and mechanic in winter."[6]

Moving from an independent lifestyle tied to the seasons to a regulated life tied to a factory was as wrenching a change for many people at that time as is our current situation. Some people became owners and managers in the new system. But most became landless agricultural laborers, or workers in the factories in new industrial towns. Initially, people often violated the new regulations imposed upon their time by leaving mills to help their families with farm chores or taking days off to hunt and fish. Sometimes entire families were brought into textile mills and employed as a work team. Farmers had to learn to adjust to industrial routines driven by overseers, bells, and the compulsions of wage labor. This new discipline ran contrary to centuries of independence. To boost productivity, owners of mills and factories imposed increasingly strict regulations on the workers. Many workers protested—both men and women. In 1849 the managers of a mill in Forsyth County,

North Carolina, painted over a window because they felt that workers were wasting time by looking out and daydreaming. The workers responded by going on strike until a clear window was installed. In 1836 women in textile mills in New England rebelled against industrial work conditions by marching through the streets singing,

> Oh! Isn't it a pity, such a pretty girl as I—
> Should be sent to the factory to pine away and die?
>   Oh! I cannot be a slave,
>   I will not be a slave,
> For I'm so fond of liberty
> That I cannot be a slave.[7]

Along with the Industrial Revolution came sweeping social, political, and cultural changes. Technology and economics were not the sole cause. Rather, a number of factors coalesced, including the rise of Protestantism and a growing sense of individualism that provoked political revolutions in America and France. There was a general sense of *splitting,* or reductionism, that occurred in philosophical thought and that spilled over into all arenas. Divisions were created between work and leisure, the individual and the family, emotion and reason. The roots of this splitting are often attributed to the 17th-century philosopher René Descartes and the English mathematician and scientist, Sir Isaac Newton. Descartes believed that the universe was an orderly system that could be compared to a clock, and that its logic could be understood through mathematics. In the generation following Descartes, Newton elucidated laws to map the workings of this clockwork universe. Nature was interpreted by applying the laws of science.

The dominant metaphor of the time was the machine. Machines are concrete and are made up of separate pieces that we can take apart, examine, and put back together. They are built for stability, predictability, and control. Descartes initially intended his comparison of the world to a machine to be a metaphor. As I mentioned in the Introduction, metaphors present a way of seeing something as if it is something else. The problem is that Descartes's metaphor lost its "as if" quality and we came to believe that the universe *is* a machine.

Consequently we thought of our early industrial organizations as machines and saw workers as cogs within the system. The machine continues to be the dominant metaphor in the workplace; hence the title and the impact of the book *Reengineering the Corporation* by Michael Hammer and James Champy.[8] When factories were first set up, jobs were defined by breaking a task down into its smallest parts. In *The Wealth of Nations,* Adam Smith gave a classic description of the new production system as exemplified by a pin factory: "One man draws out the wire; another straights it; a third cuts it; a fourth points it; a fifth grinds it at the top for receiving a head; to make the head requires two or three distinct operations; to put it on is a peculiar business; to whiten the pin is another; it is even a trade by itself to put them into the paper; and the important business of making a pin is in this manner divided into about 18 distinct operations." According to Smith, a single worker could "scarce, perhaps with utmost industry, make one pin in a day, and certainly could not make 20."[9] The new methods allowed a pin factory to produce 4,800 pins a day. Productivity increases seemed to depend on the rational organization of processes rather than on individual skill.

Human beings were also believed to reflect the machinelike characteristics of the universe at large. Descartes split people into two parts—the mind and the body—and believed that the body could affect the mind but the mind could not affect the body. People were supposed to bring only a piece of themselves to work, usually their hands. The English social critic John Ruskin said, "It is not, truly speaking, the labour that is divided, but the men." Meanwhile, the human spirit and soul were split off and relegated to the Church. Today many organizations are suffering this legacy by feeling a "spiritual bankruptcy," which Bolman and Deal say is "the deeper cost [of creating a world] where everything has a function yet nothing has any meaning."[10]

By the end of the 19th century most artisans and master craftsmen had gone the way of the wooden plow. Manual employees thought of themselves as workers, and employers became manufacturers or businessmen. As people spent more time in the factory than with the family, the importance of work grew. Increasingly it became the principal source of people's identity. For instance, in preindustrial society it was more common to identify yourself in terms of your birthplace or family membership, such as "I'm John of Winchester," or "I'm William's son." In industrialized society people began to tie identity to work, using statements like "I'm an attorney." The workplace became the main organizing feature of our life and the source of our identity, status, income, and affiliations. And by the 20th century, identity became specifically tied to *organizations*. For instance, today many people respond to the question "What do you do?" by saying something like "I work at Boeing."

Over time organizations became increasingly paternalistic. Corporate paternalism actually stems from Southern plantations after the Civil War. Textile patriarchs of the New South ruled over industrial enclaves by creating housing, churches, and company stores that produced a kind of self-contained economy and dependence. In the 20th century, organizations extended this paternalistic heritage by providing workers with health care insurance, retirement pensions, and social functions. Loyalty to the organization was rewarded with watches, medallions, and company dinners. Out of this grew the implicit and pervasive understanding between workers and organizations that is now coming apart at the seams—the belief that hard work and loyalty will be exchanged for promotions and job security.

Most of us grew up with this assumption, and many of us watched our fathers play it out. We learned to equate security with job security. Many people still believe that long-term employment with an organization is indicative of personal stability and leads to professional success. However, the Third Wave is putting an end to these assumptions. Ed Lawler, head of the Center for Effective Organizations at the University of Southern California, said, "The reason people are getting a feeling of collapse is that that's precisely what's happening."[11] During the decade of the 1980s, 46 percent of the companies listed among the Fortune 500 disappeared from the list. In 1991, nearly one out of three American workers had been with the current employer for less than a year, and almost two out of three for less than five years.[12] We are in the midst of radical change.

When our building-block assumptions are pulled out from under us, we often experience a psychological crash that feels as personally damaging as the Kobe earthquake that struck Japan in 1995. The ground gave way and left widespread damage along with a sense of chronic anxiety and powerlessness. What was learned from this disaster, however, is that wood-frame-and-stucco buildings do not survive an earthquake because they do not yield. The new generation of earthquake-resistant structures includes rubber and steel pads in their foundation to act as springs or shock absorbers. Those buildings that had this type of foundation were virtually untouched by the Kobe earthquake.

Likewise both we as individuals and our organizations will need built-in flexibility to weather the future. The machine analogy no longer holds. Our world no longer has the stability and predictability of earlier times. Workers in the information age need to use their minds and hearts, not just their hands. We need to be learners, and we need to learn how to learn. We gained much knowledge through analysis, or breaking things apart. From this we learned to put things together by using an assembly line. But now we need the understanding that comes from synthesis, or seeing the relationships between the parts. We need to be able to learn, sort, link, apply, and create intangible information.

In the 21st century the relationship between organizations and workers will be much looser and more temporary than in the past. With computer technology we can communicate as easily with someone in Singapore as with someone across town. This blurs organizational boundaries so that it no longer makes sense to organize by production lines and rigid divisions of turf. Organizations in the future will need to be more like amoebas than like machines. To survive, they will need to be able to change shape, expand, and contract to adapt to continuous environmental change. Work will be more fluid and will be organized by projects and assignments, rather than positions and titles.

Right now we are in the midst of the transition. We lag behind the new reality in terms of policies and social structures that will support the new relationship between organizations and workers. Things have changed so fast that it takes our breath away. We can no longer take comfort in following our parents' or grandparents' way of life. Many of our understandings about how the world works are no longer true, and with this comes a sense of ennui and loss. As we enter the 21st century, we find ourselves caught in a time between two worlds. So the question from the CEO's dream that I mentioned at the beginning of this chapter remains: How deep is the water and how far is the shore?

## Chapter Two

# Broken Dreams

*A person is not a thing or a process but is an opening
through which the absolute can manifest.*
—MARTIN HEIDEGGER

What is difficult about being in a time between two worlds is that
we discover that many of our familiar stories no longer hold the
same truth. When we discover that a bedrock concept or belief is
no longer true it can feel as though the rug has been pulled right
out from under us. Or it may come upon us more slowly, like a
gradual tide that brings a growing sense of disappointment, uncertainty, or confusion. We stay in this uncomfortable place until we
come to terms with a new understanding. Right now we are grappling with our understanding of job security and how to navigate
a career amid shifting tides.

We can think of job security as a myth. As I mentioned, myths
are stories that may not be literally true but that symbolically teach
us truths about human nature. The myths that we draw from
ancient literature are obviously symbolic stories filled with gods
and goddesses and magical events. But we also share current prevailing myths that bind our culture together. One of the functions
of myth is to support and validate our social order, to link us to a
larger group or tribe. They also teach us how to adapt to our culture, since a single lifetime is too short to individually learn all the
things we need to know. For instance, there are many myths sur-
rounding our notion of family. Through this mythology we learn
general ideas about what it means to be a father, mother, or child.

However, when myths are taken too literally, or when the environment changes, then they can serve a dysfunctional role.

Many of us grew up watching television shows like *Leave It to Beaver* or *Father Knows Best,* which perpetuated our 1950s notion of what families were supposed to be like. June spends the day at home, happily vacuuming in her high heels and dress, while Ward goes off to a job that doesn't seem to be too stressful and Wally and the Beaver pal around like best friends. This idealized, televised image became our myth of the American family. But times have changed and the 1950s myth no longer works. Most families require that both spouses work outside the home, almost one out of two marriages end in divorce, over 18.5 million children grow up in single-parent households,[1] and in 1989 more women were abused by their husbands than got married.[2] Even during the 1950s the televised image of families was not reality for most people. But the point is the degree to which these images became our cultural myth about family life. Our myths become dysfunctional when they are so disparate from our social reality. We take the myth literally and grow up believing that this is what our life will be like. When we fail to live up to it, we feel guilty and inadequate. Similarly, many of us grew up believing that if we worked hard and were loyal to a company, then we would be rewarded with job security and advancement. Many are now realizing that this belief no longer holds true.

This is because our environment, or context, has changed. Myths help us to bridge the particulars of our own life with our culture and in doing so they help us to adapt. When there is a dynamic relationship between our own life and the larger cultural myths that inform our life, then myths provide energy and meaning. However, when the context changes so that the myth no longer carries truth or no longer informs us, then the living quality is lost. In *Living Myth,* Stephenson Bond explains, "When a living myth dies, it doesn't disappear. What departs is the energy, the living quality. The shell remains, like a fossil in a dried-up riverbed where the water once flowed. What was once a ritual becomes a convention, a habit. What was once work becomes labor. What was once a way of life becomes a set of social expectations."[3] The myth itself becomes dysfunctional because it points us toward a way of life that no longer works. This is what has happened to our myth of job security.

Not long ago I had three conversations with three different friends—one had recently left her job, one was recently demoted when her company merged, and the third felt underemployed. What struck me is that all three of these people were in a very similar place—each touching her despair, feeling at a loss, and wondering where to find meaning and purpose.

The friend who left her job was the chief operating officer of a start-up software company. She left when a CEO was hired later, and she realized that their differing management philosophies could not be bridged. Because it was a small company, there was no place for her to go but out. This was one of those situations that was voluntary but not planned. Now that she is outside of an organization, she told me that she thinks what she yearns for is a connection to something larger. She does not feel strongly connected to her family of origin, and now she has no connection to an organization. For many of us, our companies have become the organizing feature of our life. When this connection disappears it brings a profound sense of loss—and for many, a sense of *being lost*. Particularly when we have defined ourselves by our work, when we leave that place we no longer know who we are. Our surroundings, our personal context, no longer define us. Being lost seriously calls into question our very survival.

This brings to mind a time when I got lost eight or nine years ago while cross-country skiing. A group of friends and I had traveled via snow cat to a remote cabin deep in the Cascade Mountains. The group spent the first day skiing, and in the early afternoon a friend and I decided that we were tired and would break off from the group and return to the cabin. However, my friend was a much better skier than me. I kept falling. Pretty soon she was out of sight along the trail. I called and called and got no response. I realized I was lost—seriously lost. So I started going down various trails, having no idea where I was going. I tried to look for familiar signs, but realized that I had not paid that much attention when I was skiing with the group. Nothing looked familiar. For a while I even went off the trail and forged my way up an embankment. But walking with my long cross-country skis up an entangled embankment in deep snow was so awkward that I fell many times and worried that I might twist or break my ankle. I finally came to a clearing and decided to just keep going forward. Yet I had absolutely no idea which way was the right direction. By

3:30 in the afternoon I was still trudging, thinking that I was head-
ing in the direction of the cabin. The sun began to go down. I realized that if I could not find the cabin before dark, I probably would
not survive the night—I had no provisions and the temperature
was far below zero. Then, out of the blue, I saw a group of skiers
off in the distance. We were skiing on intersecting paths. I called
to them and eventually they heard me and skied over to me. They
turned out to be my group of friends! I was skiing in exactly the
opposite direction of our cabin.

My experience of being lost was disorienting and frightening.
While in the middle of it I tried to stay calm, but later realized that
I would not have made it had I not crossed paths with my friends.
I also berated myself for being unprepared. Being tossed out of the
familiarity of organizational life feels very similar—it can be disorienting and frightening, and can lead to self-doubt and self-
blame. This is exacerbated by the larger cultural myth—which no
longer holds true—that tells us if we work hard we will keep our
job with the company and if we lose our job then we've done something wrong. Yet if we think of job loss more in terms of *being lost*
rather than simply as loss, then we may be more inclined to learn
from it. Sometimes when we are in unfamiliar surroundings we ask
more questions, or new questions. Or perhaps we pay more attention. When job loss triggers deep questions of meaning, then the
questions themselves may lead us back to our soul.

The death of job security leaves us with a gaping void where
once there was a path. Culturally we are in need of a new myth that
informs our daily life. Where is the path to security? We can no
longer think that organizations will provide it. So right now many
of us are left in the woods and not sure which way to turn. This is a
major shift, to be responsible for creating our own path.

Perhaps, as when I got lost, you have the sense of being left
behind. Among the three friends I mentioned earlier, the former
chief operating officer is on her own. The other two are still working within their companies but are not satisfied, and said that they
think if they had plenty of money then they'd be okay. But I do not
think so. This is the myth of the American Dream, another story
that binds our culture.

Many headlines are heralding the loss of the American Dream.
There is a growing sense of bitterness that opportunities for
advancement are gone and that things are beyond our grasp.

Stockholders and the few in charge acquire huge short-term profits by downsizing, while the many who are tumbled out of organizations wonder if they can make their mortgage payment or send
their children to college.

What happened to the American Dream? It split into two separate pieces, and it got distorted. It began to break in half during
the early days of this country. In 1620 the Pilgrims sailed over on
the *Mayflower* seeking abundance and greater freedom. Their first
winter was terribly difficult and about half of the original 101 Pilgrims died. That spring and summer, friendly Indians taught the
settlers to fish and plant corn. This created a bountiful harvest in
the fall. The Pilgrims celebrated by asking the Indians to share
their harvest as guests at the first Thanksgiving.

The Indians also taught these first Pilgrims something about
gifts. Lewis Hyde describes this in *The Gift,* a book that draws from
anthropology to describe gift economies, which are usually indigenous or precapitalistic cultures.[4] In gift economies there is
exchange and circulation of gifts, rather than commodities. The
essential difference between a gift and a commodity is that the gift
leaves a feeling bond, while the commodity leaves no such connection. Gifts are kept alive through their constant movement
through the community. The concept is not to create an even
exchange of gifts, as in our culture. Rather, gift giving is alterna-
tively one-sided. It is assumed that a gift will be returned sometime
in the future, because it is assumed that there *is* a future to the relationship. As gifts circulate, they bind the community and create an
"increase" that goes far beyond the material object. According to
Hyde, the cardinal principle was that "the gift must always move."[5]
The Melanesians express it like this: "Our feasts are the movement
of a needle which sews together the parts of our reed roofs, making of them a single roof, a single word."[6]

The next group of English settlers who landed on this conti-
nent arrived on a boat called *Fortune.* As more and more Puritans
came to America, they lost sight of the gift-giving culture practiced
by the Indians. This created misunderstanding. Imagine an Englishman being invited to share a meal at the Indian lodge. To help
the guest feel welcome, a pipe of tobacco is passed from person to
person. The pipe itself represented a peace offering that tradi-
tionally circulated among local tribes. It would stay in one lodge

for a while and then be passed on. The polite Indian then offers the pipe to his guest to take home. The Englishman is thrilled to receive this lovely souvenir. After a few months, leaders of a neighboring tribe might drop in on this Englishman's house for a visit. To their horror they discover that the peace pipe is mounted on the wall. The gift got stuck! The Indians ask to smoke the pipe and then carry it home with them, to keep it in circulation. The Englishman then coins the term "Indian giver" to describe the misinterpretation.[7]

The American Dream broke in half as we split the getting from the giving and focused solely on the getting. The Dream came to represent acquisition. Whenever something is severed from its opposite, it becomes distorted. The distortion of the American Dream is excessive consumption and greed. Meanwhile the positive side of acquisition—the hope for something better—is getting lost.

The half of the American Dream that we latched onto carries a certain emptiness. It holds a false promise that the more we have, the better we will feel. This makes me think of the movie *Citizen Kane,* which is based on the life of William Randolph Hearst. The story epitomizes the American Dream taken to an extreme. In the movie, Charles Kane inherits a mine worth millions of dollars as a young boy and is sent away to be raised by the trustees of his fortune. As an adult he becomes a newspaper baron. The movie makes it apparent that what Kane really wants is love—as symbolized by Rosebud, the sled he had as a child. But he cannot buy love and he does not understand how to get it because the only currency he knows how to exchange is money. Money buys him control. But it also pushes him further and further from what he really wants. He buys a huge estate and fills it with thousands of things worth millions of dollars. Still, he remains desperately lonely and his magnificent house seems empty. Kane was trying to fill a hole inside himself that can never be filled with things. By the end of the movie he looks like a stricken ghost. Kane dies saying the word "Rosebud." The last shot shows his little sled lost among a sea of things and then being tossed into an incinerator and going up in flames. Is this a dream or a nightmare?

The insatiable hole that Charles Kane exemplifies was formed by the split between getting and giving. He was preoccupied with what he could get, and did not know how to give. The American

Dream is a myth that puts us in danger of creating such a hole within ourselves. When it is associated only with personal acquisition, then it too serves a dysfunctional role. The irony is that in pursuing just this part of the American Dream, we often lose ourselves. We lose touch with our true nature and our real passion. We lose touch with the inner resources that provide us with energy and feed our soul. We lose touch with our real gifts and with the source of those gifts.

Not only do we risk losing sight of our own gifts but we find they also get lost in the sight of others. When we bring a small piece of ourselves to our work, what gets mirrored back to us is a fragment of who we are. We become our position, while our spirit quietly bleeds from inattention. When the focus is always on the return on investment, everything becomes a commodity. Stan, a man I interviewed who lost his job after twenty years with the same company, said, "The strongest feeling I had was that I wasn't going to get the Quarter Century Club and get a clock, and the company that I was working for and I thought I would work for until I retired had totally changed. And I wasn't going to be there to end my career with them. The biggest thing that I had to get accustomed to was being a commodity. It doesn't take a rocket scientist to figure out that labor is a commodity. They'll use you as long as they need you, and then they'll let you go."

We must remember, however, that a corporation is a body of people. Who are we blaming when we point the finger at a corporation? We are talking about a group of people, and a collective way of thinking. The biggest danger is when we begin to think of ourselves as commodities and to calculate our own sense of value based on what we are worth in the marketplace.

Thinking about the gift economy requires a shift in thinking as much as anything else. It requires a recognition of the gifts we have to give. Often we do not access our natural talents because it is not apparent what the financial return will be. We believe that time is money. But time is more than money—it is a gift unto itself. Giving our time is a huge gift. It is a gift we seldom give to ourselves. We live in a sense of compressed time where everything is urgent, while we lose sight of what is important. We do not attend to the seeds of our own potential, so after many years all we have is a pile of dead or dying seeds inside.

This is what T. S. Eliot described in his famous poem *The Waste Land*:

> You cannot say, or guess, for you know only
> A heap of broken images, where the sun beats,
> And the dead tree gives no shelter, the cricket no relief,
> And the dry stone no sound of water. Only
> There is shadow under this red rock
> (Come in under the shadow of this red rock),
> And I will show you something different from either
> Your shadow at morning striding behind you
> Or your shadow at evening rising to meet you;
> I will show you fear in a handful of dust.[8]

This is a place where everything is meaningless, purposeless, unrelated—the negation of life itself. This is when life feels like a dried-up fossil or dessert. Life becomes all prose, and the poetry is lost. Before writing *The Waste Land*, Eliot was experiencing this himself. He was experiencing his own void and felt that all he had was a pile of "broken images." Yet by falling into it, he came out with one of his best-known poems, a poem that paved the way for contemporary poetry. The central theme of the poem is that out of death comes new life.

Right now there are parts of the American Dream that are in free fall, and this needs to happen. A recovery requires a fall. After the fall comes winter, and then spring. We can recover our own dreams—and what got lost in the American Dream—only when we stop to examine them. The loss of a job can bring forth new questions. We ask fewer questions when things are going well, or when we are too busy to stop. Often we keep ourselves busy to avoid the void. When that busyness stops, things come out of the shadows.

It is worth examining the questions brought about by the widespread sense of losing the American Dream. What are we afraid of losing? Our dignity? Our worth as human beings? Many of us have merged a fragment of ourselves with our job and have come to believe that is all we are. The degree to which we have learned to merge our work with our entire identity has also become a dysfunctional aspect of the myth. We are afraid that if we lose our job, we will lose our self. Yet it is when a crack develops that the soul has an opening, a doorway, to get in and be seen. It is when things are falling apart that we look again.

Several years ago I read a story about a famous actress whose house was badly damaged during one of the California earthquakes. But right after the earthquake, when things were broken and strewn all around and the house was literally falling apart, all she thought about was the little kitten she had gotten the day before. She ran through the rubble searching for the kitten, and found her in one of the kitchen cabinets. This put things in perspective. Could this be a metaphor for the American Dream? Through our assumptions and stories we create the architecture of our lives. What kind of house have we built? What parts need to be dismantled or redesigned?

When things are coming apart, it feels bad and frightening, and it can be devastating. But therein lies the hope and the promise. Recovery from job loss means rediscovering our gifts. It means reclaiming the fragmented parts of ourselves that were ignored while we were working. It means healing the splits. It means putting Humpty Dumpty back together again.

In folk tales, a gift is often depicted as something that initially seems worthless, such as ashes or coal. But when carried home, the gift turns into gold. In the next section I will share the stories I heard about job loss and recovery. These stories are told by people who lost jobs ranging from vice president of a large corporation to director of a small nonprofit agency. Think of them as gifts. As they circulate they may create a widening circle of new understanding, and perhaps contribute to a new Dream.

# Part Two

# Voices of Experience

## Chapter Three

# Two Stories

*This is the best of times*
*Some say the worst of times*
*I guess it all just depends*
*Which glass you're drinking from*
*This is our only chance*
*To reverse a dance*
*That was started so long ago*
—SARA HICKMAN[1]

In this section you will read the stories of the professional people I interviewed who experienced involuntary job loss and bounced back, feeling better off than they were before. The stories reflect their subjective experience. You will notice that there is no direct route from losing your job to feeling better off.

I must point out that it was not hard to get these people to commit to a significant amount of time to talk with me, and that they were very open about sharing their feelings and experiences. Several mentioned that they believe that sharing their story is part of "giving back." This is why I think of these stories as gifts. Among these resilient people there was a definite sense of wanting to help others who find themselves in the same boat.

I began the interviews by asking my interviewees to think about how they felt from six months *prior* to losing their job to where they are now. Then I handed them a blank piece of paper and a pencil and asked that they draw a graph of their experience. They'd all had at least six months' lapse since losing their job. I suggested that they draw the graph so that the horizontal axis would represent time and that the vertical axis would represent something about where they were emotionally, such as their self-esteem or positive and negative emotions. Figure 3.1 shows some examples.

I expected to find common patterns in terms of the emotional process, but I did not. Instead each person's graph looked like a unique journey. The only thing the graphs had in common is that at the end, most—but not all—of them ended at a higher point than where they began. This shows that most—but not all—of the people I interviewed ended up feeling better off. What this tells me is that perhaps the most significant pattern is that there is no common pattern. After losing their job, people do not seem to follow a common linear process of going through various stages of loss. There are too many variables that influence the job loss and transition and thus make each experience unique. At the same time, there were some common emotional and behavioral responses—they just didn't necessarily occur in the same order for everyone. I think it is comforting to know that most people who ended up feeling better off also passed through times of anger, betrayal, depression, or darkness.

You will also notice that people varied in the degree to which they felt better off at the time of the interview. Some perceived their job loss as a major positive turning point in their life. Some felt better off but did not view their experience as a major catalyst for change. A few actually did not feel better off and longed for things to get back to the way they were. In these latter cases there was a discrepancy between how the people I interviewed came across to the person or group who referred them to me, and how they really felt. Each interview lasted for two to three hours. During the course of the interviews it became evident that some people were keeping up a brave front but did not really feel better off. When I put all the interviews together, the degree to which people felt better off fell along a continuum. This turned out to be instructive, as I will discuss in the next section.

Throughout these interviews I kept a journal of my own reflections, sparked by the stories that were shared with me. I realized that I was both shaping and being shaped by the interviews. They triggered emotions and thoughts about my own experiences, as

# Figure 3.1.    Personal Graphs.

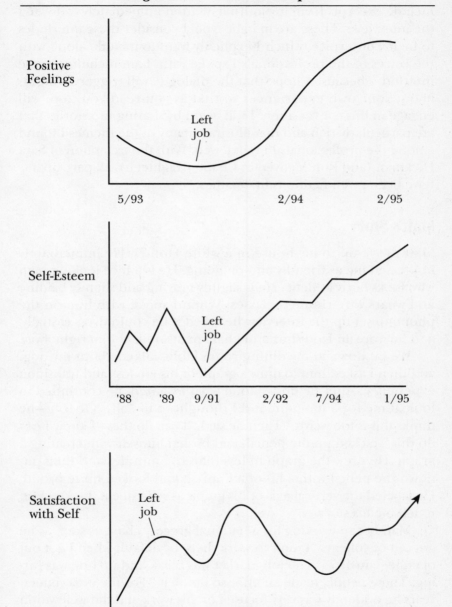

well as insights about resilience in general. In this section I will include excerpts from my journal, written immediately following the interviews. These are in italic type. I consider these interludes to be my own voice, which I explicitly want to include along with the voices of the professionals I spoke with. I am including these interludes because I hope that the dialogue will trigger thoughts about your own experiences so that as you read you, too, will engage in this conversation. I will begin by sharing two stories that are particularly rich and that illustrate many of the themes I found among the professionals I interviewed. With the exception of Sara Hickman (and Ron Medved in Chapter Eighteen), all participants have been given fictitious first names.

## Matt's Story

Matt drove up to my house in a white Honda. He immediately impressed me as friendly and outgoing. He is a nice-looking man who looks fairly athletic. He is slightly graying and slightly balding and wears wire-rimmed glasses. When I spoke with him on the phone to set up the interview he asked if he could dress casually, and he wore an Izod shirt and khaki pants. I liked him right away.

We sat down at my dining room table, talked about my dog, and then I asked him to draw a graph of his job loss and transition experience. After he understood what I wanted, he continued to look at me for a moment and I thought to myself, "Oh, oh—he thinks this is too weird." Then he said, "I can do this—I know I can do this," picked up the pencil, and busied himself with creating a graph. He drew the graph in less than five minutes and then put down the pencil with a bit of a flourish and looked quite proud. He labeled the vertical axis of his graph as self-esteem. I asked him to tell me his story.

Matt began working for a national grocery chain as soon as he got out of college. "I went to work there by default when I got out of college in 1975. The job market was bleak and no one was hiring. These people made an offer so I took it." For the next sixteen years he evidently was very focused on his work and did well within the company. In 1989 he accepted a new position as a zone manager. Because his zone did well, a year later he was given a second zone with greater responsibility. However, around January 1991 things were not going so well because of tension between Matt and his supervisor. Matt did not go into too much detail about this, except to say that he had "credibility issues" with his supervisor, which culminated in July. The initial rift occurred when Matt attempted to terminate someone within his zone who was not performing well, only to discover later that this person was a relative of his supervisor's. Throughout much of the year, Matt said, "No matter what I did, my immediate supervisor would not be happy with it." Consequently he anticipated that he might be laid off: "I'd kind of been preparing myself since January—I knew what was coming."

On Matt's graph, the time from 1989 to September 1991 shows a steady decline in self-esteem. I asked him whether he considered quitting during this time and he said that at times his wife encouraged him to do so but he was reluctant because of the financial ramifications: "I would've just left with what was in my pocket." Plus, Matt said that in terms of his boss, "I didn't want to give him the satisfaction of leaving." Matt was laid off in September. He said, "It was really a relief for me. I went in on Friday morning—Friday the 13th." He laughed and continued, "We were doing performance reviews—I'd written my own review. When I walked in my boss had it on his desk and he said, 'I don't agree with anything in this.' I said, 'I figured that, that's why I stuck with the numbers—is there anything wrong with the math?' He said, 'No, but I just don't like the way you handle people . . . I'm going to invite John from human resources in here and we have some options.'"

Because the company did not have grounds for terminating Matt on the basis of his performance, they restructured the position by eliminating his zone. No one else lost their zone. However, this resolution was advantageous to Matt because he was offered a fairly lucrative severance package. In reflecting back, Matt says, "The day I walked out of my office with my box under my arm there was a sense of relief I didn't expect. I would've thought I'd be devastated by it. I come from a family of alcoholics . . . I would've thought I'd go home and solve the problem the way I've seen problems solved, and I didn't."

Instead, Matt went home and talked with his family about it. Because he had been talking with his wife all along, it was not a big surprise to her. He felt it was also important to share things with his children, who were ten and twelve years old. At the same time he did not want to worry them: "My son is very sensitive and if he'd been concerned about money it would've devastated him. Friday afternoon when the kids got home from school I said, 'Good news guys! I'll be able to take you to school and pick you up for a while.' I didn't go into all the particulars, but I said 'I've left the company but don't be concerned, because we've got enough money to make it for a couple of years with no problem.'"

Matt decided to give himself a break by not rushing immediately into a rigorous job search. He took three months off and did not attempt to search until early December. Instead he spent a lot of time going canoeing and camping by himself. He also spent time coaching his son's basketball team. Matt says, "I did a lot of self-evaluation in terms of where I was and how marketable I was. I also read a lot of books on transition. I tried to step back and not rush into anything." It was during this three–month period that Matt experienced a major shift in his thinking:

> Something occurred in November that really opened my eyes—we were sitting down at Thanksgiving dinner and my daughter was not quite thirteen and she said, "Dad, this is the first Thanksgiving I can remember you being home all day." That hit real hard because I had not realized how much I had been gone. I realized I had a wife and two kids who were really pretty neat people. It helped me get my priorities back in line. I came to the conclusion that I wasn't willing to do this anymore. I wanted a job where my time was my time and where I wasn't on twenty-four-hour call and every time the phone rang it wasn't an emergency.

I asked Matt if his priorities shifted after that and he said, "Absolutely!" Then I asked him if he thought that would have happened had he not lost his job and he said, "No, I think I would have lost my family . . . just another five years and I'd have had two teenage kids I didn't know and a wife who'd put up with an awful lot, and having to put up with two teenage kids I didn't know, I don't know if we would've been able to live together."

Matt said that he believes losing his job was a blessing in disguise: "It was not a catastrophic event! There was a paradigm shift but it wasn't a catastrophe. Sitting at the Thanksgiving table I realized the course I'd been on and where it had left me with the people most important in my life. Yes, they had the schools they wanted to go to and they had all the other things they wanted, but I wasn't part of their life. And I realized I really wanted to be." I asked Matt what was most helpful to him during this reassessment time, and he said,

> The thing I drew on the most and got the most out of is that I became much more secure in my faith and reached a point where I really trusted that yes, there are some things I have to do but this next decision I have to make is going to be the right decision for the right reasons because the Lord has something in mind for me and I just have to find what that is. I really centered on that . . . then all the wrong things fell away, and the right one continued to stand. I guess when the stresses are greatest you can either respond to those stresses or look for additional strength. That's what I did. And it was there.

Matt said that during this time he realized that his life was out of balance and that he wanted to bring it back into balance. During his transition he did shift his priorities and evidently he has sustained a better balance since then. Prior to losing his job, Matt would have ranked his career as his number one priority. Since then, he considers his family, friends, and community service to be more important than his career. Matt said that by getting back in touch with his family he began to "realize how out of whack I was and I began looking for the spiritual side." I wondered if his sense of career success changed. He replied, "I have a whole different career. My career now is to be a husband and father."

Matt refers to his three-month hiatus as a time when "I packed my pack and hit the woods for a while." He says that after his break, he felt rejuvenated: "Once I got back and had reassessed and was recharged, I didn't have any trouble at all getting back into a business routine every day, whether I had a job to go to or not." Considering that prior to this time he had spent his entire adult life working within a corporate setting, I asked him how he structured his day. First he set up an office in his basement with a personal computer. Then he followed the same schedule every day by starting at 8 A.M., reading the *Wall Street Journal*, researching companies at the library or by talking with a stockbroker friend, and contacting companies. He worked until about 4 P.M. every day. He said that at the time he was not very conscious about creating a new structure, but says that, "If I'd gotten up and said what am I going to do today, I probably would have sat in front of the TV with a cup of coffee."

By mid-December, Matt was conducting a "grandiose search" for a new job from his home office. He was having qualms about the possibility of moving, however, because he did not want to uproot his family. How he actually got his job involved a coincidental sequence of events that further verified his sense that "there's a bigger plan in the works."

One Sunday morning he and his family attended a different church service than the one they typically attended. An acquaintance who was sitting in the pew in front of him turned around and they began to talk. She told him about a position she knew about with a company related to Matt's field, and said that she would mention Matt to her contact. When the contact called, he turned out to be one of Matt's old high school friends! Matt said that when he was thinking about networking, his church acquaintance never would have come to mind: "I was trying to establish networks, and when it all came down to it, it was the established network that I'd overlooked that really made the difference. My caution to anyone is, before you start looking for new ones, you'd better look and see what you're standing on, you may be standing on the greatest network framing you're going to find. As far as networking goes, start at home and see where that takes you."

Matt began his new job in February 1992. His new position required less travel and the company culture is less intense. He told an anecdote about the first holiday at his new company. At his previous firm, even though they said they were closed on holidays he had always worked because that was an expectation. At his new company, a letter went out announcing that they would be closed for the holiday but Matt went in anyway. (Old habits die hard!) He said that at 10 A.M. he realized that no one else was coming in so he went home: "It was a revelation—that when they said the office was closed they meant for you to take the day off!"

In July 1994, Matt was named regional manager of the year by his new company because his region had a 20 percent increase in business without adding any new markets. He believes he was able to do this through high visibility and establishing strong relationships with key people. At the same time, Matt has spent more time with his family. He is the assistant scoutmaster for his son's troop, and has attended every football game where his daughter is in the band. He says that now most of his friends are also involved with his community service, which is mainly Boy Scouts as well as some work with the American Heart Association and Muscular Dystrophy Association.

At the time of the interview Matt was working out of his home office because the company he was with now was downsizing. Though Matt's position did not seem to be in jeopardy, he had drawn up business plans to start his own company. He said, "I've come to the realization that if I'm really going to do what I want to do, I'm going to have to be working for myself." When I asked him what he really wanted to do he said, "Financially I want to do twice what I'm doing now. Mentally and emotionally I like total responsibility, and I don't like being second-guessed. I want responsibility for my own destiny instead of delegating that to an employer. If I make it, fine—if I don't, I'm still employable." When we talked, Matt was in the process of seeking financing and software support for his business concept. He said he hopes to build a business that's "radically different from the ones I'm most familiar with."

Reflecting back on his job loss and transition experience, Matt believes that it served as a major catalyst for personal growth:

> I had to come to the realization of who I was, and that there's a difference between who I am and what I do. In my previous job, I *was* what I did. I was the zone manager. I had the car and I had the clothes and everything that went with it. I became consumed with the position. It was my identity—it's what I drew everything from, it fed my ego. After I left, and all that was stripped away, I had to deal with who am I? Having done that, the job I do is no longer who I am. Yes it feeds the ego somewhat, but it's not the total me. There's more to me than that. Looking back, when I was assigned to be zone manager I would've thought my next move was vice president. At that time if someone had told me that in three and a half years you're going to be terminated I would've thought that would be the end of my life. Because it was the end of my identity. I had to discover a new identity.

The initial loss of identity that Matt experienced was replaced by a more multifaceted sense of self, which includes his roles as husband, father, and scoutmaster. Another loss that Matt was aware of during his transition was the loss of relationships with his store managers. He compared it with an experience he had in high school, when a close friend died of a brain tumor. While Matt and the other friends tried to stay close to the friend with the tumor, the friend who was dying withdrew. Matt's eyes got a little teary as he recalled this. He said, "I guess it's the same sort of thing when I lost my job. Things were never going to be the same, I was not going to be a part of their hopes and dreams and career paths anymore. That being the case, I was separating from them more than they from me."

His three-month hiatus was also a type of withdrawal and he believes that this was a good strategy. He had many people calling and asking him if he would like to go to lunch but he tried to minimize this: "I think, had I accepted all those phone calls and gone to lunch with all those people that it would've been a very depressing situation. I think I could've easily said, 'Well you're right—it's not fair.' Fair's got nothing to do with it—it happened, what are you going to do now? I just didn't feed that animal and he finally left." Still, three years later Matt says, "I still have some very good friends at my old company. There's not a month that goes by when I don't get a call asking me how I would handle a situation." He also said that a lot of people from there have called and asked him to help them make the transition into new jobs or organizations.

Matt believes that the major work-related lesson that he learned from his experience is, "It doesn't matter what the performance is, it's the relationship that will make the difference." In retrospect he realized that in his previous job, he did not manage up as well as he managed down, and that he could have managed his boss and boss's boss better: "Because they didn't know me personally—they knew my numbers, but they didn't know me personally—it was easy to make the decision and say we'll go ahead and restructure . . . rather than saying if you're going to restructure why are you focusing on him? And that's my responsibility. I didn't establish those relationships. I could easily sit back and say, well they did this to me. And if I did, I'd never grow from this experience."

Matt also learned that maintaining a more balanced life is an effective long-term way to cope with life's ups and downs: "If there's a low point in the job, there's a high point somewhere else, you've just got to find it. It may be taking eleven-year-olds who've never been out in the woods, and turning these kids into guys who would be self-sufficient if they were in a plane crash in the Northwest, and really seeing them grow. When I go off for a weekend with those guys there's nothing that's going to happen at work that's going to take that away."

When I asked Matt what he would tell others who are faced with involuntary job loss, he emphasized that first you must share it with somebody and not keep it in. He then suggested sitting down and putting a budget together to figure out what you have to make each week, then how you are going to get that minimum amount while you are working on where you want to be: "My wife and I sat down and we knew exactly what we had to have, and we stripped away everything we could strip away and came to the conclusion that I could get a job making half of what I was making before and we'd still be fine. So there was the security of that, and it took the pressure off because I knew we could make it."

Finally, Matt suggests spending most of your energy on moving forward, rather than looking back:

> You can't dwell on what happened or why it happened, you're too close to it, there's too much emotion to be honest about the situation, so don't worry about the whys or what-fors. Don't keep looking back. You can't drive on the interstate if you're always looking in the rear-view mirror—you're going to hit a wall. You may be in first gear, but at least keep moving. Then set some goals. Don't look at what you want to do, but where you want to be. And don't start any further out than three to five years, then drop back to two to three years, then the end of this year. At first, the only place you want to be is employed, you don't want to worry about making the rent or car payments. I believe if you let those things motivate you too much, you'll put yourself right back in the situation you started in.

At the end of the interview Matt and I spent some time talking about the feelings of anxiety many people are feeling toward their work these days. Matt commented, "So many people are unhappy in their jobs but they won't make the decision to leave unless it's made for them. That's the situation I was in. I was holding on to the security aspect of it and doing that was blinding me to everything else."

At this point, Matt has shifted his locus of security away from his work. I asked him where his sense of security is rooted now and he said "strictly my family," but he thinks that ultimately it might be rooted in his faith.

Matt's graph ends with a steep upward incline of self-esteem. He laughed and told me that he has always been a self-confident person, even when he's wrong—but his graph ends on a considerably higher level of self-esteem than where it began in 1988. His current perspective is that his job loss was a very significant *positive* experience in his life.

> The phrase "anchors that echo" keeps going through my mind. Anchors that echo. . . . I think about the notion of feeling anchored, of staying in one place. At what point does this represent stability, and when does it bleed into entrapment? Yesterday a friend told me that we must continuously let go so that we can be perpetually renewed. But then where does the continuity come from? Perhaps we can't expect it to come from anything tangible at all, but it seems as if that would be comforting. This notion that our continuity is in the continuous present moment seems too abstract. I'd rather have the continuity of a person, or a house, or even my dog. It's hard to be continuously receptive to change. Yet if we hold on to what's known for too long, we can get stuck. Someone once told me that he never learned anything while he stayed in his comfort zone. So where does resilience come from? Is it something we get from outside of us, or within us?

Prior to his job loss, Matt would have described himself as a typical executive who devoted the majority of his time and energy to working his way up the ladder of one company. Sara, however, had a very different path.

## Sara's Story

I first came across Sara Hickman while lying in bed listening to my radio early one morning in December 1994. National Public Radio (NPR) routinely wakes me up and usually I linger in that semi-awake stage for a while. However, that morning I was jolted awake by the story that was playing over the radio. The story was about a singer-songwriter named Sara Hickman who was dropped by her record label just as she was making it big on the music scene. She had recorded two albums for Elektra and received good reviews that applauded her impressive emotional range. Consequently when Elektra dropped her, it came as a complete surprise. She decided to go ahead and produce the album anyway, on her own. But because she had been working on this album for Elektra she was in a position where she needed to buy her songs back.

While Sara was building her reputation as a singer-songwriter, she had also built a reputation for her willingness to contribute time and talent to altruistic causes. These ranged from children's relief organizations to returning U.S. hostages to an AIDS resource center. After being dropped by Elektra, Sara turned to her fans with some misgivings and asked for help with raising money to produce the album on her own. Subsequently I ordered a copy of the NPR transcript, and this is what two of her fans said about her on the air: "We thought that it was about time that Sara got help from others, 'cause she's been doing so much stuff for other people, and that it was the right thing for us to get involved." "Usually other people when they find themselves in this position, they're doomed, it's over, they don't know what they're going to do, they're out of the business for a couple of years. And Sara was not about to take no for an answer."[2]

Ultimately she did buy her songs back and produced her own album, called *Necessary Angels,* which is selling well. Meanwhile she was picked up by another label called Discovery. Jac Holzman, the president of Discovery, commented: "Unlike so many artists who feel that once they have made the record, it's up to the record company to make all of the magic happen, Sara will do anything. She will go visit branch sales meetings. She will go to stores. She will take out her guitar and she will sing anywhere. She'll do what is necessary because she understands that she is also responsible for connecting her music with her audience." The NPR commentator ended the story by saying that in retrospect, Sara believes that Elektra "did her a favor by dropping her because she wound up with a more congenial label and got to know her fans in a way few performers ever do."[3]

I decided that I had to track down Sara Hickman because it sounded like she had an interesting story to tell. It was not easy.

After following a phone trail that went from Washington, D.C., to Chicago to Los Angeles, I finally got the phone number of Sara's manager in Austin, Texas. He was very nice over the phone but said that Sara was on an extended tour around the country with Nanci Griffith and that it would be hard to reach her. He mentioned that they were performing in Nashville in February and perhaps I could catch up with her there. That sounded dubious to me but I was willing to try. However, when I called to get tickets to the performance it was already sold out over a month in advance. I then decided just to call her manager every month or so and maybe I would eventually be able to get a phone interview. On the third try, it worked. He said Sara was home and he gave me her home phone number. I left a message on Sara's answering machine, not really expecting to hear back from her. She returned my call the following day. I explained my research and she said she would be willing to be interviewed, so we set up a phone appointment for a Sunday morning.

When I called Sara that morning, I woke her up. She said she had been up late working the night before. I said that I could call back later, but she remembered that we had scheduled the interview and said that it was fine now, though her voice was a little gravelly. Sara struck me as down-to-earth, reflective, and articulate. She also was extremely open about her experience, and at the time I noted that her willingness to be vulnerable—to be seen inside-out—probably relates to her success as a performing artist. I thought I was correct in my hunch that she had an interesting story to tell.

It started in 1992. At that time Sara lost her voice. She explains, "I had a major stress-related incident in which I felt like I didn't really have a voice at Elektra, creatively—and I was having a lot of physical and mental stress related to this, and I had internal hemorrhaging inside my throat. Symbolically, it's like my body finally said, 'No one's listening to me,' and it shut down. This was in early 1992, right around my twenty-ninth birthday. I went to the doctor due to this massive pain I was having inside my throat, and because I was having trouble even speaking." The doctor told her that she needed to stop talking for a month and to stop singing for six months, or else she might never sing again. A lot of internal hemorrhaging had occurred and she needed time to heal so that the blood and bruising would go away.

During this same time Sara wrote demos for Elektra. Demos are examples of new songs that the record company uses to determine which ones will go on the artist's next album. Sara did record some of these even though it was a real struggle because of the problems with her voice. Between songs she had to breathe into a humidifier in the recording studio to try to clear the clotting and get moisture into her throat.

In the fall, Elektra asked her to come to New York so that she could begin recording a new album. However, Sara remembers that at the time something seemed "off": "I was having . . . I don't quite know how to explain this, but I was having a lot of internal anxiety. I was hearing a lot of voices kind of warning me. I felt that things were wrong right away. When I was producing in Austin I felt that my tracks were going quite well. Then I left Texas and started working with other producers, and I felt like all these warning bells were going off but I couldn't quite put my finger on it."

Sara had originally signed with Elektra in 1989. However, by this time the relationship had reached a high level of discomfort: "Creatively, I was feeling like I wasn't being heard—I was working with some very strong personalities—so I felt as a musician and as a woman that I was not being heard, and I was in this pain. So my level of anxiety was extremely high at this point." I commented that given this feeling, it was very interesting to me that she literally lost her voice. The physical mirroring of the psychological state was quite symbolic. This symbolism had not escaped Sara.

The album got recorded but Sara did not feel good about it. She said that it sounded "like three different producers . . . like three different chefs in the kitchen had created three different soups." By now nearly a year had passed and Sara was coming up on her thirtieth birthday. She went on a vacation to celebrate her birthday and when she returned she got a call from her manager:

> I knew something bad had happened because he wouldn't drive up to Dallas from Austin to tell me something that he could tell me on the phone. So he came up and we sat down, and he said, "I have something to tell you." Basically he informed me that Elektra was

shelving the record, that I was being dropped, which meant that I was no longer going to be working with the label, and that I didn't have the rights to my songs that I recorded. This was about fourteen songs. So for five years, I could not record those songs.

I asked her how she responded at the time and she said that her first response was to go into a kind of shock: "I was actually in physical and mental shock because I'd just been through this whole year of stress and anxiety, so I think I just shut down that night." However, the next day the fact that she had been dropped by her record label began to sink in: "Physically I felt like I'd lost something really precious to me, which was my voice; spiritually and creatively I felt like I'd lost something, which was my voice, and now I also lost my job. How was I even going to express this voice because now I had no place to express it—at least at the level which I'd worked really hard to attain. So from there I went into a downward spiral. In a career mode, I felt like I was publicly humiliated."

Sara went into a major downward spiral that lasted for about three months: "There were times when I was suicidal. Because my voice was everything to me—I'm sure this is how people feel when they lose their job—you're really intertwined with what your job is and who you are. For me, it's even harder because my job comes out from inside of me—it's never really been a job. It's who I am."

What reversed Sara's downward spiral? Her mother was a major catalyst:

Basically what happened is that my mom got really angry *for* me. I'd be talking to her on the phone and I would be in this horrible painful place, and she would get angry for me. She'd say, "I can't believe that they're treating you this way, and you can't give up because one person decided to drop you!" It was really hard, but one day it kind of clicked. I would say this was June, and I'd been dropped in March—so that was three months. My mom came up with an idea. She said, "Why don't you fight back—that's what you've always done, you've always believed in yourself and you can't let these people take away what you love to do just because they don't think it's going to make them money. You never did this for money, anyway. You did this because you love it."

Around June this attitude clicked: "I started realizing, what if I got angry about this instead of being abusive to myself?" Her mother suggested that Sara negotiate a price for buying her songs back and that she raise the money to do so. I asked her if this was an unusual thing for an artist to do and she said that it had never been done before, except with a few major artists like Frank Zappa and Joe Jackson. These two artists bought their masters back with their own money for a price in the millions. However, no artists had actually turned to their fans, explained that they had a creative difference with their label, and raised the money to buy back their songs on their own. Elektra is part of Warner/Elektra/Atlantic (WEA), which is the largest record company in this country, and owns a majority of the record distribution market. So Sara explained that for her to go up against WEA was like David and Goliath. She did so by superseding her own manager and attorney and calling Elektra herself:

> I called Elektra directly and they came down from $250,000 to
> $100,000. Because, the way I explained it to their lawyer was,
> "These are my children. You go to work every day from nine to five
> and you have a photo of your wife and children sitting on your desk
> and every day you get to go home and blow off time and have fun
> with your family. That's a choice you made. I'm not married and I
> don't have children because I made a choice to be committed to
> music. Those are my children, and in that sense you are holding
> my children hostage. This is my livelihood. If you withhold my right
> to rerecord my songs, how am I supposed to make my livelihood?"
> He said he would need to call me back.

When he called her back, he told Sara that they would come down to $100,000. Afterward Sara called her mom and her mom replied, "Well I know you have at least a thousand fans—why don't you do something where if they donate $100, you come up with some concept." Sara continued, "My mom reminded me of a hostage named Thomas Sutherland who I'd spoken about, and I'd worn an ID bracelet on his behalf for four and a half years. She said, 'What if you got bracelets made that say Necessary Angel on them and for this donation of $100, people would get a bracelet and they could wear it until the songs—that is, the hostages—are released.'" This idea is what got Sara moving forward again. As she explains it,

> The fact that I started to replace this angst, this anxiety—which I was still feeling, I was still dealing with self-esteem issues—but for me to start getting to be creative, to find a creative solution to a very detrimental problem, really helped me because I was able to be creative again. And I was also doing something that evoked a bit of danger because I was putting my career even further out on the line by taking this risk. I just come from a very creative family, where if you believe in yourself, what's going to keep you from going even further out on a limb because sometimes that craziness is just that amount you need to put in the recipe to make it work.

Sara explained that she does indeed come from a creative family—her mother is a weaver, painter, piano player, and photographer, and her father is a professor of art at the University of Houston. Her parents are divorced and her mother now writes computer programs for a large company; so, Sara said, her mother also has a sense of business.

To begin raising money to buy back her songs, Sara wrote a letter that she sent to her fans, friends, and family. Her concern at this point was that she "didn't want this to be a pity party for Sara Hickman." In the letter she explained her situation and said that people who made donations toward her album would get their names printed in the new CD and cassette liners, an invitation to an exclusive record release party, and a hand-numbered Necessary Angel bracelet that would serve as an admission ticket to the party. This entire scheme kept Sara quite busy because she essentially was now running a business, which involved a great deal of record keeping. Her first task was to figure out how to get the bracelets made and she spent $3,000 of her own money to do so. "It got me moving because I had something to do. There was that inner voice, again. The inner voice kept saying, 'Do this. Trust me. It seems crazy, but do it.' And I think that little inner voice—you can call it God, or call it your own instincts—*really* was what I had to start listening to. Underneath *all* this pain, and turmoil, and confusion, I really tried to start listening to that little voice."

Her fans started sending her money. Sara notes, "The amazing thing was not the money. The amazing thing was the spiritual side and the amount of time and love and outreach that complete strangers were giving me." Meanwhile, Sara had sold her home and everything she could think of, including her dining room table and chairs and an antique salt and pepper shaker, to help raise money. She put her remaining things in storage and lived with friends.

I asked Sara what it was like for her to go so far out on a limb in terms of her own money. She said that she went through all of her assets and even had to dip into her retirement account, but that she was able to do so because of something her dad once told her when she was younger. When she was sixteen she had saved $2,000 in the bank and wanted a car. By that time her parents were divorced. Her mom told her that she would sell Sara her car for $2,000. Sara was lamenting to her dad that her mom wanted all the money she had for a car and her dad said, "Well do you think that's the last $2,000 you'll ever have?" Sara says, "From that moment on I realized money is a way of not only moving forward in life, but it only can make you more money if you let it go. That's been a truth for me. Even when I think I'm going to be broke, somehow money comes from somewhere if I don't get all worried and stressed out about it. So I think that was part of the cockiness involved in thinking 'Oh, I can do this.'"

Meanwhile, Sara was still performing: "I was having to perform in front of people and not feel ashamed about the fact that all this stuff had gone on." Sara also continued with her negotiations with Elektra to try to bring the price down further and got them to agree to $50,000. She had raised $40,000 but the price was still just beyond her reach. While Sara was trying to come up with the remaining $10,000, she met Jac Holzman, president of Discovery. Ironically, Jac was the founder of Elektra in the 1960s. Other labels had approached Sara but they wanted her to drop the "necessary angel baloney." Jac was supportive. He suggested that she renegotiate with Elektra once again. She did so with some reservations, and they came down to $25,000.

In December 1993, Sara bought her songs back. They arrived on Christmas Eve. With the remaining $15,000 she produced her album. She rerecorded and remixed songs and dropped some songs altogether. She finally made the album as she always imagined it. The album came out in July 1994 and with its release Sara had a big party and invited all of her "necessary angels."

When Sara reflects on this entire experience, she compares it to a rebirth:

> I suppose that it's what it's like to be born—you're inside, you're all warm, you're in this substance that's surrounding you, protecting you, and you can hear your mother's heartbeat. And the next thing you know, you're out in the cold world and somebody is slapping you. And everything is bright and confusing and loud and noisy, and there's no heartbeat anymore. That's the way I look at it. My inner voice was the heartbeat that got lost in this bright, spanking world, where all of a sudden it really, really hurt, and I was cold, and I felt like I was abandoned. That's what I relate it to—an awakening.

Certainly the dominant theme of this story involves losing and finding her voice. The voice can be interpreted on many levels:

> I think before I got dropped, part of why I was feeling I didn't have a voice was because I'd lost my voice. I lost my voice creatively, I lost my voice because I lost my way. I felt really confused and overwhelmed. I just didn't like what I was becoming and who I was. I think secretly I was wishing I didn't have to be with Elektra anymore and I think my wish made its way to the path of my little voice, and my little voice said, "Oh, that's right, that's Truth—and I'm going to make this happen." The old saying, be careful what you wish for, I think is very true. I think that wish grew and grew and it was splitting me.

In many ways the voice seems to represent Sara's authenticity. Though she was losing it, she believes that she never completely abandoned it. Evidently there were times at Elektra when she stood by her voice before she was dropped:

> When the label really wanted me to do things way different from myself, I said "No," and that hurt me in the long run with Elektra. But I'm glad because I stood by that voice—I stood by who I was— and I could've said yes to what they wanted and I probably would've been more famous and in the end I wouldn't have been dropped, but in the end I wouldn't be making the music I'm making. That inner voice would really be dead now. And though the struggle was

extremely painful and to this day there are moments of self-doubt, my voice has gotten stronger. I have a truer sense of who I am as an individual, and where my songs are going. It's almost as if I had to go through this little war to find a bigger path. And it was really worth it.

I asked Sara if she thinks of that voice as God and she said, "I definitely do—I think it's your transmitter to God." Thus the voice is Sara's truest self and at the same time it is beyond Sara, bigger than Sara. The experience strengthened her spirituality so that she believes she can better weather ups and downs: "It's gotten to a point where I could get dropped again and this time I would know that there'd be no self-doubts, that this is what I'm supposed to be doing."

I asked Sara what she would tell people who are faced with involuntary job loss and after a long pause she said, "I would say, allow yourself to feel that pain, which is in essence what I did during those three months. I allowed myself to grieve, and feel sorrow and confusion and hopelessness." She added that this dark time was also a very creative time:

> Actually I was writing some of the best songs I've ever written in my life. I didn't think I would . . . I was kind of surprised because I thought I would be writing sad, horrible songs and instead I was writing moving, beautiful, uplifting, positive songs—so go figure. I think that a part of me wants to be a caretaker, and in a way I was doing what you're asking me—what would I say to people who are going through this? And that's what these songs were doing—they were saying it isn't easy but here's what I'm doing. This is when I wrote that song, "The Best of Times."

Finally, Sara added that she thinks it is important to always try to find "the little happiness":

> The name of my new publishing company is Le Petite Bonheur, which means "the little happiness." I call it that because I read a little saying that I cut out and put in my journal that says when you are at your saddest place remember *le petite bonheur,* which means find the little happiness. If you can hardly get out of bed, just get up to take that bath. Take every small thing and find joy in it. And

that's what I had to start doing, even when I didn't feel like getting out of bed, and I didn't want to wash my hair, and I was depressed . . . I would go sit in the front yard and think how lovely the grass was.

Sara says that overall, "I've learned a lot about myself, I've learned a lot about my fans, about the people who love my music, I've learned a lot about what I can handle—which is an extreme amount—and I've learned that I have a great mother who will stand by me."

She adds, "I've learned a lot about being committed to what I believe in." She has a better sense of where she wants to go musically and professionally. She says, "My path is very clear—all the shrubbery has been removed from my path. I can see down the path, I can see where I want to go." She feels that her humor and stage presence have strengthened, and that her sense of doubt is greatly diminished. Her voice is back and healthy again: "I think my voice actually sounds better now than it's ever sounded. I think in my next record, my voice is going to be really beautiful, and I'm really excited about it. I think confidence has something to do with it—the way I'm approaching singing, and approaching the microphone, and where the voice is coming from inside of me, instead of where I think it *should* be coming from."

Thus in many ways Sara has grown from this experience, though she does not diminish the difficulty of the process. I asked her if she feels better off than she was before and she replied, "The first day I told my mother I got dropped she said, 'A year from now you'll be glad this happened.' I wouldn't use the term '*glad* that it happened,' but I am appreciative that it happened, and I'm thankful—even though it was the lowest period in my entire life. I'm thankful because it taught me a lot about me. It made me stop and think about where I was going with my life as a person."

While writing this story I played Sara's *Necessary Angels* album in the background. I realized how much a "voice" can transmit—especially when we have found our own voice, the truest expression of our self.

*I believe that what I am hearing is the resilience of the human spirit.*
*Because if we bring spirit down to earth and think of it as something that is*

*not distinct from the human being, then in all cases there is a strength and resilience of spirit that keeps these people moving. In Sara's case it is explicitly spiritual, and the voice inside her, which she hears as God's voice, is the beacon. Evidently it has become stronger as a result of her experience; she hears the voice more clearly.*

*Something about these people gets inside of me, and I believe that it is something about their spirit. Something calms me, and causes me to feel more at peace with where I am and where I'm going . . . perhaps it is God coming through, perhaps it is that electrical arc Martin Buber writes about, the arc that sometimes occurs between two people and where God comes through. When Buber was asked, "Where is God found?" he gave the idea that God is not a place—but a moment. When two people act in a truly human fashion, God fills the space between them and therefore God is not so much in either person as in the relationship that connects two people to each other. This does transcend physical distance because it even happens over the phone. Perhaps it has something to do, too, with the way in which these people open and share their vulnerabilities. And I open to their experience. And spirit comes through.*

Now I would like to turn to the experiences of all the professionals I interviewed. Among them there are many interesting stories to tell, but I do not go into the amount of detail with the others that I did with Matt and Sara. Instead, I cluster their comments and anecdotes according to how they felt and what they did after losing their job.

## Chapter Four

# Shock and Betrayal

*Call the world if you Please "The Vale of Soul-making."*
*Then you will find out the use of the world. . . . I say*
*"Soul making" as distinguished from an Intelligence—*
*There may be intelligence or sparks of the divinity in*
*millions—but they are not Souls till they acquire identities,*
*till each one is personally itself. . . . Do you not see how*
*necessary a World of Pains and troubles is to school an*
*Intelligence and make it a soul? A Place where the heart*
*must feel and suffer in a thousand diverse ways . . . !*
—JOHN KEATS

When I asked people how they felt when they first learned that they were losing their job, these are the kinds of responses I heard:

"Totally shocked. Disbelief. How can this be?"

"I felt hugely betrayed, hugely betrayed that they didn't offer me another position. Very very very betrayed by that."

"It was anger, betrayal, humiliation . . . I wanted to go uhhhh [like a baby crying], but I thought, I'm not taking this lying down. So I went into my full-blown defense."

"I never dreamed that this would be directed at me. I never predicted that. It was like a bolt of lightening."

Although initial feelings varied among the people I interviewed, over half mentioned that they felt surprised, shocked, or betrayed. For some, losing their job came as a complete surprise.

A few, like Matt, anticipated that it was coming and this tended to soften the blow. Yet most did not expect it. Even people who worked in companies engaged in major downsizing, such as IBM, AT&T, or Digital, tended to think that it "would not happen to me."

For instance, Jean joined a large corporation in the computer industry in 1967. She was among the first women to be employed there as a computer programmer. Over the next twenty-six years she moved around quite a bit within the company, always seeking out new projects where she could learn and expand her skills. Consequently she knew many people and was highly respected. But over the last five or six years the company culture dramatically changed. Jean says, "For the first twenty years I was there it was extremely unusual to have someone leave or be fired. I fired someone once, and it took over a year and a half. But there's been a massive culture change." Still, she did not expect that it would happen to her.

She got her first inkling that it might happen in June 1994, when she realized that her division was being hit with downsizing. Her company uses the term *surplused*. Her boss notified the department that they were at risk and then a few months later found out that he was being surplused. A few weeks after that he asked Jean if she had her résumé and then the next day he asked her to come to his office:

> I went to his doorway and said, "You wanted to talk with me." I could tell by the look on his face that I must be on the list and I said that. So he handed me a package that the company gives you. I'm sure he explained it but I don't remember because I was quite upset. What he read identified the actual termination date and he said I was free to find another job within the company. I knew from other people that he would take my company badge and credit card. I had a choice of collecting my personal belongings that day or coming back. That's the only time I've ever cried at work.

She returned to her office to collect herself and to call her husband. Then she went down the hall to the conference room which was staffed by outplacement counselors. Jean said that the counselor she spoke with was a very nice woman who gave her information about her severance package and also asked her what she planned to do for the rest of the day. Jean says, "I think she had a dual purpose for asking me about my plans. One was to make sure I was OK, but the other was to make sure that I didn't have a gun out in the car and was going to come back in with it." I asked Jean if losing her job was similar to anything she had experienced before and she said, "My sister died of cancer six years ago and it's similar in terms of the grieving—the shock, and distraction. After losing my job I found myself being incredibly distracted and very tired, and it felt odd that I was not in a routine anymore."

In these cases of large downsizing, most of the people I spoke with felt betrayed by the *company* but not by the person who decided to lay them off. In Jean's case her boss was also surplused and the day he told her that she was losing her job was his last day. She said, "He was very upset by our conversation. I was actually surprised at how upset he was. I imagine that some of that is because he was going through the same thing." Jean felt sympathetic toward her boss but disillusioned with the company.

Stan left a large firm after twenty years in various positions involving sales, marketing, and finance. I asked him how he felt when he was asked to turn in his company badge and was escorted out: "Oh . . . disappointed. I knew they were doing what they had to do and it didn't pay to have a lot of animosity. I was disappointed with the organization, disappointed with the management of the organization that I'd left because the process they used to select people to surplus was flawed at best. Rather than applying a logical process it was more a case of picking the people that you wanted to keep and letting the rest of them go. Seniority, performance, skills, your pay—none of them played. It was random."

Tammy also worked with a large company for twenty years in customer service and marketing. She and her family had moved across the country for her job and then she was let go just one year later. Tammy said that when she was asked to turn in her company badge it was "like they were asking me to chop off my hand."

What *was* severed in all of these cases is the psychological contract. A psychological contract is an unwritten, unofficial agreement between two parties that is based on implicit assumptions and expectations. For instance, all marriages have both a legal agreement and a psychological one. The psychological contract is made up of all the underlying assumptions and expectations that each spouse has of the other, though these are often not explicitly discussed. This is an emotional tie rather than a legal one and it is tenacious. The psychological contract that evolved over the past century between organizations and workers is that if employees work hard and pledge their loyalty to an organization, then in exchange they will receive job security and promotions.

The glue of the psychological contract is good faith, so when it is violated it often results in long-lasting feelings of mistrust, betrayal, or resentment.[1] The violation is a jolt, and its biggest victim is trust. People involved in large company downsizings, who watch others around them getting laid off, usually experience a more gradual erosion of trust. For instance, Stan expresses how this sense of violation seeped through his company: "And now, after going through the process of having them tell me that they literally don't want me, they'd just as soon usher me out the door, they lost all loyalty. There isn't any loyalty there anyway, even among the people who are there, because they know there are live rounds being fired and they could just as easily be next. Once you've experienced that, you have no more loyalty."

Notice how Stan uses the phrase "there are live rounds being fired." In companies where there is widespread downsizing, death imagery is common among both the "survivors" (those who aren't laid off) and the "victims" (those who are). In his book *Healing the Wounds,* David Noer links the death imagery he has heard among survivors of downsizing with the work of Robert Lifton.[2] Lifton is a psychiatrist who studied resilience among people who survived extremely traumatic events, such as the Holocaust or Hiroshima. One of the terms that Lifton uses in his research of survivors is "death imprint." The death imprint is associated with the event that triggers the extreme threat or end to life. Death imagery comes up because when we experience such a trauma, we relate it to actual death or death equivalents such as a sense of extreme separation and disintegration. The death imprint allows us to revisit the trauma until we have assimilated it and come to terms with its larger meaning. By noticing how frequently people involved with downsizing use language or images associated with death, we get some sense of the emotional severity of the experience.

As much as we might read or hear that the traditional contract between organizations and workers no longer exists, it is hard to believe until it happens to you. One person I interviewed began her story by saying, "At that point in my career, reality set in. I was working with old paradigms—I worked in a company that was blue-chip, I'd gotten promoted regularly, gotten advances, gotten more people. The old paradigm was working—you work harder and you get rewarded."

Even after losing a job, some people do not believe that the employment contract has changed. They hang on to their old assumptions and try to fulfill them in the next job. When assumptions about the psychological employment contract do not change, it seems to be more difficult to leave the sense of betrayal behind.

Some of the people I interviewed were not involved with the kind of widespread downsizing that has occurred in organizations such as IBM or AT&T. Being specifically singled out carries additional ramifications because it feels more personal. Everyone I spoke with believes that performance was not at issue in terms of the job loss. Those who felt singled out believe that their job loss had more to do with organizational politics or personality clashes with specific people.

Bonnie is one who had such an experience. Bonnie has a good sense of humor and we laughed a lot during her interview. She was director of operations for a fast-growing medical services company with about three hundred employees. When talking about the job she lost, she said, "I liked my job—it was a great job. I was doing all the things I liked to do and I was good at it." One of the things Bonnie liked about her job is that she had a lot of autonomy. However, after working for this company for about three years she acquired a supervisor she did not get along with: "It was very traumatic for me. I was no longer able to do my job without a lot of explanation and questioning and second-guessing." Even though she liked her job and the company itself, she felt trapped: "I was working in a department that was headed up by the founder of the company's brother, so politically that was part of it. And I was working for his pet. The politics of it had me trapped." The company reorganized. The general policy was to eliminate jobs but to keep people by moving them or not replacing them. During this reorganization, Bonnie was one of two people in the company who got laid off: "I think the shock that came was that I knew I was valuable to the company, I knew that I was good at what I did and that I served them well, and I thought I would get restructured more than fired. Basically, I think that when push came to shove this woman chose not to defend me at all, and so I got fired."

Even though her last months with the company had been uncomfortable, Bonnie still felt a deep sense of betrayal:

> I was truly very miserable, and very unhappy, and very stressed out about that. It paralleled being in a bad relationship that you knew you would be better off if you were out of, but it's not that easy to just walk away from it. Some of it came from my loyalty, some of it came from knowing it was a great job for me, and some of it came from—you just don't want to cut yourself off financially—even though I had resources, they were meant for something else. So it's a lot like being trapped in a bad relationship. Since they broke it off first, it was very painful. It was very painful for me. And those same kind of feelings—betrayal, and panic, and fear, and I had a lot of tears around it. I remember calling friends and saying "Oh my God—I've been fired." I mean, I was *fired*!

When I asked Bonnie if this experience felt like anything she had experienced before, and she said that in college she lost a part-time job at a day care center because she was a personal friend of the director's, and the director got fired. As fallout from that, Bonnie got fired also: "Again, the issue was not so much about money—or anything else—it was, *'How can you fire me*—I'm a good employee. I'm a good employee and I work hard for you—how can you do this to me?' So again, I think that sense of betrayal even then was probably foremost."

Even though Bonnie did not expect to be laid off during the reorganization, she had started looking for a new job while she was still there: "Then too, I had to laugh because here I was interviewing for another job—who betrayed who! I can always be rational—oh that nasty company—they betrayed me before I could betray them!" This job came through rather quickly after she left, so she actually did not have a long period of time between jobs. She is now working for someone she likes very much, and believes she is learning a lot.

> *Initially when I thought about betrayal, I thought of it in external terms—the sense of being betrayed, or feeling betrayed by an organization. But few people think about whether or not they've been betraying themselves. It is much easier to notice when it happens to us. Most of the time we don't even*

*realize when we do it to ourselves. Usually all the anger and disappointment gets focused outward. Ironically, though, being betrayed by an organization might reveal to us that meanwhile, we've been betraying ourselves. Perhaps getting in touch with that feeling of being betrayed will lead us back to ourselves; it may serve as a mirror or a reminder about what we've been doing to ourselves all along. How do we betray ourselves? It is when we lose ourselves; it is when we distract ourselves and cover our ears and pad our heart so that we no longer hear that small voice within. It is when we know that we're out of touch or out of sync but are afraid to take steps to move closer to who we are. We feel that dissonance at some level but rather than facing it, we cover it up with activity to muffle that voice even further. We betray ourselves because we're afraid—afraid that by listening and following our true nature we'll become different, we'll stand out, we'll be irresponsible, or perhaps we'll hurt or surprise people around us—those who carry their own expectations of who we are. We betray ourselves because it is easier to keep that voice muffled. If we don't hear it, we can pretend that it doesn't exist.*

The surprise factor was greatest among the people I spoke with who felt singled out. For most of this group, losing their job came as a complete shock, and the feeling could take a long time to dissipate. For example, Will was still recovering at the time I spoke with him, six months after he lost his job. He did not feel better off. He impressed me as a strong, stoic, kind man who had difficulty leaning on others or asking for help. Will was fifty-three when he lost his job as vice president of finance for a small, privately held company. He said that his job was fairly satisfying and he had no indication of any problems. Will said that he thought he was doing an outstanding job in terms of divestitures and handling some difficult situations. He was also receiving bonuses on a regular basis.

Then one day the president of the company called Will into his office and said, "We're just not going to be able to make it work." Will asked him how he had reached those conclusions, but the response was vague: "The area he seemed to be unhappy with is probably my strongest suit. I think it's a case where corporate politics were involved and therefore I did not have sufficient knowledge of it. I went through a period of time where I couldn't understand why I was out—what did I do? What did I miss? What subtle things? Are my perceptive skills not up to speed? My conclusion was that no, there really wasn't a concrete reason that I can understand."

Will said that when the president told him this he struggled very hard to be professional and not take it personally. But he told me, "It was a shock—it really was," and speculated that it must be what a divorce feels like. He said that he was having trouble reaching closure because he was so unclear on why it happened. He was plagued by a cloud of unknowing.

Doris also felt singled out and was left with lingering effects. It seemed painful for Doris to tell me her story and I sensed both sadness and anger. She has scaled her lifestyle back more than anyone else I interviewed and believes that because she is fifty-one years old, the change in her circumstances is permanent.

Doris had previously owned her own catering company. Then in 1989 she decided to take a job in human resources at a large and successful retail store in her community. She thought that she would have better benefits and opportunities for advancement with this company than working on her own. After three years, she was asked to be in charge of a café that was located within the store. She took the position and said, "It wasn't my cup of tea but I saw it as my only opportunity to advance in the corporation—to take an area that wasn't doing well and turn it around." Doris did turn it around. The café had been losing money but under her management she reduced waste and increased profits. Then a new chief operating officer was brought into the store who had a very different management philosophy from Doris's previous boss. She said, "The day he came, he was horrible. But I thought, I've dealt with this sort of thing before and I can win him over."

Though this man was hard to get along with, Doris felt that things were going OK and she focused on increasing the profitability of the café. She said that her new boss set a goal of $500,000 for the café and that she exceeded this goal by bringing in $750,000. Then one day she was asked to come to the corporate headquarters: "The day I went over to corporate I thought I was going to get a raise—I really did." But instead her boss said, "This is it—we can't work together anymore." Doris asked him about a severance package. He told her that there would be no severance but that she could come to the corporate office and work for an additional three months to plan a new café for a store in another city. He added, "You can't come unless you have a good attitude."

Doris told me, "I was in a state of shock. I couldn't believe it, and neither could anyone else. I thought it was a bad dream." She went home and called a few of her close friends who advised her to take this three-month position. She felt that she had to take it because "I didn't have a plan B; I didn't have a backup or contingency plan." Doris said that the first day she worked in the corporate office "was probably the worst thing I ever did in my life. It was humiliating, it was awful."

What got her through it, however, was the support she received from the corporate administrative staff, who were all women. She also frequently talked with another person who had recently left the organization. She explained, "What my friend and the women at the corporate office did was validate my feelings—*this is wrong*. If no one had been there to tell me that we see this and we know that this is not right, I might've thought that I was cracking up or something. You know what I mean by validating? It's explaining that this is the way you should be feeling; that this isn't right."

Doris looked for another job while she was planning the new café. However, she could not find anything. Several months after leaving the corporation she was getting down to the last of her money. So she did something that she always wanted to do but never thought was practical—she went to travel school. She said that as a child she used to dream of being a travel agent but it hadn't seemed feasible once she grew up because she was a single parent raising two children. She decided that "at some time in your life you need to do what you love—just once," and that this was the time. Doris's unemployment compensation was going to run out in January and she was feeling very anxious about her financial situation: "I'll never forget this because it was Christmas week, and nobody else would even return my phone calls. On a whim I went downtown and stopped at a travel agency and filled out an application. I got home and the human resources person called back and said I want you to come in for an interview. They were starting a training class the ninth of January. So I went in and interviewed, and I got the job the next day. It was the day before Christmas eve—and I got a job!"

Doris is now making less than half of her previous salary. To help make ends meet her daughter and son-in-law recently bought into her condominium so they could establish a credit rating, and moved in with her. This has helped, but she still feels a financial strain. She also was left with lingering anxiety because her job loss came as such a shock. She said that in her new position, "I *still feel,* when the vice president or somebody comes by, I get this catch in my throat. And I think I'm going to be fired. It is awful! Because it was so unexpected. I never *dreamed* of something like that happening to me."

At the time of the interview, Doris was still grappling with coming to terms with the psychological contract: "Well, it's hard to separate people's work from their being and I identify with, if you're doing a good job you'll get a raise, and if you keep doing a good job you'll get another raise and you'll make money, and that's why we work." Yet recently she has felt that "I have this *tremendous load* off myself" because she is enjoying her job and not taking it home with her. Through her job she even won a trip to the Bahamas, which she had just taken the previous week. Still, she said that before she could begin to heal she needed to let herself off the hook about losing her job: "There's so much negativity with it that I don't think you can do anything—I don't think you can interview, I don't think you can live, I don't think you can do anything positive—until you let yourself off the hook about it. And that is the hardest thing for a work-oriented society to believe. Because I'd always heard, 'You do a good job—you'll get promoted; you do a good job—you'll get a raise.' And you can do a good job and get fired. I'd never heard that—*never,* not ever."

*The psychologist James Hillman sees betrayal as an archetypal motif, and ties it back to Judas's betrayal of Jesus. Because of that betrayal, Jesus experienced a death and transformation—death and rebirth, or reawakening to a higher level of development. So why does betrayal lead to such a potentially transforming response? Perhaps it's because it cuts so deeply to the heart. And when our trust is violated, is cut away—a part of us dies. I wonder if the part of us that dies is a certain innocence. We are rudely jerked out of our Garden and forced to acknowledge that those whom we love most have the greatest capacity for our betrayal. Trust always carries the seed for betrayal. And I suppose that conversely, betrayal carries the seed for trust. So if betrayal is linked archetypally with death and transformation, then how does this apply to job loss? Perhaps the betrayal motif relates to the death of our identity. And also, to the death of a certain naïveté. Something in us does die when we place our trust and spend hours of our days in the belief that our hard work will be exchanged for loyalty and longevity, and realize that this belief is an illusion. And something in us does die when our work identity provides us with a sense of importance, urgency, and value—and suddenly that identity is gone. Yet if betrayal is an archetypal pattern, then those deaths are necessary for the experience to have a transforming effect.*

*But I think for that to happen, the sense of betrayal must be allowed to get through to us. Those who cover it up don't experience the experience. They don't feel the cut. They don't bleed. And consequently I think it may be more difficult for them to be awakened to new parts of themselves. Then, of course, there are those who feel the betrayal and rather than allowing that betrayal to have a transformative effect they become stuck in bitterness and cynicism. Perhaps they too are fending off death. Rather than letting go of an illusory psychological contract they armor their belief system and hold rigidly to it.*

When Doris finally left the organization that let her go she said, "When I stopped working—I'll never understand exactly what happened—but it was so euphoric to not have to face it every day. It was *such* a relief!" Though many of the people I spoke with initially felt shocked and betrayed, a significant number also felt relieved.

## Chapter Five

# Relief

*I live my life in growing orbits*
*which move out over the things of the world.*
*Perhaps I can never achieve the last,*
*but that will be my attempt.*
*I am circling around God, around the ancient tower,*
*and I have been circling for a thousand years,*
*and I still don't know if I am a falcon, or a storm,*
*or a great song.*
—RAINER MARIA RILKE[1]

At some point, many of the people I interviewed felt a sense of relief after losing their job. Some felt relieved as soon as they left and others experienced relief after going through more negative feelings of surprise, anger, or betrayal. Sometimes these various emotions came all at once: "Given the fact that I wasn't equipped to enter the freelance world, it was like being thrown to the lions. At the same time I felt a wonderful sense of exhilaration because I thought, 'Man, you could go anywhere from here!' It is kind of like there are no road signs so you can go anywhere you want to go."

Feeling a sense of relief is a difference between the "victims" of downsizing and those who "survive" by not losing their job. The survivors seldom experience real relief. This is because relief has to do with feeling freed or released from an obligation or restriction.

It is understandable why there would be a sense of relief for those who leave. As in any relationship, the end of a job is often preceded by a lot of anxiety and discomfort. Actually being laid off ends an anxiety-filled time of wondering when or if it is going to happen to me. One person I interviewed said, "I was dying over there, just like a little bit every day." He elaborated by saying, "You remember *Joe Versus the Volcano,* do you remember that movie? There was a great scene in there where a guy is plodding to work. It's an old factory. He goes down in the basement and everyone is green because they haven't been outside in years, and the fluorescent lights are going bzzzzz. My job had that kind of feel to it and I was miserable."

Many people have a sense that they ought to leave an unhappy work situation but they can't bring themselves to quit. This was the case with Bonnie, who knew that her negative relationship with her supervisor was making her miserable. She still believes she probably would not have quit. In retrospect she says, "Part of it was, you just need the doctor to come in and cut off the aching limb." She drew many comparisons between losing her job and losing a relationship. In her case, she passed through intensely negative emotions quickly and then felt great relief: "The parallel is with breaking off a relationship—but certainly it is much more intense than breaking off a relationship. Actually, the pain of it was similar to breaking off a relationship, but the relief afterward was not the same! Maybe with the process of breaking off a relationship, the emotions last longer. This was real intense—straight down and straight back up over probably a two-week period."

In an interesting book called *Quitting,* Dale Dauten discusses his findings from interviewing 120 people who were faced with quitting something, usually a job or a relationship. He found that the underlying dynamics of quitting are the same in all major quitting decisions, whether it is a career change, a divorce, or a particular action. Dauten found that the most common regret from the people he interviewed was that *they had not quit sooner.* In other words, most regretted their earlier decisions to stay in a situation.

Many people do not quit because they are afraid they might make a mistake. They are afraid they might become more unhappy. Dauten considers this a paradox: "Individuals fear becoming what they already are. When individuals are in unhealthy relationships, they frequently respond not by running for freedom but by fearing freedom."[2] Dauten found that an average of five years elapsed from the time the relationship or situation became unsatisfactory to the time of the actual quit. One-quarter of those who quit believed they did make a mistake by doing so, but over half felt they made a mistake by not quitting soon enough.

The other dynamic that keeps us from quitting is the difficulty of acknowledging that we've made a mistake, which is fortified by social sanctions against quitting. Quitting is often perceived as a weakness of will. Those who successfully quit a situation and later felt that they made the correct decision tended to focus not on the problem itself but on the realization that they could not resolve the problem. Later, they still believed that they were correct in their assessment. When they quit, it was a sad giving up rather than an angry denunciation. They also were able to believe that "You are not what you quit."[3]

In terms of job loss, the most common reason I heard for not quitting was financial. When you get downsized or laid off the decision is made for you, and many people in managerial or professional positions receive a severance package. As with Matt, leaving with a severance package affords an additional cushion—and therefore freedom—not otherwise available.

Henry, an industrial engineer, knew that he needed to make a change a year or so before losing his job: "My blood pressure was up. I wasn't suffering any long-term effects at this point but a lot of tension in my stomach and stuff like that. I'd get home at the end of the day and have that feeling where you're tied in knots, and just uncomfortable. Something inside of me said, 'You can't keep doing this year after year—you've got the stamina to do it now but in five to ten years it's going to wear you down.'"

Henry had worked for this corporation for about two and a half years. He lost his job in 1992 and since that time he has been self-employed. Several months before losing his job, the company began restructuring. They were not downsizing—they were actually in a growth phase. But a new plant manager came in who replaced most of the top managers. Henry's boss lost his job and then, two months later, Henry was called into the plant manager's office: "I was asked to go to the plant manager's office. I had another item I wanted to discuss with him and had been trying to see him for about a week. But he was never available, which made me a little suspicious. I figured something might be up. When we finally met and I went into his office, he shut the door and said,

'We're going to make some changes and you don't need to come in tomorrow.' I said, 'I've got to think about this.' But before I left his office I knew what I was going to do."

Henry had thought about becoming self-employed for a long time. About a year prior to this, he and his wife attended a franchise show and identified a business that they thought would fit well with Henry's background. They bought the franchise, Henry got training, and he began to lay the foundation for going into business for himself. However, he was having a hard time getting it off the ground while working full-time. Getting laid off was actually the best solution for him: "I hadn't had the time to make this thing work, and here he handed it to me." When I asked him how he felt at the time he said, "Uncertainty was probably the dominant feeling, but there was a touch of honest excitement that here's your opportunity—seize it, don't waste time. If they hadn't let me go at that point it probably would've been another year before I took that step, and I would've missed out on some opportunities that I discovered that year." I asked Henry if it seemed as though the decision to work for himself was forced on him and he replied:

> I didn't see it as a forced choice at that point. I knew I needed to eventually get out of that environment, and I always had aspirations to be self-employed. Both my parents were self-employed—my father was a farmer and my mother was a landscape architect. I realized that I was not going to be satisfied until I was going to be in a situation where I could control my own destiny and do the level of workmanship that I want to do rather than having someone give me a deadline where I can't possibly do what I'm capable of doing in an acceptable fashion.

I must point out, however, that Henry's graph was not a straight line upward from the time he left his job. Instead, it looked more like waves. I asked him what the ups and downs were tied to and he said they mainly related to the financial ups and downs of his business. For a while this was cushioned by his wife's job, but in 1994 she left her job and joined Henry so that they could work as a team. The following fall the business went into a slump and Henry said, "I started picking up the want ads and looking through the paper and thinking, 'Do I really want to go back?'" Then around Christmas they landed a large account, which put their business on a whole new financial level.

My first impression of Henry was, "This guy is really up!" His eyes sparkled, he had a bounce to his step, and he exuded positive energy. In the course of the interview he explained that earlier that day he deposited the biggest check into his business that he'd received since it began, one that allowed him and his wife to pay off their house mortgage. I understood why he was so up.

I asked Henry how he coped with the stress of being self-employed and how he would compare it with the stress of his previous job, and he said, "Running in the morning is the time when I do some of my best thinking. But before, there was more stress to burn. I found myself running harder and swimming harder because I was fighting. Now I run at a pace that I feel comfortable with. When I was dealing with that work situation, I was trying to burn that knot in my stomach. That's what I was trying to do." He added that he prefers making his own choices about how to deal with situations and that when he was part of a larger corporation he was frustrated by being pigeon-holed into a slot. Owning his own business certainly was not stress-free, but the stresses were easier for him to deal with because of a greater sense of control.

*Yesterday while I was walking, I was thinking about the way many of the people I've talked with have felt a great sense of relief once they finally left their jobs. I looked up the meaning of relief and one definition is "delivery from a place under siege." I wonder how many people feel that they are under siege in their work environments? Another meaning of occupation is the conquest and control of a territory by military force. It's as if our occupations are under military control. And in keeping with that, we defend our jobs and our turf as if our life depends on it, often forgetting why we are there in the first place.*

*This makes me wonder how many of us are always under siege, no matter what our circumstances are. I'm not sure if it is a defense against ourselves, or if it is a defense against the world. Perhaps it boils down to people who think of the world as a safe place and people who don't. Or perhaps it boils down to a certain comfort level and confidence with ourselves. But I'm not sure if I think that the world is a safe place to be. My own sense is that we find pockets of safety. Last night someone was telling me that she calls a special friend of hers "arbor" because she thinks of a childhood game she used to play where the tree was the safety zone. As long as they touched the tree, they were safe. I suppose we all need our arbors.*

Henry's comment about feeling "pigeon-holed" was echoed in various ways by other people I interviewed. So much so, that the sense of coming out of a box and its accompanying freedom became a major theme of my research. Several people actually used the phrase "coming out of a box." Van expressed this idea quite eloquently:

> One of the things that my job loss forced me to realize is that— well, the way I describe it is, I was living in a box, and the box was prescribed for me by the church. I had a preconceived notion of what a church person ought to be and that translated to what *I* ought to be, and when I lost my job I realized that the church held no authority for me anymore. All of a sudden I saw that I was living in a box. I couldn't believe that I was that person who I was a few years back, which was even a tighter box. When I finally realized that my work wasn't necessarily who I was, and that my workplace did not have to define who I was, it was an awakening for me. I had an "out of box experience!" And I forced myself to do some things that ordinarily I never would have done.

Van was not a minister, but he had attended seminary and then got a master's degree in religious communication. When he lost his job he was working as a producer for a large publishing house owned by a church. He had been feeling increasingly confined by the precepts of the church as a whole and also by a negative relationship with his supervisor. His job loss situation was similar to Matt's, in that the supervisor reorganized to move Van out of his position.

After losing his job, Van went through a difficult time where he barely made ends meet by freelancing. His wife did not work outside the home and they had two small children, so he felt a lot of financial strain. After a year and a half, Van got his current position, where he has been working on a contract basis. This relieved a lot of the pressure, and he has been in this position for three years. He told me that after getting back on his feet financially, he felt much freer than when he had worked in the previous job. He also said that he did some wild things that he never thought he would do. For example, he and his wife took a vacation to St. Martin island, where they visited a nude beach. He explained that when he was very involved with the church, he was afraid to buy wine in a grocery store for fear that a church member might see him. Now he and his wife were enjoying a nude beach! While sunbathing he realized, "There are wonderful people here who don't live under those rules." Van had a photograph taken of him and his wife on the beach and had it made into a painting, which hangs in their bedroom.

Losing his job changed many things about Van, including his spirituality. He explained:

> The loss of my job is really a loss of a part of my life that I'm glad is not there anymore. I'm a much happier person. And a lot of it is not living in that box; it's letting myself try new things. My greatest spiritual growth lately has come from studying art, literature, and philosophy. I don't pray, in the traditional sense. I sort of meditate. I enjoy interacting with life more. Once I said to my mentor that I don't have time to pray because my children need me all the time and he said, "Well, that is going to be your prayer for the next few years."

Stan, who had worked in one company for twenty years, also expressed the idea of getting out of a box but he used a different metaphor. Stan compared his job to being confined by a glass ceiling. However, since Stan is white and male he was not using "glass ceiling" in the traditional sense of the term. He was recalling a story about fleas, which I use when I teach, and I was both surprised and delighted to find that he knew the same story. This is a true story: Did you know that fleas can actually jump quite high? But if you put them in a cage and place a piece of glass over the top of the cage, they will learn to jump only as high as the glass. If you lower the glass down as low as six inches from the bottom of the cage the fleas will jump six inches even though by nature they are capable of jumping several feet. The point of the story is that if you remove the glass ceiling, the fleas will continue to jump only six inches. Stan said that this is how he felt at his company.

Stan explained, "Opportunities were typically segregated—if you had an administrative background you didn't do the marketing or product development work. That's just where you were, and there wasn't much getting out of it." Since losing his job, Stan has pursued opportunities he would not have considered before. He says, "I have grown tremendously. I am much more comfortable

with myself. I've been required to do a lot of introspective thinking about my skills and abilities, and what I can do and can't do. I
didn't realize that I could jump past the glass ceiling. But now I am
realizing that I guess I do have some good marketing skills—I'm
even surprising myself." I commented to Stan that it seems ironic
that he actually gained confidence by losing his job.

> *I hadn't made this association with being in a box before, but I just recalled
> a dream that I had a long, long time ago. All that I can remember about it
> is that I was ready to be shipped out from the shipping department and I
> had to fit into this box, which was too small for me. It was extremely uncom-
> fortable. Yet I don't think I questioned it at the time because I was so busy
> trying to contort my body to fit into this box. I wanted to please.*
>
> *This makes me think of Doris's comments about living life "on auto-
> matic" before she lost her job. We automatically steer ourselves into these lit-
> tle boxes, often without even thinking about it. They may not be comfortable,
> but they feel safe. Perhaps we build little prisons without even knowing it.
> Doris did not really enjoy her job—it did not nurture her spirit—but even
> after losing it she would find herself unconsciously steering her car back to
> the company parking lot because she had gone there almost every day for six
> years. Consciously, she felt enormous, enormous relief when she was let go
> and did not have to go back to work every day. But something else kept her
> tethered . . . and so we tether ourselves to our workaday structures because
> they provide us with something to return to. How do we reconcile these two
> needs? The need for a base, a moorage—and the need to be free. What do we
> do with the boxes in our lives when we grow out of them and they no longer
> meet our needs?*

Again, I want to emphasize that the people I spoke with traveled different journeys to reach a point where most of them ended
up feeling better off. I have identified the most common responses
to involuntary job loss, but the people I spoke with did not necessarily have these responses in the same order. In some cases the
sense of relief was preceded by a very dark time.

| | |
|---|---|
| *Chapter Six* | |

# Dark Times

*The crisis consists precisely in the fact the old is dying and
the new cannot be born. In this interim, a great variety of
morbid symptoms appear.*
—ANTONIO GRAMSCI[1]

Debra's story reminded me of this passage from Dante Alighieri's
*Divine Comedy:* "In the middle of the journey of our life I came to
myself within a dark wood where the true way was lost." Debra has
a sparkle in her eyes and a lot of vitality. At the time she lost her
job, she was a thirty-two-year-old general manager of a large retail
store. She had moved quickly through the ranks, attaining a high
level of responsibility at a relatively young age. However, the owners of her company added a new position between themselves and
Debra so that she acquired a new boss. Debra and the new boss
had extremely different management philosophies, which created
a cultural change within the company and a great deal of discomfort for Debra.

Soon after she acquired this new boss, Debra went for a day
hike in the mountains. It was October. She and her friend literally
got lost in the woods because their map was not clear. They went
for three days sleeping outside without food, and finally found
their way out: "All we had was the willingness to keep at it, and get
up in the morning and recognize that the sun does rise again. I'd
recognized my own mortality; there were times when I wondered
whether we'd get out of the forest alive."

Debra did find her way out of the woods, but it precipitated a dark and tumultuous time: "My Dad had passed away in April of the previous year. The next year my new boss came and things got *really* rocky. Then we got lost in October of that year. I had these questions about my mortality, I was still grieving, and my family was going through these changes. And then my brother-in-law got diagnosed with terminal cancer. It was like taking a dump truck and putting it in reverse."

The pressures at work became intolerable, culminating with an incident that caused Debra to leave her job the following July. Her initial thought was to open her own retail store, something she had always dreamed of doing. While planning this, she also did things that nurtured her such as frequently visiting her family and getting together with an old group of friends who were very supportive.

Debra planned to open her own store by September. However, when she attempted to lease the space she wanted, she and the owners could not come to an agreement. Meanwhile, friends and professional colleagues had been suggesting to Debra that she start her own consulting practice. After the lease negotiations fell through, she shifted gears and instead ended up getting a very large consulting contract. She said that at first "I wondered if I would make it on my own—if there would be enough out there to really support me. But I continued to do projects here and there." I spoke with Debra after she had been working independently as a consultant for three years. She now says, "Even though I had this big job, and big money, and managed lots of people, I feel that the things I've learned, and the things I am involved with now, and the way I use my creativity is *much more* than I ever imagined! I just didn't realize the possibilities beyond where I was." When Debra looks back on that dark time of her life, she says:

> I think I learned to be on the dark side—again. When I went
> through my divorce, I remember crying so hard that I never recognized that I could cry so hard. I went through this dark side again,
> through the struggle and the loss and the grief. I think that was a
> real important time for me because I am positive and I am full of
> energy and I am enthusiastic and I tend to look on the bright side.
> Those skills have served me well, but I probably needed to recognize the balance in my life. And the downturns have taught me to
> be more comfortable—I'm still not comfortable with it, I don't

know that I'll ever be comfortable feeling bad—but during that time I knew that I would not feel this way forever.

Now Debra has a national reputation as a consultant in her field. She feels much better off than she did before losing her job.

Debra's dark time actually began before she left her job. More often, as with Jeff, the job loss is what triggers a dark time. Jeff was in the banking industry for thirteen years when he lost his job as a vice president. Throughout his interview, he told a lot of funny stories. But I thought that his eyes seemed moist and I sensed a sadness below the surface. This was six months after he lost his job and I think that Jeff was still in his dark time but was putting up a brave front. His graph did not end on a higher point than where it had been when he was employed. When I asked Jeff if he felt better off than before losing his job he replied, "I can't say that, yet." He lit up the most when he talked about some of the things he had accomplished while working at the bank.

Most people in the banking industry have been through lots of acquisitions, mergers, and downsizing since the late 1980s. Jeff watched this happening and, like Henry, anticipated that if he lost his job he would go into business for himself. However, unlike Henry, he did not have a solid foundation laid when it actually happened. Still, Jeff decided to use this time as an opportunity to go into real estate.

After losing his job, he found the first two months exciting and stimulating as he explored the real estate field and got lots of positive reinforcement about his skills. But at this point on his graph there is a sudden, extreme drop to the lowest point. I asked him what happened, and he said, "I just crashed. I just woke up one morning paralyzed and said, what if I can't do this, what if we're not successful . . . and I just started to feel those feelings of failure." I asked him if he has ever felt that way before and he replied, "I don't think that I've ever felt that." That morning he called his outplacement counselor and the counselor suggested that he come right in. Jeff said that it was helpful to talk with the counselor but also embarrassing because while he was talking he started getting flashbacks, which brought tears. As he told me this, he again fought back tears and I realized that he was getting more flashbacks. Clearly, his job loss was still very painful for him.

At the time that I interviewed him, Jeff was struggling to get his real estate business off the ground. Since the time he "crashed," he has had a lot of ups and downs. The initial euphoria of being in business for himself has worn off: "The last two months I feel I keep getting tested, and then I keep saying, 'I'm not going to quit, I'm going to make this work,' and then boom I get hit in between the eyes again and knocked down and then you go through the emotions."

He continued by saying, "I feel like Job sometimes. I know that I have more things in life than 99 percent of the people in the world. But I think this is my trial, these are my tribulations. I think they'll make me a better person. I'll just have to rise to the occasion and see what I can do." The Book of Job is about a pious and faithful man who incurs the wrath of God because Satan insinuates that Job had a doubting thought. Furious, God puts Job through continuous trials—robbing him of his herds, slaughtering his servants, killing his sons and daughters—and the man eventually winds up sitting on a dung heap and suffering from a plague of boils. Job does not even receive the support of his friends, who declare that he must have done something evil to have so many afflictions heaped upon him. Job patiently and courageously withstands his suffering without losing his faith. Although ultimately God restores the lost prosperity, Job's name is typically equated with suffering. Needless to say, the reference to Job reflects a dark time.

Many Tibetan statues and paintings of gods and deities look like demonic beings. Yet even though they look frightening, these wrathful creatures are not seen as bad. Their grotesque outward appearance is really a disguise adopted by deities embodying wisdom and compassion to help us attain greater understanding. To do so, it is necessary to face the darkness. Mythically, entering the underworld refers to the transition from a materialistic point of view to a soul point of view. This is what the psychiatrist Carl Jung meant when he said that as consciousness expands, it also darkens.

Joseph Campbell refers to this time as the "belly of the whale," referring to the story of Jonah, who was swallowed by a whale and then came out again, transformed.[2] In the Book of Jonah, God gives the prophet Jonah a destination to go to deliver his message, but Jonah decides to go elsewhere instead and takes off in his boat with his crew. A great storm ensues and Jonah responds by falling asleep in the bottom of his boat. Meanwhile his sailors consult an oracle and conclude that Jonah is to blame for the storm. The captain wakes him up and asks him about his responsibility for this mounting calamity. Not only does Jonah accept responsibility for the storm, but he also suggests that the sailors throw him overboard as a sacrifice if they want to survive. Eventually they do so and the storm subsides. Meanwhile, Jonah is swallowed by a whale who then spits him out on dry land three days later. From here, Jonah carries on as a prophet with a greater sense of depth and wisdom.

The storm is a metaphor for what happens within us when we split ourselves off from our real nature, which causes a sense of inner turmoil and disjunction. Jonah tries to deny this and alleviate his distress by falling asleep in the midst of the storm. Being asleep symbolizes not being conscious. But when the others awaken Jonah, he actually shows a lot of courage and integrity by acknowledging his responsibility for the storm. He offers himself as a sacrifice so that through his death the others might live. When Jonah falls into the sea he sinks into a dark and mysterious place. Inside the belly of the whale, he actually has a safe place for transformation. It is enclosed, protected, and secure. Thus his tomb becomes a womb, and from here he is delivered to a new life.

The theme of this story is that out of death comes new life. But first, it is necessary to go through what mystics call the dark night of the soul. This is a necessary time of withdrawal that precedes transformation. Sometimes it is described as a maze, or labyrinth, where the trails are deliberately confused. Campbell says that this is what happened in the *Divine Comedy:* "Dante says that, in the middle year of his life, he was lost in a dangerous wood. And he was threatened there by three animals, symbolizing pride, desire, and fear. Then Virgil, the personification of poetic insight, appeared and conducted him through the labyrinth of hell, which is the place of those fixed to their desires and fears, who can't pass through to eternity. [Ultimately] Dante was carried to the beatific vision of God."[3]

Creation myths from all cultures, including Christian, Hindu, and Taoist, begin with chaos or a descent into the dark. Chaos is depicted as a murky condition teeming with life. Creation begins with the resolution of chaos into order. Mythically, chaos is not considered to be a threat to life but the only premise on which life can take place. Out of chaos comes creation and transformation. For instance, the steps of shamanic initiation take the shaman to the realm of chaos, or the Land of the Dead. Shamans experience symbolic death through the process of sacrifice and dismemberment. Only then can they walk with the dead and acquire direct access to the spirit world. Through this opening, compassion and empathy are born.

Joan Halifax references the Chukchee expression, "soft to die."[4] This is when we are most open and vulnerable. It is also when the deepest structures of our psyche can reorganize. All of this reflects a central theme which is that *through destruction comes instruction.* When things fall apart, when they seem chaotic and confusing, we are more open to questions and to new learning.

> *Last night I was talking with a friend about the idea of having a second skin, or a thicker skin that provides buffering. She asked me if I thought that resilient people acquire this, or if it is already there. I thought that was a good question. Some, like Sara, seemed to acquire it but for others it was there. This raises the issue of whether or not resilience can be learned. And does it come from the inside-out or the outside-in? It seems that it's a combined effect. Because the things that are going on inside have an effect on the outside, and what's going on outside nurtures the inside. In the outside-in category I would put relationships (family, friends, network), and in the inside-out category I would put faith, hope, and imagination. It's the combined effect that seems to "thicken the skin."*
>
> *How is this fostered? I think it is fostered by being confronted with our limitations, our finitude, our pain. I think it is an acknowledgment of the life-death-life cycle that is fundamental to life. Avoiding death is an avoidance of life. And avoiding pain is an avoidance of growth. But most of us can't continue to avoid pain, anyway. God might start off by whispering in our ear, and if we don't hear that we might get a shout, and if we don't hear that we're likely to get clobbered on the head. Or, if you don't take the hint you'll get a hit. But many of us respond to the hints by battening down the hatches, closing the windows, and refortifying. This is a stasis that denies the movement of life; it is a dead-ended death.*

Becky's dark time came *after* she was reemployed. For five years, Becky worked as a manager for a large aerospace company. When the company began major downsizing several years ago, she had a dawning realization that she would likely lose her job. With this came an emotional low: "Not real low, but a realization that it could be me. Then it became more apparent that it would be me and that it was only a matter of time. Then when I realized that it *was* me and only a matter of time I thought, 'No problem—this is an opportunity to look at some other things.'"

Becky was confident about her skills and that she could find another job: "It was never an issue of, could I find a job or not. My fear was not finding a job that was challenging enough, in a place where I liked the people—where the culture was a match." For a year and a half between jobs, she got enough project and consulting work so that finances were never very strained. She enjoyed this period, especially the summer. During this time she spent more time in her garden and with friends. Through winter, however, she did experience "little valleys": "What started to kick in is that my affiliation needs weren't being met. I felt alone. I was by myself. I wasn't collaborating with anybody, there wasn't the regular work thing where you go in every day. And then it was winter. It wasn't horrible. I did consulting projects where I got energy renewal, but in between I was aware that everyone else was going off to work."

Because of these affiliation needs and also because she had concerns about supporting herself long-term with consulting, she took another job a few months before I interviewed her. According to her graph, she is now at her lowest point:

> It's funny because you'd typically think, "Oh if I get a job, that's great!" I've never had an experience like this before. Normally when you get a new job there's a honeymoon period, when you're learning and meeting new people. But my low feelings started at the beginning, and I think it's because I saw this other piece. It wasn't the consulting projects per se, it was the realization that there is another way to be. There's another way to be and I was happy doing that most of the time, and then I'm back into a regular job again.

Becky commented, "I looked so happy!" in photographs from Christmas a year ago, when she was on her own. The following Christmas she had been reemployed for three weeks and she said, "In photographs I looked like I had a glaze on my face." I asked her what she thought was the real source of her depression and she said, "I'm feeling loss now. My lost dream. I also think that during this transition period for some reason I got on more of a feeling level, so that's another reason why. Those feelings aren't new but now they're brought closer to the surface and they hurt more. I'm more aware of them. Maybe it's good that I'm in pain because maybe the pain will be strong enough that it will propel me to do something. So I don't think any of these things are totally new. They've always been there, but they were pushed down."

Becky anticipates that she will stay in her current position for about a year and then go off on her own. She says, "This is just a stopping point, like a bus stop. If I'm still here a year from now I'll be surprised." Her biggest concern is having clarity about what she wants to do. She believes that once she has clarity, she will figure out how to do it.

As you can see, going through a dark time around job loss and transition is common. However, there does not seem to be a particular pattern around *when* this occurs. I think Becky may have put her finger on something when she said that those disturbing feelings were there anyway, and her transition allowed them to surface. Often we keep our lives so busy that we are unaware of our own rumblings below the surface. We avoid any sort of respite so as to keep those uncomfortable feelings at bay. Losing your job, however, can create a break in the pattern and allow for a moment of pause.

## Chapter Seven

# Soul Searching

*The human soul is always moving outward into the
external world and inward into itself, and this movement
is double because the human soul would not be conscious
were it not suspended between contraries. The greater the
contrast, the more intense the consciousness.*
—WILLIAM BUTLER YEATS[1]

Cheryl was referred to me by an outplacement counselor who told
me that he watched her change dramatically and positively after
losing her job. She is tall and attractive, and has an air of confidence. Cheryl received her MBA about twenty-three years ago, was
hired by a bank, and stayed with it until she lost her job in 1993.
While working there she rose very rapidly, breaking the glass ceiling in terms of position and pay. During her last four years, she
weathered three acquisitions; by the third one, she had become
one of sixty thousand employees. The culture of the company
changed a great deal and she acquired a supervisor she did not
like. She says, "At that point they brought in their own people to
take my job and basically gave me a job with less responsibility,
probably hoping that I would leave, which I thought about, but I
couldn't imagine working anywhere else."

About a year and a half later Cheryl's boss told her that she
should take the next six months to find another job. He said, "You
don't have to tell anybody, you can save face, you can just resign
one of these days and be working somewhere else." Cheryl said that
he also added, "You'd better continue to do your job and do it well

because you'll be on thin ice." Cheryl laughed and said that at the time she thought to herself, "How does it get any thinner than this?"

Cheryl realized that her boss was trying to avoid terminating her so that they would not have to give her a severance package. She ignored his request to look for another job, but meanwhile she talked with a few attorneys about her situation to find out how she should handle it. A few months later, her boss sent the head of human resources in to talk with Cheryl. Cheryl said that she and the human resource director had worked together for over ten years. Cheryl explains,

> He said, "I understand you've been asked to leave and I want to know if there's anything I can do to help in that regard." And I said, "Oh, absolutely!" then pulled out my sheet of paper where I had written all these things down. I told him everything I wanted and he replied, "Based on your years with the company, the level you reached, and the contributions you made, I'm not embarrassed to ask for any of this." So when he came back everything had been approved and the only catch was that they wanted me to leave right away.

Cheryl's severance package, combined with her savings, gave her a great deal of financial freedom. After leaving the bank, this was her initial response: "For twenty-one years, ever since I left college, I'd gotten up and gone to the bank every day—for ten to twelve hours—and I thought, 'It's going to be really hard to not get up and go to the bank.' I needed to do something I've always wanted to do, and I've always wanted to spend a month on the beach. My uncle has a house up there and I called him and asked if I could use it and he said 'Yes, for as long as you want.' Then things started getting a lot better."

It was hard for Cheryl to tell her parents about losing her job, but when she did she was gratified by her father's response: "I took my father to lunch and told him that the thing I was most worried about was their reaction. He called me back that afternoon and said, 'I think your plans for the future are great.' I said, 'But I don't have any plans for the future,' and he replied, 'I know.'" Cheryl speculates, "I think he realized that during his thirty-eight years at RCA he never had the liberty to do what I was getting ready to do—to take off and decide how I wanted to spend the rest of my life."

Cheryl spent a month at Cape Cod thinking about where she wanted to go from here:

> I think the most important thing I did when I left the bank was take time and think about what are the things I've always wanted to do that I haven't done. And I just really gave that a lot of thought. And then I asked myself, "Okay, what's keeping you from doing these things now?" It was so satisfying to be able to give myself those gifts that I'd always pushed away and said, "No, the bank is more important, your job is more important," and now I said, "But these are things you really want to do, and you've never done them."

Cheryl made a list of things she had always wanted to do but did not have time for, which included—in addition to a month on the beach—taking tennis lessons, having cosmetic work done on her teeth, losing weight, and doing volunteer work. She also decided not to return to a corporate setting. This decision stemmed partly from what she learned through outplacement counseling:

> I had always felt that I could never work for myself. I didn't understand how anybody could be, like, a real estate agent—how do they live from month to month when they don't know what their income is going to be? I did a lot of reading and I became convinced that the most secure job there is right now is to work for yourself. I read something that really stuck with me. It said, if you work for yourself, you can never lose your job—you can only lose your clients. And then, what's the big deal—go get another client! I decided that that's what I wanted to do—to work for myself.

At the time that I interviewed Cheryl, she had done everything on her list. She put together several sources of income, including working as a part-time chief financial officer for several smaller companies that could not afford a full-time position. She says, "I'm happier than I've been since I was about twenty-three!" and adds, "I know now that I worked too hard. I think when you're single it's harder to have balance in your life. The positive side is, I didn't have the expenses of supporting a family. So I was able to save a lot of money, which is helping me now. But the negative side is I didn't have any other distractions in my life. That's all I did—my job. And I'm extremely grateful that I got this wake-up call. There's more to life than your job. It is not the most important thing."

I interviewed Cheryl two and a half years after she lost her job and I detected no bitterness or anger toward the bank. She said that for the first year or so she received many job offers, including several calls from the top search firms in the country. She said, "It would have been very easy for me to get another job like I had—I could've done it instantly." However, during her break she realized that it was time to try something new: "I said to myself, 'Well, I already had a career with a bank. It's been a very good one and I've been very successful, and I don't think I can top it. I don't see why I'd want to do that again.'"

An added twist to Cheryl's story is that about a year after leaving the bank, she became an aunt to a little niece who was born deaf. Her family, which lives in the same town as Cheryl, wants to teach the niece to speak so that she will be able to attend schools and so forth. Helping with this effort is currently Cheryl's top priority. Because the niece's mother has to work full-time for now, Cheryl attends all the meetings at the hearing and speech center and spends a great deal of time with her niece. Cheryl says, "For someone who always wanted children and never had any, it's a real opportunity for me."

I asked her what she would tell other people who involuntarily lose their job and she said, "Well, to me the main lesson is that this is your life we're talking about, not your job or career. You need to make sure that you're getting the most out of it and putting the most into it from all aspects, and not just focusing on the job. To me this whole career thing is like a Monopoly game, and if you're competitive you want to win. As long as you're playing you do the best you can so you can win—but you also need to know when to stop playing."

I did not especially anticipate that taking a break, or a "retreat," would turn up as a theme in my research, but it did. The retreat was not simply time off—it was a time of soul searching. Remember that after losing his job, Matt took a three–month hiatus where he spent a lot of time hiking and canoeing by himself while he thought about his next step and the changes he wanted to make in his life.

At first I thought that the ability to take a break would depend completely on financial circumstances. Many of the people I spoke with lost professional positions and received a severance package that gave them a financial cushion. But this was not always so. Doris, the former café manager, had virtually no financial cushion. However, she took two months off after leaving her company and felt this time was necessary: "I just thought, fine—I look bad, I don't look like I feel confident—this isn't good for me to be interviewing in this state of mind. You project. So I just took two months off. I got my house in order, I got my hair cut and got a new look, and just had a great time. I went to flea markets, I did things I'd been wanting to do for years. See, I worked six to seven days a week for them, and this was like a rebirth."

It was interesting to me that Doris chose the term "rebirth," because in many ways that is what a retreat allows. The stories of all great heroes include a retreat—or separation from the world— prior to the hero's transformation. Again, this is the time that Joseph Campbell refers to as the "belly of the whale." In mythic terms, this withdrawal is necessary so that the old self can die and be reborn to something new. This involves a rebirth to a "higher" self that is in closer accord with the person's inner and truer source.

Carl Jung noted that many of us go through this process at midlife. Jung had this experience himself. By 1913, at the age of thirty-eight, Jung had married, fathered a family, and established himself as a world-renowned psychiatrist. He and Sigmund Freud had been closely collaborating to develop a new science of the mind. However, Jung's ideas began to diverge from Freud's and he felt increasingly compelled to express his own individual point of view. Doing so led to a traumatic break with Freud, which was followed by Jung's own midlife crisis. During this time he experienced intense and disturbing dreams and visions. In 1922, two months after the death of his mother, he decided to leave his family for a while to build his own retreat site at Bollingen. He built a stone tower by himself and kept it as simple as possible. Later he wrote, "From the beginning I felt the Tower as in some way a place of maturation—a maternal womb or a maternal figure in which I could become what I was, what I am, and will be."[2] It was during this period in his life that Jung's richest contributions to psychology came together: "The years when I was pursuing my inner images were the most important in my life—in them everything essential was decided."[3] Jung continued to retreat to Bollingen throughout the rest of his life, spending more and more time there as he got older. He wrote, "Solitude is for me a fount of healing which makes my life worth living." He believed that his retreat site was essential to his work: "Without my piece of earth, my life's work would not have come into being."[4]

Based on his own midlife experience, Jung became primarily interested in how adults develop at the midpoint of life and beyond. He believed that we spend the first half of our life adjusting to the social world by establishing a career, getting married, creating a family, making money, and so on. However, in doing so many of us stray further and further from the path Nature intended for us to follow. The midlife passage involves a separation from the self that we spent the first half of our life creating. It is a very disturbing time. It is also a humbling time. In *The Middle Passage,* James Hollis describes it like this: "The experience of the Middle Passage is not unlike awakening to find that one is alone on a pitching ship, with no port in sight. One can only go back to sleep, jump ship or grab the wheel and sail on."[5]

Retreating in some way from the social world gives us the chance to more clearly hear our own inner voice, so that our lost soul can rediscover its proper path. Jung calls this process *individuation,* which means becoming more fully ourselves. If we go through a midlife passage, then we are more likely to individuate throughout the second half of our life. Our sense of power and authority becomes more inner-directed and in touch with its spiritual source. Jung believed that *resisting* a midlife passage becomes a growing problem as we age, and culminates in a fear of death. If we do not die to our first life, which is usually dictated to us by our parents and social institutions, then we are likely to be haunted by the impending reality of death and the fear that our lives have not been meaningful.

The people I interviewed took these soul-searching retreats at various times and for various lengths of time. For some, the actual retreat lasted no longer than a three-day weekend. For instance, recall the story of Bonnie, the woman who used to work for a medical services company and felt very betrayed when she was one of two people reorganized out of a job. At the time, she was living in

California. The next job she took involved a move across the country to Maryland. Bonnie is single and did not know anyone in Maryland prior to moving there, so it was a big move for her. Before leaving she signed up for a retreat in California that took place about six months after starting her new job. She says, "So I went back to California, saw some of my friends, and had a weekend away. The weekend was about centering and spirituality and that stuff—it was a very good experience. That break helped."

A retreat helps to create a break from the past. But the time itself may be less important the journey inward. Often the people I spoke with had a desire to spend some time alone. They had a need to reconnect with themselves by removing themselves from the distractions that typically filled their time and their thoughts.

Though many actually did take a break from work or looking for work, some simply could not afford to do so. For instance, from the moment he lost his job at the publishing house, Van said that his search for work was "unrelenting": "I had to be unrelenting—do as much as you can every day to work toward where you want to be. My greatest stress reliever was making ten phone calls or writing a letter, somehow setting things in motion. I pursued it as relentlessly as any goal that I've ever had." Van's soul searching occurred simultaneously with his job search. He thought deeply about what he learned from losing his job, and about his values and priorities:

> That was a big turning point in my life because I realized my goals were very career-oriented and my family was important and I was kind of lucky that my family was just a good family. I have since come to believe that those career goals don't mean anything—my career is for my family, and it's for me too, but they deserve more of who I am. I also realized that it's not the work we do that's important, it's what the work does inside of us that's important. Those times when I have felt devalued, that I'm not important, that it's the *job* that's important—there's something that's not right about that.

As I mentioned, Van was the sole support for his wife and two young children at home. Yet he was able to do his soul searching in the midst of activity. This meant that he had to block out distractions so that he could go inward. He was able to be solitary while staying involved with his job search and family. The ancients believed that "purposeful solitude was both palliative and preventative. It was used to heal fatigue and to prevent weariness. It was also used as an oracle, as a way of listening to the inner self to solicit advice and guidance otherwise impossible to hear in the din of daily life."[6] The key to soul searching, then, is the ability to block out distractions and go inward.

Elaine chose a radical change of scene instead of a solitary period. Elaine impressed me as quick-thinking and tenacious. She told me that she had been director of a small but visible nonprofit agency. Various political maneuverings resulted in someone being placed above her, between her and the board of directors. This person completely changed the culture of the organization and took it from being nurturing and dedicated to its cause to being fear-based and divisive. This person also set Elaine up to get fired by the board. Elaine was a former member of the board and several of the people on it were friends of hers. Being fired not only felt unjust, but also humiliating. She said that her impulse was to flee: "I didn't have a place. I didn't know what to do with myself. And I felt that everybody in town knew about this humiliating thing that had happened to me, which is not true—but I thought it at the time. I didn't know what I was going to do with myself, and I was trying desperately to think—what to do. *What* could I do?"

Prior to working in the nonprofit agency, Elaine had gotten a nursing degree. She always had a yen to go into the Peace Corps, and she decided that this was the time to volunteer overseas. She checked out Bosnia and Rwanda but both of those places already had enough volunteers. Eventually she found a place as a volunteer in Guatemala. Before leaving, she made arrangements with an editor of the local newspaper to write a series of articles from Guatemala about her experiences. This temporary resolution to her situation allowed her to do something she always wanted to do. It also got her moving forward: "As soon as I could start talking about it I did, because it distracted everybody from the past." Elaine really enjoyed her experience and the break allowed her to get a new perspective: "It was *so* different. Once I was in Guatemala, everything at home faded away completely. As soon as you see those people down there and the way they live, and how much they appreciate you, and everybody liked me—they were glad I was there. I knew, in my heart of hearts that I was still devastated about losing my job and that I didn't know what my reputation was at home, but as far as being absorbed—I never thought about it. Never."

Elaine said that in Guatemala, "I realized that people are more important to me than anything else and that I'd been neglecting my family—I'm such a workaholic—and I'd been neglecting my friends. So I made plans to visit my daughters, and to visit my father whom I had not seen for several years." When Elaine returned from her break she decided to go back to school to get a nurse practitioner degree. Although she would like to continue volunteering overseas, she decided that she must do something practical that will let her earn at least $45,000 a year. With this degree she can also do additional volunteer work in foreign countries in the future.

Sometimes the need for a retreat comes long after the job loss itself. Carol delayed it until she had worked on her own for about a year. Carol had been an internal consultant for a global hotel corporation. She was asked to manage a project that involved bringing a new information system into the corporation. Unfortunately, she was brought into the project late. After being put in charge, she realized that the project was ill defined, had no corporate sponsorship, and the wrong people assigned to it. It seemed destined for failure. On top of that, Carol's boss mandated that the project be completed within an unreasonably short period of time. All of this culminated when he surprised her by calling a large meeting that included everyone remotely related to the project—including outside vendors and contractors. Carol said, "The vice president said that the project had to be finished by December and that everyone needed to get on board, and if we didn't have the energy or passion or commitment to be involved with this project then let him know. He left the meeting and I left with him and told him, "I don't have the passion for the project and would like to resign as project manager." This is not what he expected! A few days later he told Carol that if she resigned from the project it meant she was resigning from the company. She resigned.

Carol then contacted a former boss and within two weeks of leaving her job she had lined up a large consulting project. Projects continued to come her way so that she never really had a gap where she was concerned about work. But after a year, she decided that she needed a sabbatical: "While I was consulting I put some money away. So I saw this as an investment in myself—to take some time and not worry about money. Friends called me about doing additional projects but I turned them down. I knew I could do the projects, but something was missing. I was looking for work to satisfy a deep longing, and I realized it wasn't there."

Carol planned to keep her sabbatical simple, unstructured, and open-ended. She took time to garden, walk, read, and write. Then she took a course at a local Catholic retreat center and while there she met with a counselor. When Carol pulled out her calendar to set up a second meeting, the counselor said that it would have to be delayed because she was going out of town. Carol asked her where she was going, and the counselor said that she was leading a retreat to Nepal in ten days. Carol laughed as she said, "I asked, 'Got any room on the trip?' The counselor looked at me as if she was thinking, 'You can't be serious!' One thing led to another and I went to Nepal. We stayed in a Jesuit ashram outside of Kathmandu, and the focus of the trip was to explore Hinduism, Buddhism, and Christianity. It was the trip of a lifetime! It was so rich."

Carol stayed on her sabbatical for a total of about six months. Then she got another call for a good project and this time accepted it. It seemed that it was the right time for her sabbatical to end, though she suspects that she will continue to balance her work with retreats in the future.

*Last night a friend talked with me about leaving his job, and I told him that I thought it took a lot of courage. It did. It takes courage in the sense of standing by your heart. To have courage is to stand by your heart. Perhaps this is what it really means to reclaim your soul. It is not just getting in touch with your essence. It is having the courage to act, and to stand by yourself. And also, listening to your Self. My friend said that he had dueling voices. There was the little voice that he knew was Truth—that told him he had to leave. But he also heard the other voices, the voices of his mom or dad or society or whatever—about how it's weak to quit, that it must be his fault, there must be something wrong with him, and so on. Which voices do we listen to? Often it's hard to know which is our own voice.*

*Most of the time we can't hear it because we don't clear the space. In this case he cleared out his bookshelves. His books are important to him. He said that for the first time he started pulling books off the shelves and was*

*on the verge of getting rid of them all. Then he waited a day, and ended up*
*keeping them. He said he didn't know what got into him—he's never*
*cleared his bookshelves before. I think he was creating space for something*
*new, and symbolically wanting to leave his past behind.*

Soul searching involves an introspective time, a movement into
the self. What is going on inside takes precedence over what is happening on the outside, in the larger world. At some point, however,
this movement needs to shift. It is like an ebb-and-flow movement.
Eventually, everyone I spoke with felt the need to move forward.
As one of the inspirational quotes Cheryl told me she kept in mind
goes: "When there's no wind—row."

## Chapter Eight

# Moving Forward

*Far out on the western ocean man has drawn an invisible*
*dateline where instantaneously today becomes yesterday*
*and the westward voyager crosses into what the world*
*behind him calls "tomorrow." Whether he crosses that line*
*in calm seas or raging storm makes no difference. For him*
*it is still tomorrow—for he journeys with the sun.*
—WARREN SCHMIDT[1]

A retreat provides a pause in activity, a time to rest and regroup. However, all the people I interviewed also had a strong sense of momentum, of forward motion to their lives. Nearly everyone commented on spending most of their energy looking forward and not looking back. Remember that when Matt returned from his three-month hiatus he chose to "leave bitterness behind," and launched his search for a new job. Henry, the industrial engineer who started his own business, said, "When I walked out that door, that was it. I wasn't going back. I basically put that behind me and said I learned some things, I made some friends there. But I wanted to move on—my focus was forward, not backward." Stan, in coming to terms with losing his job after twenty years with the same company, said, "You've got to put it into perspective, don't take it personally, pick up and move on and don't look back. You asked about coping—I don't look back, ever—you can't look back. If I started to look back at all the opportunities I missed, I could drive myself nuts. I'm only looking forward. That has permitted me to cope."

Moving forward after losing your job is one of the most important aspects of resilience. Among the people I spoke with it was catalyzed for different reasons. In some cases a person's financial situation simply leaves no choice but to move as quickly as possible. Again, this was the case with Van. When he lost his job he was under a lot of financial strain because he figured that he only had three months where he could make his house payments without additional income. I asked him how he would rate his financial anxiety when he left his job on a scale of one to five, with five at the high end of the scale: "I walked out the door thinking three months is not a long time. However, it does give me a chance to get into fourth gear, really moving. By the end of the first month my financial anxiety moved to about four and by the end second month I was on a high five. It scared me to death because we had no other income. I was it and I was frightened to death." For Van, generating activity to find work and move forward helped to relieve the stress of his financial anxiety.

People moved forward at different rates. Van felt good about generating a lot of activity. Some, especially during their dark time, could only take one step at a time. Jeff, who was having a hard time getting his real estate business off the ground when I interviewed him, said, "I just keep putting one step in front of the other and brush myself off and say, I can't let it beat me. I just keep moving forward. I look at my kids and say to myself, 'Hey I've got to do this for them.'" Others needed to move quickly. Elaine, who went to Guatemala for three months, said, "I think I had to move fast. The alternative would've been to sit around in the fall, twiddling my thumbs. And I couldn't think of what I wanted to do with my life, so this was a great thing for me to do for three months. It was voluntary—I didn't have to find a job right away—and it was away from my home town, and it was doing something that I always wanted to do."

A few people learned to move forward more quickly as they gained experience with job loss. This is the case with Dan, an engineer who has been through several downsizings over the past six years. He left his first job in 1989. The division within the organization where he worked at that time used to employ ten thousand people and does not even exist today. After leaving that position,

Dan worked on a contract basis for about two years before landing his next job as director of engineering for a large medical manufacturing company. This was a major increase of both pay and position from his previous job. After two years he lost that job due to downsizing, but then landed a position at another firm—again with a substantial increase of pay.

I interviewed Dan rather late in the evening. He came straight from work after a very busy day. He said that he appreciated the way others have helped him in the past, and he wanted to do the same. Dan seems like a cheerful and optimistic person. He has a great deal of savvy about how to find a job in today's market and has come to terms with the new psychological contract: "The time of having a career for life has come to an end, no doubt about it. You've got to be flexible. I mean, no place is forever—whether you like the house or don't like the house, or like the job or don't like the job."

Dan has found that it is important to think of the new contract as being two-way and negotiates certain things as he goes into a new position, such as a salary package, insurance, and letter of reference if he is let go for no fault of his own. Dan's father worked for three companies in his lifetime and held his last position for twenty-nine years, so Dan has had to learn new ways of thinking about work. Yet he seems comfortable with it:

> In today's environment there are no guarantees; it can be here today and gone tomorrow. Like in my last position—I usually worked sixty to seventy-five hours a week—but there's no guarantee that will be there tomorrow. When you're working, it's an opportunity to build your résumé, make more contacts, and do more networking. It's the old adage—when you're handed a lemon you make lemonade. What you put into it is what you're going to get out of it. In terms of my last job, it didn't cost me a dime. They paid for my relocation, and I appreciated the twenty-one months of training—and now someone else is benefiting from that.

I would describe Dan as mainly pragmatic. He understands and accepts that lifelong job security is gone. Yet the basic pattern of moving continuously upward to higher positions with higher pay has not changed. Dan is simply doing this across organizations, rather than within a single organization, and this fits his goals and desires. So whereas Dan has experienced several job losses, it does not sound as though the rhythm of his life has changed.

> *I was talking with a friend the other day and she made a comment that I liked. She said she believes that there's nature, and nurture, and choice—and that too often we are in so much of a debate around nature versus nurture that we forget about choice. It seems to me that nature and nurture are both rooted in the past, and choice is rooted in the present and future. There are lots of choices we can make around involuntary job loss—choices involving attitude and actions—that determine our resilience. It goes back to the idea of our response-ability. Do we choose to leave bitterness behind? Do we choose to see the learning inherent in the experience? Do we choose to be true to ourselves? These are choices that everyone can make, whether or not they have an optimal genetic make-up or upbringing.*

It was hard for me to tell whether Dan moved forward out of habit or out of choice. I think it was out of choice. There is a subtle difference, however, that comes down to whether we *react* or *respond* to change. When we react, we might think of the notion in physics that for every action there is an equal and opposite reaction. A mechanical reaction causes an object to be forcefully propelled in a particular direction—as with the propulsion of a jet engine. Our reactions are often automatic, emotional, and rooted in past experience. By contrast, responding to change implies a more thoughtful process. The word *respond* means to answer, correspond, or reciprocate. It is an interactive process that suggests a dialogue with the environment. It is more like rafting a river. When you raft down a fast-moving river you need to be very attuned to the environment and respond to upcoming obstacles, like rocks. The biggest danger is a *sleeper*—a rock hidden just below the surface of the water. Sleepers usually reveal themselves only through a slight ripple or change of current, but if *you* are asleep and fail to steer away from the sleeper then you are likely to tear or capsize the raft. This is why rafting down a fast-moving river requires focused attention.

We respond out of choice. We react out of habit. Sometimes moving forward can simply mean learning to move beyond our habits. Robert Sardello describes this in his book *Love and the Soul:* "Moving does not necessarily mean moving away or moving out. Moving means moving out of the fixed patterns of habit. All fear is the fear of doing, for doing may take away what one already has. And it does—it takes away the illusions that one has; it may take away the comfort that one has; it may take away the conceptions of who we think we are."[2]

Ellen Langer has researched the idea of acting out of choice versus habit and explains her findings in *Mindfulness*. She contrasts mindless and mindful approaches to living. *Mindless* behavior is when we react to things automatically, based on our previous habits, and are locked into a single perspective. For instance, she describes Napoleon's invasion of Russia as an example of mindlessness. As Napoleon advanced, his adversary, the Russian general Kutuzov, allowed the Russian army to keep falling back. Meanwhile Napoleon was obsessed with his goal of taking Moscow, but when he did so he found that the city was empty and that the Russians had set it on fire. Now Napoleon was far from his supply lines and the harsh Russian winter arrived. This is when Kutuzov attacked and defeated the French army. Langer points out that Napoleon's obsession with conquering Russia blinded him and led to his mindless defeat. All he thought about was conquering enemy territory and he ignored incoming information. Meanwhile, Kutuzov responded creatively to news of Napoleon's advance. He evacuated the city so as to set a trap, and knew that the Russian winter would serve as his ally once Napoleon was far from his supply lines.[3] Thus, *mindful* behavior involves being open to new information, able to create new categories, and aware of more than one perspective.

How do we cultivate mindfulness? The first step is to catch ourselves before we react automatically. When Dauten studied people who successfully quit something, he found that their decision to quit was a thoughtful and measured response to a situation that they could not change, rather than an angry, impulsive reaction. Automatic reactions are physical as well as mental and emotional. When events arouse us, our autonomic nervous system often drives the body into a stress reaction—the heart pumps quickly, the hands sweat, the stomach churns, and so forth. Many of us keep ourselves in this heightened state of arousal during most of our waking hours. It is now well documented that the result of living in this chronically stressed state leads to a vast array of physical problems, such as high blood pressure, indigestion, chronic headaches, and back pain, and the list goes on and on. This is why

Jon Kabat-Zinn, founder and director of the Stress Reduction Clinic at the University of Massachusetts Medical Center, distinguishes between the mindless stress *reaction* and the mindful stress *response*.[4] Stress reactions happen automatically and unconsciously. Choosing to replace this automatic reaction with the stress response involves paying attention to what's happening within us, physically, emotionally, and mentally, moment by moment. The key to doing this is simple, but not easy to remember. When we feel the impulse to react, we need to catch ourselves and instead take a few moments to notice and deepen our breathing. This grounds us by redirecting the mind and quelling our emotional and physical reactivity.

Choosing the stress response, however, does not suggest that we extinguish all feelings of anger, fear, or distress. Among the people I interviewed, a few initially did move forward out of anger. The emotion provided the energy—the fuel—for forward momentum. This was the case with both Sara and Elaine. Fighting back is what got them moving again; their anger moved them beyond their despair. Elaine was angry about being set up to get fired as director of the nonprofit organization. She took steps to vindicate herself and ultimately succeeded. Yet I think that being in a foreign country and doing something completely novel is what inspired her imagination and helped her to sustain forward motion. Elaine strongly emphasized not looking back: "Resilience for me is the ability to change directions and go on, and look toward the future, and not to live in the past. There's nothing to be gained from living in the past." However, she later added that she believes her healing came from feeling sad and angry, and then looking back to consider how she got where she was and what she would do differently in the future: "I just don't think you can heal unless you can do that. And I don't think you can let it go until you've done all that stuff. You can put it behind you—but you can't let it go. I said in the beginning you can't look back—forever—but you have to look back in the beginning . . . I was miserable, and I was angry—thank God I was also angry. Because of that, I think I could heal better. It was like cleaning out a wound, then it could scab over."

Sara also needed to get in touch with her anger to stop her fall into depression after she was dropped by her record company. But it was the creativity ignited by her mother's suggestion to produce the album on her own that pulled her forward. Anger may provide the initial impetus, but the more adaptive long-term response is to then transform the anger into creativity or new activity to sustain the forward momentum.

> *I think hope is very related to the theme of moving forward. Hope is rooted in the future, it pulls us toward the future. And it must be mingled with imagination. Hope and imagination go hand in hand. Our imagination provides the possibilities, and hope provides the energy that moves us toward those possibilities. I think that hopelessness comes from feeling trapped in the box and hope moves us out and beyond the box. Where does hope come from? It is fed by imagination. Where does imagination come from? It is fed by hope. Without both there is no energy, no incentive for moving forward.*
>
> *Wait, I have to contradict myself. I think we can also be pushed forward. I think that when we're pushed forward, the energy driving us is fear. Being pushed forward is like running from the fire as it is catching up to you. This definitely creates forward motion. When I started my first business, I think it was born out of hope and imagination. But after those first few years that energy diminished and was replaced by something that felt more like drudgery and I was pushed from behind. I lost my inspiration. But by then I had a house and other bills and needed to make money. The forward motion was more from having that money monster right behind. It would be nice to always feel pulled forward rather than pushed. I wonder how often this happens?*

Many of the people I spoke with said that they focused on the future rather than the past to gain a sense of control over what they could change. For instance Bonnie, who lost her job at the medical services company, said: "I don't do guilt, and I don't do regret." She added with a laugh, "Certainly I do do review! I may look back and say I could've done something else that would've been smarter, kinder, wiser, whatever—but I review it and then hopefully put it into my fund of knowledge and move on. It happened. I can't change it. All I can do is change things from that point on." Henry, the industrial engineer who went into business for himself, also talked about the importance of controlling his attitude:

When a person is let go—and it's different for everybody—look forward and don't look back. Your focus needs to be on looking forward. Don't take it as a failure or a personal defeat. Whatever the case is, a month or two down the road you're going to be the only one who remembers it so don't hold a grudge. If you take it as a personal defeat it will drag you down and limit your potential to get another job or get a business off the ground. It becomes a game of controlling your attitude, and that's not easy to do when you're going through a traumatic change.

You can see that the people I interviewed moved forward at different rates and for different reasons. But in all cases, they did move forward. To do so they eventually let go of emotions like anger or bitterness that would have trapped them in the past. The graphs they drew that tracked their journeys all went up and down to varying degrees. No one drew a graph as a flat line. This reminds me that in medicine, "flat line" means death. Movement is essential to life. Several thousand years ago Aristotle taught that the natural state of living things is to be at rest and quiet. Today we know that this is not true. Quantum physics informs us that the natural state of all matter is continuous jiggling motion. We see this in nature. I look outside my window this spring day and see the budding growth of new leaves. The word nature comes from the Latin word *natura,* which means birth.[5] Life is movement, and when we are aware of the mystery of life we realize that we are constantly becoming.

# Part Three

# The Journey Home

## Chapter Nine

# A New Map

*We shall not cease from exploration*
*And the end of all our exploring*
*Will be to arrive where we started*
*And know the place for the first time.*
—T. S. ELIOT[1]

Ptolemy is the father of modern geography. Nearly two thousand years ago, he invented a framework and a vocabulary for mapping the world that is still used today as the basis for cartography. The common image of the world during Ptolemy's time was that of a known land mass surrounded by uninhabitable ocean. But Ptolemy rejected this image and instead drew a map of the world that included vast, unknown lands that were not yet discovered. His map was based on some serious miscalculations that greatly reduced the distance between the eastern tip of Asia and the western tip of Europe. Using this map, Columbus set off across the ocean and eventually landed in America. What if Columbus had known how large the world really was? Would he have made the trip at all? Perhaps the most important point is that by creating a new map, Ptolomy prepared the world for exploration. He suggested that there were lands that had yet to be discovered, and thus opened minds to receive new knowledge.[2]

I like this story because it shows how a new map can guide us toward new vistas. In this case, the accuracy of the map was less important than the fact that it created a new way of conceptualizing the world. It gave explorers like Columbus enough courage to seek unknown lands. The trip was not exactly what Columbus expected, but it did lead to new discoveries.

Right now we need new maps to help us conceptualize our changing relationship toward work and organizations. When we think of a map, we typically think of geography. Yet maps can be used more broadly and take a variety of forms. In a sense, maps can be thought of as metaphors that allow us to exchange information so that we share common perceptions. They provide a concrete image of information. For instance, an X ray can serve as a map of the human body and an organizational chart is a map of a company. The most interesting maps I have ever seen are in a book called *Maps of the Mind* by Charles Hampden-Turner. Hampden-Turner created graphic representations of sixty complex theories from philosophers, psychologists, and writers. In a remarkable way he uses maps to explain theoretical ideas, such as existentialism or anxiety, without reducing these ideas to oversimplification. He points out that maps have strengths and limitations. For instance, take a look at Figure 9.1.[3] If you take a cylinder, a cone, and a sphere and shine a light on them from a particular angle, you can create a "shadow map" wherein they all cast identical shadows. If you change the angle of the light, however, you can create a different image in which a cone may appear to cast a square shadow. Depending on your perspective, maps can show similarities and also create distortions of the original objects.

This reminds me of the stories I heard from the people I interviewed. Each traveled his or her own unique journey. You might say that each of the journeys had its own shape. But if you shine a light from a certain angle, you can also see that they had much in common. Most of these people initially felt some combination of shock, betrayal, and relief. Most experienced a dark time, and then retreated from their usual activities to allow their feelings to sink in and to think about where to go from here. Then they all moved forward toward new goals and possibilities. At the same time I realize that taking a snapshot of an ongoing process is a distortion. None thought that they were finished, or had arrived at a final destination when I interviewed them. They were all at various points along the way, and had taken different routes to get there. The danger of creating a map of these journeys is that it provides a

**Figure 9.1.    Shadow Map.**

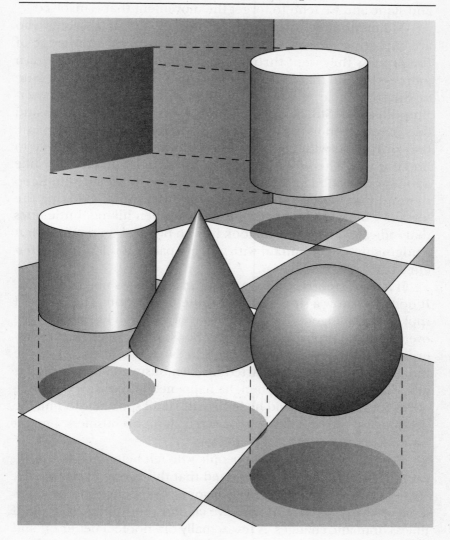

snapshot when really we need a movie. A map is two-dimensional and static and we tend to forget the movement that is involved.

As I mentioned earlier, I think of these people as scouts who are exploring new ways to navigate their careers. Knowledge of the process they went through can help us illuminate our own journey. I found that I was not able to map their journey as a four- or five-step linear and universal process. That would be an over-simplification. Still, a map is useful. Maps help to orient us and they may beckon us with the spirit of adventure. When we are lost, they provide us with confidence and hope that we will be able to find our way. Therefore I have created a model that is more like a topographical map, showing a broad view of the terrain. Keep in mind that looking at a map is a lot different from hiking the terrain. I have used topographical maps when hiking. Little lines that indicate elevation gain look like no big deal on the map, but trudging up the mountain with a heavy pack on is a whole different story.

It is also important to keep in mind that this is not a *road* map. It does not show a single correct route or location. The people I spoke with changed their perceptions of their job loss experience over time, and probably their perceptions are still changing. Recovering from job loss is an evolving process. Remember Henry, the industrial engineer who started his own business after losing his job? The day I talked with him, he happened to receive a very large check for his business and he felt great! Had I spoken with him the previous fall, when he was discouraged about his business, I might have heard an entirely different story.

Even though I sought out people who felt better off after involuntarily losing their jobs, I realized that this group of people felt "better off" to varying degrees. For some, losing their job served as a major catalyst for transformative change. For others, it resulted in less dramatic changes. A few actually did not feel better off and wished that they could find a job just like the one they had before. When I put all this together, the changes fell primarily along two dimensions: the degree to which people changed assumptions about themselves, and the degree to which they changed assumptions about their work. Mapping the two dimensions of change results in four quadrants, and each quadrant represents a different response to job loss (Figures 9.2 and 9.3). This model distills

## Figure 9.2.    Career Resilience: Mapping Your Journey.

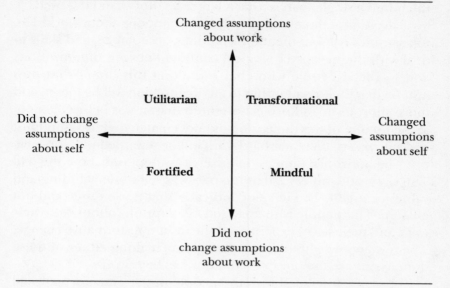

## Figure 9.3.    Responses to Job Loss.

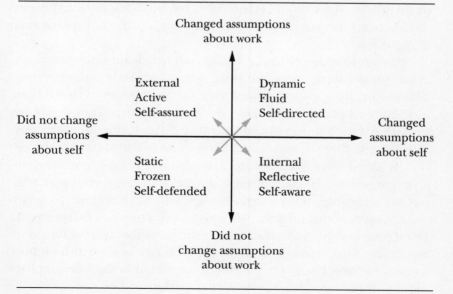

the stories I heard from the people I interviewed and combines them into a single map so that a larger territory can be viewed.

The vertical dimension involves assumptions about work. The top signifies gaining the understanding, acceptance, and skills to deal with the new psychological contract between organizations and workers. People who changed along this dimension now assume that their relationship to an organization will be looser, and more short-term and project-oriented than it was before. People at the bottom of this dimension did not change their assumptions, and still believe that their hard work will be rewarded with job security. The horizontal dimension involves assumptions about the self. The right side indicates that the person's self-understanding and values changed. The left side indicates that these things did not change. The people who changed assumptions about *both* their work and their selves experienced the most transformative change. The few people who did not change much along either of these dimensions are the ones who did not feel better off.

I became intrigued with the people in the Transformational quadrant, and will spend much of this section discussing what they had in common. First, however, I will give you some examples of people representing the other quadrants. Again I want to emphasize that a person's placement within a quadrant is not definitive or invariable. This model is intended to show differing responses to job loss, but most people move through different quadrants along the way.

People representing the **Utilitarian quadrant** changed their assumptions about work but were not particularly introspective. This means that prior to losing their job they believed that if they worked hard and were loyal to their company, then they would be rewarded and their job would be secure. After losing their job they questioned their assumptions around this and developed new beliefs about work, its place in their life, and their relationship to an organization. Dan is a good example. Dan is the engineer who has been through several downsizings, and has developed a great deal of savvy about finding new jobs in our current environment. But it was hard to get Dan to talk about himself—most of his focus was on his work. His advice to others is "buyer beware and be prepared." He now has a very pragmatic approach to the new employment contract, and he is comfortable with this:

Today, having a job means you're on an assignment—whether that assignment is six months or six years. The most recent statistic is that a graduate graduating today will have thirteen to seventeen different jobs and several different careers. That's a lot of moves, a lot of changes to make. If you're not willing to move and be flexible, and if you don't have self-confidence, then you have a problem. But if you are willing to be flexible, and you know what you do well, and you know how to package it and sell it, then life goes on.

Julie and Henry are two people who changed many of their assumptions about work and after losing their jobs, decided to work for themselves so as to have more control over their career destiny. Both were more introspective than Dan, but did not feel that their job loss brought about significant personal change. When Henry reflects on his experience he says, "Before my career was something I had to put up with to get a paycheck, and now it's a vehicle to get me where I want to go. It's a tool to open doors instead of something to go fight and get paid for." I said to Henry that it sounded to me as though his definition of career success had not changed, but that he had modified his route and he replied, "I have an entirely different vehicle—I'm driving a new car."

Julie had been self-employed for four years at the time that I interviewed her. Julie is a CPA and also holds an MBA degree. She experienced an upheaval three years prior to leaving her job, when her organization spun off a company that Julie worked for, and then merged this spin-off with another company. At that time, Julie and her husband moved to a new city to take a job with the newly merged company. When this company was bought out by a new company Julie said, "I'd been through this upheaval before, the upheaval of having your job change drastically and the threat that it would be pulled out from under you. At that time I waited around to see if indeed they were going to move me. This time I didn't want to go through that again. I didn't want to feel as if somebody else was in control of what I was going to do with the rest of my life."

Like Henry, Julie started her own consulting business prior to actually leaving her job but did not have much time to get it going. It helped that when she lost her job she received a severance package, and then could devote all her energy toward building her own business. I asked Julie how she felt when she left her job. She said,

"I was scared, but I also felt a sense of bravado. I remember saying to my husband at times when we commuted together that I had butterflies in my stomach and felt on the edge. Those went away the day I went to work for myself." When I asked Julie if she feels better off now than she did before losing her job she said:

> Let me count the ways—I don't have the commute to a congested metropolis, my home is my office, I can look out the window and see the geese in the pond and the horses in the pasture. I set my own schedule, even though it's rigorous some days but some days it's not—if I eat lunch and can't stand it I can go take a nap. I can fire a customer—and I've done that; I can stop that situation without stopping my career. It all boils down to the fact that I control my own time—time is so precious—now I'm the one making the decisions.

I asked Julie if she thinks she would ever go back to a corporate setting and she replied:

> It's conceivable, but I'd rather move to Cheyenne, Wyoming, and work in a gas station and go home at five and live in a one-room house. I'd rather have a job I could leave. The other side is, I have a new contract where I've gone back to a corporate environment part-time. They treat me differently. They've hired me as an expert and they trust me to give them the outcome they need. If I don't, they won't pay me. That's the way it ought to be. But I don't have someone coming in every five minutes saying, "Is this done, or why don't you do it this way."

You can see that both Julie and Henry place a great deal of emphasis on determining their own career destiny and they feel that they have more control over this by being self-employed. Both also mentioned that being in business for themselves allows them to have more of a mergence between different parts of their life that were previously segregated. Julie expressed this by saying, "Believe it or not, right now my career is my recreation—I really enjoy it. And as I've said, I've begun to think of my clients as my friends, and my friends as my clients." People in the Utilitarian quadrant take a lot of responsibility for directing their own career, and they are confident that they can do so successfully whether working within or outside of an organization.

People representing the **Mindful quadrant** were more introspective after losing their job and the experience changed some
of their assumptions about themselves and their values. However,
they were less inclined to change their assumptions about the psychological contract between organizations and workers. Fred
exemplifies the Mindful response. He has an MBA, but it took him
a long time to find a new job in his field. His former employer, a
large hospital corporation, sent him to Singapore to set up a data
processing center. The company was caught up in a leveraged buy-
out just before his return to the United States. When he got home
he found out that his entire division had been eliminated—along
with his job. His wife, who had stayed in Singapore with their two
children so they could finish the school year, asked for a divorce a
few months after he lost his job. Consequently, Fred's transition
problems were compounded by this double loss and it took him a
while to recover emotionally. For five years he worked as a custo-
dian for his church and a house painter, while continuing to search
for a job in his profession. He said, "I remember painting a house,
standing on a ladder in ninety-six-degree weather with the sun
beating down on me and I'd think to myself, 'Boy—glad I spent
that money getting an MBA.' That was very difficult. It was a very
humbling experience. It's given me a whole new perspective on
hourly workers and other people. I now go out of my way to say
something nice to the guys who are working on the lawn, the guys
who are picking up trash."

During this time Fred went to counseling and also became
much stronger in his spiritual faith. He experienced much personal growth. However, he did not really change his assumptions
about work. Several months before our interview Fred turned fifty.
He had told himself that if he did not have another job by the end
of that year, he would just accept the fact that he was not going to
be employed professionally again. Fred finally found a new job in
his field in December and I interviewed him about three months
later. He is thrilled with his job and this is what he said about it:

> I told my boss that one of the reasons I'm interested in this job is
> because number one, you're not going to get acquired, and num-
> ber two, you're not going to go out of business. So there's security
> here. At the time I debated whether it was a stupid thing to say or a
> smart thing to say. Now that I've been working here for three

months I think it was a smart thing to say. I told him I was looking for a place to work where I could retire, and he said that's what he was looking for—someone who had that commitment.

I hope Fred is right and that he will be able to retire with his new organization, but as you can see his transition process did not seem to result in questioning his prior assumptions about the psychological contract and work.

One of the questions I asked people was how they would rank what is most important in their life among career, family, friends, community service, recreation, and spirituality. For many, the importance they placed on their career dropped after losing their job. Many also placed a greater priority on their family, friends, and spirituality after their job loss. When people lose their jobs, their career is apt to recede into the background while other parts of their lives come forward. The importance of the career does not disappear, it merely becomes smaller relative to those things that seem more enduring such as family, friends, or faith.

In some cases job loss created greater clarity, rather than a change, of values and priorities. Several people had ethical issues or a clash of values with the organization they left and they plan to screen more carefully along these lines for future positions: "I now know where most of my values are, though they're not bound in concrete. But knowing that, I've decided that I would rather not give someone else control over my values unless I choose to give it to them."

Bonnie, who felt so betrayed by her job loss, talked about struggling with her values and her anger toward the company:

I was in the middle of a project and my supervisor wanted me to write a report so she could take over. Part of that was the struggle of, how am I going to choose to leave this company? Am I going to wipe all the stuff off the computer? Am I going to blow off the report? It was my values. I was mad at them, I felt betrayed, but I took the high road—which is truly the only thing I could do. I wrote the report and told her everything I knew. I left everything on the computer and turned in all the equipment. I did what I had to do for me. It had nothing to do with her or the company. The wonderful part of doing ethically what I needed to do for me was that she had everything she needed and still couldn't figure out what to do!

Some might wonder whether a lack of loyalty between organizations and their employees will cause employees to abandon any ethical behavior toward the company. I did not find this to be true among the people I spoke with. Like Bonnie, they chose to be loyal to themselves and in doing so they maintained high ethical standards to preserve their own self-respect.

Not only did people change or clarify their values, they also changed some assumptions about themselves. Many learned to separate their identity from their work role. This is what Matt referred to when he said, "I had to come to the realization of who I was, and that there's a difference between who I am and what I do." Bonnie echoed a similar sentiment when she said, "My job is important to me and doing a good job is important to me. It's certainly more than what I do for money, but it is not who I am."

In separating themselves from their work, many discovered new aspects of themselves so that their self-esteem and self-image no longer hinged solely on their work performance. After losing her job, Cheryl (the former bank vice president) lost weight, took up tennis and cooking, and had cosmetic work done on her teeth. All of this was to improve her self-image: "Leaving your job after you worked as hard as I had is terrible on your self-image." Cheryl talked about another friend, who left the bank without separating her identity from her work: "One of my friends, who left the bank because she basically didn't like the way they were treating people, now has her own company. She's very successful, but she's working too hard and traveling too much. I said to her, 'Why are you doing this? One of the reasons you left is to have more time for yourself.' She said, 'I want to know where you're getting your self-image when you're not working.'"

Part of the new source of self-esteem may be from an increased sense of authenticity. Sara described this very clearly when she said, "My voice has gotten stronger, I have a truer sense of who I am as an individual, and where my songs are going—it's almost as if I had to go through this little war to find a bigger path." I think it also may come from having a more multifaceted sense of self so that you are drawing your self-esteem from more sources, like drawing water from several wells. Several said that because their sense of self became more broadly based, they felt more balanced.

People representing both the Mindful and Transformational quadrants found that their job loss triggered introspection and self-examination. Many changed or clarified their values, and increased the priority that they placed on family, friends, and faith. They also acquired a more multifaceted sense of self, greater authenticity, and a distinction between themselves and their work role.

People representing the **Fortified quadrant** seemed to change few assumptions as a result of their job loss. They also did not feel better off at the time that I spoke with them. For instance, Will was looking for a job very much like what he'd had before and had a hard time imagining himself doing anything different. Unlike Cheryl, who became a part-time chief financial officer for several smaller companies, Will's attitude was, "What would get my life back to normal is if I had a job, whatever that job may be." However, Will's experience has dispelled his belief that "it can't happen to me": "I think it's brought home that jobs are very transitory. Although I felt that I was being professionally challenged and contributing, out of the blue I'm no longer employed. It says that can happen. One day I was talking with a fellow who's president of a very large corporation, and he said 'It isn't a matter of *if* you get fired, it's *when* you get fired.' I think the higher you are in the organization, the more true that is. So that's kinda come home to me."

Will seemed guarded, but he did not come across as defensive. To his credit, talking about his job loss was uncomfortable for him and I think he did his best to respond to my questions honestly. But clearly, this was a topic that he did not discuss with many people—including his friends or his wife. Because Will could not picture himself doing anything other than what he had done before, he seemed to lack a certain cognitive flexibility, or perhaps it is simply imagination. Some of the people I spoke with felt boxed in by the organization and once they left, they experienced a sense of freedom and a lot of growth. But Will carried the box with him in terms of imaginative and emotional constriction.

For people representing the Fortified quadrant, losing their job did not lead to personal change or changes in how they view the new employment contract. These people tended to respond to their difficult situation by *steeling* themselves. This is a way of defending yourself from threatening situations that was described in early research on resilience by the term *invulnerable*.

Much of the research on resilience has been on children who are able to function in a healthy way despite very aversive conditions such as abuse, poverty, or a mentally ill parent. In the 1970s these children were called Invulnerables. The analogy was made that you could line up three dolls—one made of glass, one made of plastic, and one made of steel—and give each doll the same blow from a hammer. When exposed to the same risk the glass doll breaks down completely, the plastic doll carries a permanent dent, and the steel doll merely lets out a metallic sound.[4] The children who were compared to the steel doll were called Invulnerables and considered to have extremely tough constitutions. They seemed to have an outer, protective layer that provided buffering—a sort of protective shield against the world. This buffering is important, but the danger is that it will rigidify over time. When it becomes like a protective coat of armor that is worn by adults all the time in all circumstances, then it can get in the way.

Today most researchers use the term *resilience* because invulnerable implies a fixed quality. Resilience is more akin to buoyancy or elasticity. Whereas a steel doll serves to illustrate invulnerability, a rubber doll more aptly illustrates resilience. As adults, our resilience actually varies with different times and circumstances. Sometimes steeling yourself is necessary, but often yielding is a more adaptive response. People who are resolutely invulnerable or impermeable close themselves off to emotional vulnerability, and it is emotional vulnerability that fosters relationships.

The people I interviewed who represent the **Transformational quadrant** appeared to have an unusually high capacity for cultivating both intimate and professional relationships. They also demonstrated a fluid, rather than fixed, response. They opened themselves to the experience and the accompanying pain or discomfort and consequently they learned from it. Thus I would say that all the people I interviewed were resilient to some extent, but not everyone experienced transformative change. Those who did combined both the Utilitarian and Mindful responses by radically changing both their relationship to their work and their sense of self. They now seem to be comfortable with who they are and feel the best about where they are. They appear to have an inner compass that directs them despite changes in their environment. These people may be the real scouts as we try to understand how to best navigate our careers and our lives in the information age.

## Chapter Ten

# Transition or Transformation?

*Only birth can conquer death—the birth, not of the old
thing again, but of something new. Within the soul,
within the body social, there must be—if we are to
experience long survival—a continuous "recurrence of
birth"* . . . *to nullify the unremitting recurrences of death.*
—JOSEPH CAMPBELL[1]

Everyone who loses a job goes through a transition. It is impossible to avoid. We go through transitions throughout our life; they accompany the passage of time. Transitions always involve a loss. Something must be left behind in order to usher in something new. This is why endings and beginnings are two sides of the same coin—you can't have one without the other. An ending is a beginning, and a beginning is an ending. Sometimes the span of time between the ending and beginning is long and sometimes it is instantaneous.

But transformation is something else again. We can go through life without experiencing a transformation. Transformation is associated with radical change. The word *transformation* means movement across or through forms. It is a more mysterious and less linear process than transition. It is quite a different experience from the typical developmental changes we go through when we grow taller or lose our hair. A common symbol of transformation is the butterfly. The butterfly is also a symbol of the human soul.

In ancient Greece the word for soul was *psyche,* and it was often imaged as a butterfly. Butterflies are born out of a transformation that occurs within the protection of the cocoon. Once the caterpillar spins its cocoon it begins a transformative process where most of its organs literally dissolve, so that if we were to cut the cocoon open at this critical stage we would see something that looks more like protoplasm. The fluids eventually come together to form the tiny wings, eyes, and muscles of the butterfly. When it emerges from its cocoon the new butterfly can spread its beautiful wings and fly where before it could only crawl. The transformation, however, is not the butterfly itself but that magical and mysterious time between forms.

The Greeks had two different words for time: *chronos,* the linear passage of time as measured by a clock, and *kairos,* or meaning-filled time. Meaning-filled time often demarcates a significant "before" and "after," such as before Christ and after Christ, or before and after the birth of a child. Chronos time is time as we know it; it cuts a horizontal plane through life. Kairos time is time in its depth dimension. It takes us beyond linear time toward the transcendent and eternal and toward that which endures. It cuts a vertical plane through life, and connects us with our spirit and soul. The significant crossings in our life are when both kinds of time cross. At one level we experience the loss we are leaving behind, and usually we come to terms with this loss through the passage of time. At another level, we become like a vessel that has all kinds of energy pouring into it. This is archetypal energy that is beyond our particular experience. We have a heightened sensitivity and awareness that is often accompanied by dreams, new images, and coincidental experiences. We are apt to feel anxiety, fear, rage, passion, and excitement. This does not feel like a neutral time—it is often disturbing, chaotic, and intense. We may feel as though we are cracking up. But some kind of a crack is necessary to create the opening for this depth experience.

It is easy to become frightened, to clamp the lid shut, hunker down, and march forward. This is the conventional path. Creating a hermetic seal around ourselves cuts us off from this new energy. It may feel more safe. But a safe is also a locked container and the danger is that we end up locking ourself outside of our Self. Jung used the word Self to describe a larger spiritual connection, a vital potentiality. When we cut ourselves off from this we eventually reach a dead end, and this is when life feels empty and meaningless. The transformative response is to open ourselves to the discomfort and surrender to the experience. Jung said that the path to individuation is one in which many are called but few are chosen. The choice, however, is ours to make. Can we hold the tension at the crossing until our life transforms into something new?

All the people I interviewed lost their jobs, and for the most part it was not by choice. When describing the process of job loss and transition, most of the models are a derivation of the work of Elisabeth Kübler-Ross. Kübler-Ross made an enormous contribution to our understanding of grief and loss through her research on terminally ill people and their families. She found that when coming to terms with loss most people pass through the stages of denial and isolation, anger, bargaining, depression, and acceptance.[2] Although Kübler-Ross's original work was about death and dying, her model has been applied to most losses or changes that we face in life, including divorce or loss of a job. This model mainly describes the emotions involved with the process. The people I spoke with did not necessarily fit this model. They may have experienced these various emotions, but it was not very evident that they shared a common emotional process. What was more evident is that in all cases their job loss caused them to question previous assumptions.

Ironically, the word assumption shares linguistic roots with the Latin word *sumptus,* which means to undertake by choice. Yet many of our assumptions are formed without any conscious awareness. Most of our assumptions are tacit, or hidden below the surface. We form our assumptions from our experiences and from what we are told. As children we learn by turning our experiences into stories. As we grow and learn we catalogue these stories into the gist of the story, or scripts. For instance, we may have a script about how to behave in a restaurant, or how to act with a new boss. Scripts provide us with a basis for automatic behavior so that we can function in the world without thinking about every little experience that comes our way. Our world becomes increasingly familiar and more predictable. Block by block we combine our assumptions and our scripts to build what Murray Parks calls our assumptive world.[3] Our assumptive world is created by all of our assumptions from our past experiences as well as our expectations for the future. It is the only world we know and includes everything we know or think we know. It is also unique to our experience and cannot really be known by another person.

An unexpected change or loss feels like pulling blocks out of the foundation of our assumptive world, and it can create a sense of collapse and meaninglessness. Job loss often triggers such a collapse. It calls into question our source of money and security and the familiar structure of our daily life, and may signal the loss of a cluster of hopes and expectations about our future. One reason why looking for a new job can be exhausting is because as we anticipate the new job we recreate a new set of hopes and expectations, and then if the job does not come through we experience another loss. A job search involves a continuous collapse and rebuilding of our assumptive world until we reach a new point of stability.

James Fowler, a theologian and educator, refers to "*Homo Poeta,* man the meaningmaker, the singular animal burdened with the challenge of composing a meaningful world."[4] With the collapse of our assumptive world comes a loss of meaning. Old assumptions no longer make sense and it feels as though we have lost our bearings. Meaning is the crucial organizing principle of our behavior. It links our feelings, intentions, and expectations, and gives us reasons for taking action. We cannot act without interpreting what is going on around us and predicting what we think might happen. We interpret our experience by matching it to something familiar. Each discovery is the basis for the next, until a series of interpretations gradually consolidates into an understanding of life. Karl Weick calls the loss of meaning a *cosmology episode*: "A cosmology episode is when people suddenly and deeply feel that the universe is no longer a rational, orderly system. What makes such an episode so shattering is that both the sense of what is occurring and the means to rebuild that sense collapse together. Stated more informally, a cosmology episode feels like vu jadé—the opposite of déja vu: I've never been here before, I have no idea where I am, and no idea who can help me."[5]

Peter Marris believes that the process of loss and change essentially involves the loss and recreation of meaning.[6] His original research was based on studying bereaved widows. He found that we become attached to the people or things or circumstances that make our life meaningful and losing these attachments provokes grief. An interesting point is that the intensity of the grief mainly relates to the intensity of involvement, and not to love or satisfaction. In other words, widows grieved the loss of an unhappy marriage just as much as a happy one because in either case it provided the organizing structure for their lives. This is why losing a job that we do not like can be just as distressing as losing a job that we love. Whether a job makes us happy or miserable, its loss can collapse the meaning system that we rest our lives upon.

This reminds me of something Doris said about how she felt after losing her job. Doris is the former café manager who was so surprised by her job loss. Even though she had not been happy in her work situation during the last few years, and even though she eventually felt "a tremendous load" lifted after some time had passed, immediately afterward she found herself automatically driving to the parking lot if she was not thinking. I asked her if she felt more of a sense of loss or change right after losing her job and she said, "For me it was loss—the biggest was loss. Because it was in all areas . . . to work that many hours and feel that sense of commitment, you're there too much. I mean, I would be driving and forget what I was doing and I would wind up in that parking lot. I'd driven it so many days and so many nights—if I wasn't paying attention my car would just go there. So that is a big loss."

The point is not to avoid attachments, but to realize that loss of our attachments triggers grief and loss of meaning. We love particular people and places and kinds of work. Failing to make enduring attachments creates underlying yearning, loneliness, or doubt about who we are. Yet when we lose these attachments, we can end up in this same place. We may turn our grief inward by becoming apathetic, depressed, cynical, or guilty. Marris believes that when we experience loss, it is very important to feel our grief and to bring important parts of our past forward: "People who compensate with busyness and don't grieve seem hollow. They appear to've found new purposes, but they're not rooted in the past and represent a disintegration of identity more lastingly damaging than the painful retrieval of purpose from the wreck of dead hopes."[7] The process of reformulating meaning takes time. We must leave some things behind and carry other things forward. We can move forward with renewed purpose and hope only after we reweave strands of meaning from our past, present, and future. In doing so we reconstruct an assumptive world that is usually larger than what we had before. This is conveyed by the Native American saying: "We are an old people, we are a new people, we are the same people—only deeper than before."

Transition, then, involves the loss and recovery of meaning. It is both an emotional and cognitive process. Our very survival is thrown into doubt because life has lost its predictability. If we think of our assumptive world as the framework of the house where we live, then it is as if a portion of that framework collapses and must be rebuilt. Some of the people I interviewed made only slight alterations as they made the transition away from their old job toward something new. But some of the people built an entirely different house. These are the people who had a Transformative response.

Transformation also involves questions of meaning, but in these cases the meaning becomes linked to something larger than the individual's particular experiences. It is a deeply inward process. When we go deeply inward, we get in touch with thoughts, feelings, or images that are part of our basic, shared humanity. This is like an underground stream that we all can access. When we do so, the deeply personal becomes universal. This connection is revealed in a story of the Hindu god, Krishna. One day when he was an infant his mother—who did not realize that he was a god—took him to the beach to play. Like any typical two-year-old, Krishna ate some sand. But when his mother looked into his mouth to wipe out the sand, she saw the entire universe.

As I mentioned, myths are stories of our search through the ages for meaning, truth, and significance. Joseph Campbell spent his life studying the myths of all cultures and showed us how much they have in common. This is because mythology accesses this common stream and uses images, which Jung called *archetypes*. Archetypes are basic patterns or elementary ideas that show up in all cultures even though they may be wearing different guises. For instance, Mother and Father are two archetypes. When people think of the archetypal Mother, Christians may think of a loving Virgin Mary, whereas Hindus may think of the destroying Mother Kali, and Greeks would have thought of Demeter, Mother Nature. The different costumes worn by archetypes result from different historical and environmental conditions.

Archetypes carry an energy and power that is bigger than we are, and this is why it is important to pay attention to our own images and dreams during important crossings. Images come to us as gifts, and we use them to create our own myth. Archetypes link us to the mystery of life, and in doing so they provide us with energy for renewal and transformation. When we are cut off from this energy, life loses its mystery and a spiritual aridity sets in. Campbell said that at their deepest level, archetypal myths offer us the experience of being alive: "Mythology *is* the song. It is the song of the imagination, inspired by energies of the body . . . myths are metaphorical of spiritual potentiality in the human being, and the same powers that animate our life animate the life of the world."[8]

By linking what is most intensely personal to what is universal, myths help us to see things from a new perspective: "Thinking in mythological terms helps to put you in accord with the inevitables of this vale of tears. You learn to recognize the positive values in what appear to be the negative moments and aspects of your life. The big question is whether you are going to be able to say a hearty yes to your adventure."[9] Stepping into a mythological perspective helps us to put our travails, including job loss, into a different and larger perspective.

As I thought about the people who had a Transformative response, I realized that they were on the hero's journey. This is not an interpretation that I had preconceived. It only came to me after spending many hours thinking about the stories I heard. The journey metaphor is used in all cultures to describe life and the quest for meaning, and probably the best-known journey motif is the hero's journey. The hero's journey always involves departure, initiation, and return.

The hero's journey reminds us that many heroes have come before us, so we need not travel this path alone. The basic motif of the hero's journey is leaving one condition and touching the divine or supernatural, which brings forth a richer or more mature condition. In *The Hero with a Thousand Faces,* Campbell recites numerous stories and myths from different cultures that express this universal idea. The hero's quest involves leaving the familiar world to go to a depth or distance, encountering a source of power and learning a fundamental Truth, and then returning to the world with this new learning. It always involves a wounding, but because of this hole the hero is made whole and discovers what was missing in his or her previous world. Remember the CEO's dream that was described at the beginning of Chapter One? For him, leaving his job was like jumping into unknown waters. Water is an archetype for the unconscious and emotional realm. It often appears in fairy tales and myths as representing an unfamiliar but powerful place, such as the sea where Jonah was swallowed by the whale. Usually the biggest challenge for the hero is returning to the world he or she used to inhabit and trying to hold on to what was learned.

One example of the hero's journey from classical Greek mythology is the story of Persephone. Persephone is the goddess of the underworld. She was the daughter of Zeus, Father god of the sky, and Demeter, Mother goddess of the earth. As a maiden goddess Persephone was light-hearted and naive. One day she and her nymphs were picking flowers in a meadow. Persephone strayed from her companions, reached for a beautiful narcissus, and the earth split open. Out of a dark chasm came Hades in his chariot. He abducted her and carried her back into the underworld to be his bride. Demeter was distraught by the loss of her only daughter. The earth became dry and lifeless while she searched and grieved. Eventually the state of the earth became so catastrophic that Zeus ordered Hades to bring Persephone back to her mother. However, while in the underworld Persephone had broken a fast by eating a pomegranate seed and this was enough to tie her to the underworld forever. Zeus struck a compromise with Hades: Persephone could return to her mother if she spent four months of every year in the underworld.

When Persephone returned, Demeter became so joyful that the earth broke into abundance and flowers and life. However, Persephone was not the same carefree maiden of her earlier days: "After the lord of the dark world below carried her away she was never again the gay young creature who had played in the flowery meadow without a thought of care or trouble. She did indeed rise from the dead every spring, but she brought with her the memory of where she had come from; with all her bright beauty there was something strange and awesome about her."[10]

This myth represents the yearly passage of the seasons. Winter is the time when Persephone is in the underworld, and spring marks her yearly return. It contains the universal elements of the heroic tale because Persephone experiences a departure (abduction), initiation (marriage to Hades), and return. Similarly, many of the people I interviewed had the experience of departure (losing their jobs), initiation (a dark time), and return to a stronger sense of self.

Persephone's abduction came as a complete surprise to her. It was more than a surprise—it was a shock! In *The Goddess Letters,* Carol Orlock gives us a lyrical and imaginative treatment of this myth through letters between Persephone and Demeter. Persephone begins her correspondence from the underworld to her mother with: "This can't be earth. Or Mount Olympus either. I'm not sure where I am any more, if I'm anywhere at all, or even if I'm Persephone any more. I dream of warm wind and fire, then I wake up all cold and shivering."[11] Persephone is lost. Similarly when people involuntarily lose their jobs there is often an initial sense of loss and of *being lost.*

In myths, the adventure frequently begins with a blunder or surprise that reveals an unsuspected world. Campbell said that these surprises are "ripples on the surface of life, produced by unsuspected springs. And these may be very deep—as deep as the soul itself."[12] More literally, James Hillman wrote of the *ha-ha.* In the 18th-century, ha-ha's were surprising sunken fences, hidden hedge, or boundary ditches. While walking it was easy to fall into one of these, bringing forth a "ha ha" that stopped your progression, thus "forcing the foot to turn and the mind to reflect."[13] While in the underworld, Persephone spent a great deal of time reflecting, and through her correspondence she shows a growing wisdom.

In the hero's journey, the accident or surprise that reveals a new world is considered to be "the call." Something breaks suddenly into our life and disrupts our normal pattern. The word *vocation* actually comes from the Latin word *vocatio,* which means "calling." Jung believed that many of us receive such a calling at midlife and that it marks the beginning of a second adulthood that is more attuned with our true self. Sometimes when we stumble, we end up falling into our calling. It is not so much that we have chosen our vocation but that our vocation has chosen us, and it may have nothing to do with how we earn money. Our choice is in how we respond. Refusing to answer the call can damage the soul. It turns the adventure into a negative. Campbell said that when the hero refuses to answer the call, "His flowering world becomes a wasteland of dry stones and his life feels meaningless—even though, like King Minos, he may through titanic effort succeed in building a empire of renown."[14]

Sometimes the call sneaks up on us quietly and sometimes it clobbers us over the head. Persephone got clobbered, and I believe that involuntary job loss may feel the same way. Answering the call means opening to the experience. Most profoundly, it means opening to death. Persephone's journey is really about the life-death-life cycle. This cycle is fundamental to transformation. Symbolically death is not an end, but it signals a profound change. The Land of the Dead represents the inner world of the soul, and the deepest meaning of death is transformation.

Involuntary job loss does involve death. Often we experience a death of our identity. Like Persephone, many also experience a death of their naïveté around the notion that "it can't happen to me." Further, many of us experience a death of the myth we were living. This is the myth that was largely lived by our fathers—the belief that hard work and loyalty will result in job security. The important point, however, is to face these deaths rather than deny them. Denial is what leads to a dead end.

As the hero moves from one world into the next, he or she must always cross a border. In Persephone's case, she was snatched and carried across. Often the hero stands on the edge of a forest, lake, or cave, wavering about moving forward into the darkness. Another word for "border" is the Latin *limen*. A *limen* is a doorway or threshold. The word liminality is used to describe the psychological state of being in this borderline place. Liminality occurs "when the ego is separated from a fixed sense of who it is and has been, of where it comes from and its history, of where it is going and its future; when the ego floats through ambiguous spaces in a sense of unbounded time, through territory of unclear boundaries and uncertain edges; when it is disidentified from the inner images that have formerly sustained it and given it a sense of purpose."[15]

When we lose our job we cross a border. We often feel unmoored, floating. Usually this is a border we did not expect or want to cross. I had this experience myself. In 1990 I received a large consulting contract that was expected to last for three to four years. It seemed both stable and flexible, so I thought it would be a good time to return to school and pursue my doctorate. But about a year into the project and into my doctorate, my marriage fell apart. A few months later this project that I now counted on for my sole income was surprisingly and abruptly canceled. These losses came so close together that it felt like a tornado had swept away the structure of my life and that I was left standing alone on the sidewalk. I had an enormous sense of being unrooted. I felt like the old Skittles game that I used to play as a child, like a top rapidly and randomly skimming across the surface in all directions. There were so many decisions to make that I became paralyzed, unable to make any decisions at all. I couldn't even order from a menu at a restaurant—which is not typically a problem for me! I realized how easily I moved into a sense of complacency about my work, and that losing a large contract that I counted on was much like losing a job. This double loss pushed me over the border, into a time of liminality. Yet Campbell tells us that mythically passing over a boundary is when the adventure begins: "You get into a field that's unprotected, novel. You can't have creativity unless you leave behind the bounded, the fixed, all the rules."[16] When job loss takes us across and outside of the organizational threshold, we move beyond the box. As Debra mentioned, we may discover a world that is *much more* than we ever imagined.

What distinguished the people who had a Transformative response is that they consciously crossed this border and stepped into the unknown. They stepped into the void. This involves a certain surrender because the outcome is unknown. For a while we must abandon our former identity and live with questions that do not have any answers. All we can do is trust. A journey through the wilderness is an archetypal experience. It is associated with the hero's journey because those who undergo a dark, painful journey are also those who experience marked psychological development. But suffering in itself does not lead to development. It is important to have the right attitude toward it, and that attitude is psychological honesty. This is the same point that Matt emphasized when I asked him why he thought some people bounce back from job loss better than others. He said, "Your ability to be honest with yourself because I've got to say that I was ultimately responsible for my job loss—no one else was—it's whether or not they can be honest with themselves about what happened."

Learning to trust the life-death-life cycle moves us out of fear and into meaning. By struggling with the mystery of death—in all its manifestations—we discover the meaning of our life. Many people in our culture insulate themselves from death in all its forms and consequently inhabit a world of quiet despair. Like Charles Kane in the movie *Citizen Kane,* we create well-defended castles around ourselves that let us feel secure but ultimately become our prisons. Living within the castle results in loneliness, anxiety, and depression. Especially in our work lives, many of us connect to others through small and remote windows and feel safe revealing only a sliver of ourselves. The only way out of the castle is to "die voluntarily" so that a new life can be born that is more creatively linked to something larger than itself. The ego moves over and allows for the birth of the Self. In terms of dimension, the ego is to the Self as the earth is to the sun.

From a mythic perspective, involuntary job loss opens us to the possibility of finding meaning through the hero's journey. We stumble across a ha-ha and are brought face to face with the myth we have been living. The journey is not easy or comfortable, but ultimately it has the potential to infuse our life with new meaning. We may come out of our castles and discover our souls. We must remember that the mythic world and our own world are actually the same. Myths use archetypal images to help us touch the divine. If only for a moment, they take us away from worrying about how to pay the bills and lead us back to our soul.

Just before he died in 1961, Jung—who may be the world's most influential psychiatrist—said that he believed he failed in his life's mission. He believed that the message he was meant to convey is that people have a soul and that we have lost touch with it. But we do not need to retreat to the mountain top to find it. The world of myth and spirit is right here. As Van said: "The spirit of God can really be found in a few saints and common people . . . people who get up in the morning and care for their children and work hard and love their wives and husbands." Martin Buber called this "the hallowing of the everyday." It is a stubborn affection for finding Spirit in ordinary life.

In the following chapters I will describe what people in the Transformative quadrant have in common. This includes a network of relationships, a shapeshifting ability, and a synergistic combination of faith, hope, and imagination. Because we are dealing with transformative change, I will begin each chapter with a story that brings us back to this mythic perspective.

## Chapter Eleven

# Relationships

*How should we be able to forget those ancient myths that
are at the beginning of all peoples, the myths about
dragons that at the last moment turn into princesses;
perhaps all the dragons of our lives are princesses who are
only waiting to see us once beautiful and brave. Perhaps
everything terrible is in its deepest being something helpless
that wants help from us.*
—Rainier Maria Rilke[1]

Before the caterpillar moves into its transformative time, it spins a
cocoon. The cocoon is a sort of tough second skin that provides
protection. It also serves as a container. Transformative change
requires something to protect it and to hold it so that the magic
can do its work. The strongest theme revealed among the people
who experienced transformative change is the degree to which
relationships can provide this important holding function.

The Hindu myth about Krishna and Mount Govardhana shows
the importance of a protective canopy in making a safe transition
from one worldview to another. It involves the Hindu concept of
*bhakti,* which stresses personal and affectionate relationships
between people and the divine. In this story, the youthful Krishna
came across some shepherds preparing to give homage to Indra,
lord of thunder. Krishna suggested that rather than worshiping
Indra, they should worship Mount Govardhana since it provided
nourishment for their herds, and that they should worship the
herds themselves since they provided milk for the shepherds. Indra

was infuriated by this because Krishna was interfering with sacrifices Indra regarded as his due. If the shepherds failed to make the sacrifices, Indra would lose power as a vital spiritual force. Indra therefore decided to drown the shepherds and their cattle by creating a terrible storm of thunder and rain. However, Krishna uprooted Mount Govardhana and held it up with one finger as a giant canopy, protecting the shepherds and their herds. The storm continued for seven days and seven nights, until Indra finally gave up and removed the clouds from the sky. He was so impressed by this encounter that afterward he came down from the sky with his wife and both asked Krishna to befriend their son.

Indra represents the old social order, which is characterized by an absolute and authoritarian power. This story is about the transition from the worship of Indra to that of Krishna, who represents compassion and human relatedness. The transition comes about smoothly because Krishna has enough vitality and power to protect the people and to supplant the old god. Krishna shows that the divine is capable of love and affection.[2]

Krishna initially challenged the shepherds to consider the real source of their nourishment. The people I talked with who experienced transformative change found that relationships provided a more enduring source of nourishment than their job. For many, their net of relationships—both personal and professional—served as the holding container for their transformation. In *The Space Between Us*, Ruthellen Josselson paints a very vivid picture of holding as the most primary human need: "Of all the ways in which people need each other, holding is the most primary, the least evident, and the hardest to describe. Holding contains the invisible threads that tie us to our existence. From the first moments of life to the last, we need to be held—or we fall."[3]

The sense of being held takes us back to our earliest experiences as babies. It is the sense that someone has their arms around us and that we are safe. One time when my niece was about a year old we were sitting on a bed and suddenly she rolled right off of it. First she was startled (so was I!), then she was afraid and started to cry. I picked her up and encircled her in my arms and I could feel her little body relax. This is the experience of holding. The degree to which we feel held as infants influences how we feel supported as adults.

Falling is one of the most terrifying sensations. One person I spoke with told me that after she left her job, she initially felt exhilaration, freedom, and euphoria—but this was followed by a decline: "It was like I let go of the vine and was in free fall. Where was I going? I had nothing to hang onto. Basically I had to learn to live with that feeling of free fall all the time." She told me that what helped her get through this time were two older women who were both her close friends and mentors. It is this sense of support from others that keeps us from falling too far. We feel supported when we believe that someone believes in us, that someone will *be there* for us. Sometimes it is a family member—a parent or spouse, or a long-term friend. But sometimes someone appears on the scene at the critical moment and offers just the right words to give us courage. When no one is around, even a memory, a place, or a reassuring phrase can provide this holding function.

The kind of holding I am referring to is like the protective container of a cocoon. Yet paradoxically, all transitions also require letting go. The analogy of a trapeze artist can be applied to losing or leaving your job, or to any transition. We have to let go of the bar, or whatever we are holding on to, and then there is a moment of suspension before the next bar comes toward us. To let go we need to trust that the other bar will swing our way. But if I really think about swinging on a trapeze—which I've never done—for me the *net* would be the critical factor. It would be much easier for me to let go if I knew that a net was below that would catch me should I fall. Then even if the other bar does not come, or comes too late, or I'm not able to grasp it, the results would not be catastrophic. The fall might be embarrassing, but would not lead to permanent crippling. Fear of falling is what often keeps people from leaving bad situations. Many people who have not lost their jobs fear that being downsized or surplused would be humiliating. People hold on because they are afraid they will be mortified. Mortification comes from the Latin word *mors,* which means death. Some people hold on tighter and work harder to keep their fear of death at bay. This is the death of their public persona or identity.

Recently I had an interesting conversation with a woman on a plane. She used to work at a managerial level for AT&T and I asked her about people she knew who had lost their jobs. She told me a story about a former manager who was not doing well. As downsizing spread throughout the company, creating more and more insecurity for those who were there, this manager's fears constellated around a fear of flying. One time he was at a meeting in Detroit with my seatmate and several others, who all needed to get back to Cincinnati. He suggested that they just rent a car and drive. Everyone else said, "No way!" The others took a short flight but this man rented a car and spent hours driving home. Eventually he did lose his job and now, several years later, he still has a lot of bitterness toward the company. I thought about fear of flying as a metaphor. At night when we dream about flying it often connotes a real sense of freedom. But a fear of flying means that the focus is on the crash. It is a fear of crashing, and dying. I think this man had an impending sense of death that was accurate on one level, because he did lose his job. Yet he also clings desperately to his old identity and refuses to let it die so that it can be reborn to something new. By bitterly clinging to his past he is forfeiting his present and perhaps his future. His fear of death has brought him to a dead end.

People who experienced transformative change after losing their job had less fear about dying to parts of their past. They probably felt safer. Both the men and the women had constructed a net of support that provided buffering. Prior to beginning this research, I would have guessed that during hard times women would rely on relationships more than men. But this was not true among the people I interviewed. Both men and women talked about how much their family, friends, and professional contacts helped them through this time. The men who experienced transformative change placed just as great an emphasis on this as did the women. For instance Matt commented, "If it hadn't been for my relationships there's no way I could've made the transition."

Freud noted that we all need to have a certain amount of buffering to protect us from the constant bombardment of stimuli in our environment. Children who seem "thick-skinned" are usually more resilient to adversity. Those who seem "thin-skinned" are more sensitive to stimuli; they literally feel what goes on around them more acutely, as if there were more nerve endings on the outside of their skin. Of course, adults have these differences as well. Those of us who were not born with a thick skin can compensate by buffering ourselves through the support of others. This provides a sort of net or container where we feel safe and can relax. The amount of support that people need varies, but it is important in all cases and especially during difficult times. The people I talked with who felt the best about their job loss and transition experience all talked a great deal about how important their relationships are to them. As I mentioned, this was as true for the men as the women. The only difference is that the men were more apt to come to this realization during the course of their transition.

This issue about relationships suggests a chicken-and-egg question: Are people resilient because they have good relationships or does having good relationships make people resilient? In her book *Resilient Adults,* Gina O'Connell Higgins describes her research with forty people who had very difficult childhoods but grew into adults who love well and work well. She did find that throughout their lives, despite the most oppressive or abusive conditions, these people all had a "homing device for good relationships."[4] They had the ability to find and attract good people into their lives, and as children many were taken under the wing of a surrogate parent or teacher.

George Vaillant, director of the Study of Adult Development at the Harvard Medical School, has also found that relationships, or social support, are an important component of resilience throughout our lifetime. His work is based on longitudinal studies that have followed selected groups of people for a fifty-year span of time. Vaillant stresses the importance of being vulnerable enough to let the hope, strength, and experience of others inside. He also stresses the importance of reciprocity, of giving and taking in relationships, and compares this to breathing: "Inspiration . . . is a metaphor for the way ego strength is acquired—by taking people inside."[5] I noticed this reciprocity among the people who experienced transformative change. They realized that it is important to put time and energy into relationships as well as allowing them to provide support. Especially among the men, they placed a greater priority on their family and friends after their job loss and transition than they had before.

Both Higgins and Vaillant point out that resilience is not simply something that we are born with; it can be cultivated and learned throughout our lifetime. It is a combination of attitudes and skills that help us to heal and bounce back from adversity. The ability to form and maintain relationships is clearly an important skill that contributes to resilience.

I would like to point out that while seeking people to interview, I did not pay any attention to whether they were married, single, or divorced. It turned out that at the time I spoke with them, most of the men I interviewed were married while most of the women were not. Yet more important than a person's marital status was the quality of relationships that they cultivated around them. For instance, Cheryl said, "I have incredibly wonderful friends. And not really having a family with children, my friends have been my family for most of my adult life. They really were great to me when I lost my job. My friends are very very important in my life." Those who were married received a lot of support from their spouse: "My wife, she really kept me pumped up. I don't think there was a doubt in her mind that I would find something better and pull through and it was going to be all for the better."

Let me remind you that the people I interviewed were not a random group. Job loss often precipitates marital discord or divorce and for those who are sole breadwinners, a family inevitably adds pressure. I spoke with professionals who were characterized as resilient in the face of their job loss. Those who experienced the most transformative change had a strong support network built around them before they lost their jobs, and they maintained or strengthened this network during the transition and afterward.

A few people did not have such a support system in place, and the men who were divorced probably had the least. Both the men and women who lived alone mentioned that loneliness made the process more difficult. However, the women were more likely to have someone to call. Several mentioned that they realized the importance of friends or family from an earlier difficult time, most often a divorce: "I think through my divorce I realized how important friends are—that you can't count on one person to be everything, that it's important to have a lot of good friends. That probably changed my whole life. My friends are very important to me, and I do everything to maintain good friendships. I always want to have a lot of friends around because you help them and they help you."

Ross is someone who did *not* have a support system in place, but was particularly resourceful in dealing with this issue. Ross lost his job as vice president of professional development at a large insurance company. This was actually the second time he lost his job within the last four years. He moved to Nashville to take this position and then the company restructured two years later. His marriage was rocky throughout this time. An additional stress came when his wife discovered that she had ovarian cancer. He said, "The day she came home from chemo was the day I lost my job." When he told her that he had lost his job she replied, "Well I was going to file for divorce on Monday." Because Ross was new to the area, he did not have many friends in the community. Ross said that at times, "I was at my rock bottom lowest . . . lower than a snake's belly."

Ross left his job in July and as winter approached, he was concerned about the upcoming holidays. He said, "I was going to outplacement for a couple hours every day, and then going back to an empty apartment. And there's a major loss here, in terms of losing a job, getting divorced, the health issues—it was disaster." Ross told me how he dealt with his loneliness and the upcoming holidays by prefacing it with, "Promise not to laugh?" Then he said, "I worked in Opryland at Christmas in the Park for $4.40 an hour from November 16th to New Year's Eve. That's how I got through the holidays." He explained, "I worked out there as a host, from 3 p.m. to 10, and they give you a costume and the whole nine yards. I didn't make any money, by the time I bought some turtlenecks and some shoes and ate out every day, but I had someplace to go. I'd do my outplacement during the day and at 2:30 I'd head over to the park and I wouldn't get home until after 10. That got me through six terrible weeks."

Ross sought out this situation because he realized, "I needed to be with people, and you never know who you're going to talk to who might have a job for you." No jobs came out of it, but being around people in a more uplifting atmosphere really did help. Ross worked the model train display, and it reminded him of something he used to do with his dad when he was a kid. I asked him if he had ever done anything like this before and he replied, "Crazy like that? No! I've never done anything like that, and it felt so good."

Outplacement can also provide a support function during the transition. Some companies hire outplacement firms to help people move on and find something new. For some, outplacement provides a place to get up and go in the morning while seeking a new job. Most of the people who received outplacement support found that it was helpful, especially if they did not have a strong support system in place or clarity about their next step. Many said that what was most helpful was the emotional support they got from meeting other people who were in the same boat. For the same reasons, joining a career support group can also help: "There were six of us in the group who were all in the same boat—all the same age, same type of background, and we had a special relationship. We would meet once a week in the morning and have coffee and doughnuts and talk about how we were doing."

A network of relationships was the most frequently mentioned item that helped people through their job loss and transition. This includes professional relationships. Prior to losing their jobs, those who experienced transformative change had all cultivated a very large professional network that was at least national in scope. Most of this group remained self-employed, and were able to get their businesses off the ground because of their professional contacts: "My support network goes from Virginia Beach to San Francisco. I have an old boss in San Francisco and old friends in Los Angeles. If I moved to San Francisco tomorrow I could just pick up the phone any time and call my friend and ask, 'What's the latest joke?' If you have developed a good-sized network, you have it wherever you go. It truly is transferable. It's not like, I sold my house and it's not mine anymore. A network endures." Professional networking is considered to be the most effective method of job hunting, and it is estimated that 70 percent to 75 percent of people in job transition find new jobs this way.

Matt is someone who experienced transformative change. He has very good networking skills and used them while searching for a new job. But remember that the way he actually found his job was by talking with a woman at church who reconnected him to an old high school friend. I was struck by his comment, "You'd better look to see what you're standing on. As far as networking goes, start at home and see where that takes you." At the time I told him that this reminded me of the Polynesian saying, "standing on a whale, fishing for minnows." Through our relationships we weave a safety net that holds us, and it may be bigger than we realize. When we stumble, this is what keeps us from falling too far.

Many of the people I spoke with found their relationships to be more enduring than their job, which now seems transitory. A friend of mine from India told me that in his country security is linked to family and community and not to money or material possessions. Our country is sadly lacking in this form of security and this may be why we are feeling so insecure right now. Yet I think this type of security is something we can and must create for ourselves. In her book *All Our Kin,* Carol Stack explains that in some cultures kin is not just blood relations but "those you count on," whether or not you are related.[6] This was echoed among the people who did best with their job loss and transition: "Knowing, *knowing* that my friends and family are here, it makes the world a less scary place. It's that security that whatever the worst was, I would be OK. I have a number of friends who would send me an airplane ticket and take me into their home. My parents certainly would. I have friends and family that if I were truly sick, they'd come out here in a moment. And I just *know* that."

Not only do relationships provide support, but they also serve as a holding container that allows for personal development and change. They both hold and contain us. When transformation occurs there needs to be some sense of boundaries. Unbounded or uncontained change can be too frightening, or simply too much. When a magician wants to work magic he puts a circle around himself so that powers can be contained that would otherwise be lost. Transformative change has more to do with this containing notion than with the passage of time. Like a pot of soup, the ingredients need to be held so they can meld into something new. The challenge is having a container that holds us firmly but also loosely enough for change to take place. Sometimes people in our lives hold us too tightly; they box us into a container that is too small or too rigid. This makes change very difficult.

## Chapter Twelve

# Shapeshifting

*To exist is to change, to change is to mature, to mature is*
*to go on creating oneself endlessly.*
—HENRI BERGSON[1]

People who have experienced a transformative change were fortunate to have a holding container that was not too big and not too small, but just right. Consequently they were able to make significant changes in their lives and they had the support for doing so. Rather than responding to their job loss by holding on to what they had or were in the past, they used the loss as an opportunity to experiment with new possibilities. Instead of clinging to what they'd lost, they ended up feeling much better about what they found. I call this ability *shapeshifting*. It is a fluidity of thinking and acting that allows for continuous adaptation to change.

Proteus was a sea god described in the *Odyssey* who was known for his shapeshifting ability. He lived near the mouth of the Nile and was charged with tending seals and other sea creatures belonging to Poseidon, who presided over the sea. Proteus had the ability to change himself into whatever form he desired, including any animal or element such as water or fire. He also had the power of prophecy, but he used his shapeshifting ability whenever he wanted to elude mortals who sought answers from him. One time Menelaus and his ships got stuck in a becalmed sea near the Nile, and he sought Proteus's help. Proteus tried to elude Menelaus by changing into a lion, serpent, panther, bear, water, and finally a tree. But Menelaus did not let him escape, so Proteus finally divulged how Menelaus could continue his journey, which involved returning to Egypt and offering sacrifices to the gods.[2] Because of Proteus, in mythology shapeshifting is equated with wisdom.

Robert Lifton uses the Proteus myth as the springboard for his book, *The Protean Self*. Lifton is the psychiatrist I mentioned in Chapter Four who has spent over forty years studying survivors of extremely traumatic events such as the Holocaust and the nuclear bombing of Hiroshima. He believes that the most resilient survivors are those who have come to terms with death, play, and transcendence. In *The Protean Self*, Lifton argues that today, a shapeshifting capacity is also adaptive and necessary. He describes a protean person as someone who is capable of assuming multiple identities without splitting into pathological fragmentation. An example is Vaclav Havel, the first president of the Czech Republic. In the course of his life, Havel shifted from being a playwright and disciple of Samuel Beckett, to becoming his country's leading dissident and political prisoner, to becoming the first post-Communist president of Czechoslovakia. Lifton quotes Havel as saying, "How does this all fit together? Why don't these paradoxical qualities cancel each other out instead of coexisting and cooperating with each other? . . . How can I—this odd mix of the most curious opposites—get through life, and by all reports successfully?"[3]

The traditional view of a healthy personal identity is one that is characterized by inner stability and constancy. Lifton makes the point that because change is so prodigious in our modern world, this is no longer a functional way to be. It is more functional to have multiple involvements, images, and skills that allow us to adapt to changing circumstances. The people I interviewed who experienced transformative change do have these protean characteristics. Remember that the central idea of transformation is movement across or through forms. These people were imaginative in applying their skills to a variety of situations. They were not stuck in thinking that they could only work in one type of setting or role. Think of Cheryl, the former bank vice president who could have returned to a job just like she had for twenty-one years, but instead opted to work as a part-time chief financial officer for several companies and to change the balance of her life. By contrast,

Will, who was also a chief financial officer, believed the only thing that would get his life back to normal was finding a job like the one he had before. Will defined himself and his career too narrowly.

In 1975 Theodore Levitt wrote what is now considered to be a classic business article called "Marketing Myopia," published in the *Harvard Business Review*.[4] This article talks about how entire industries have gone out of business because they defined themselves too narrowly. For instance, had the railroad industry realized that it was in the business of transportation, rather than the more narrowly defined railroad business, it probably would have diversified into automobiles or airplanes. Instead the automobile and airline industries advanced and grew, while the use of rail transport drastically declined so that the railroad industry nearly became defunct. Similarly, when people define themselves too narrowly in terms of their career, it can lead to career stagnation or even obsolescence.

In my research, the people who felt the best about their situations had a broad view of their career and entertained many possibilities. It is interesting to me that I asked everyone I talked with whether they thought of their job loss more in terms of loss or change, and everyone who experienced transformative change put the emphasis on *change*. In fact Cheryl said, "I don't feel any loss." I replied, "Well, you did lose something—I mean, you lost a job," and she said, "Right. But I've never missed it for a day." Then she laughed and said, "The only thing I've missed I only had for a month anyway, and that was e-mail. That was fun—I'd zap little messages to my friends in Miami or wherever." These people experienced their loss as an opportunity for change, and they were creative in imagining new possibilities.

Not only did they demonstrate a shapeshifting ability in terms of reinventing themselves after losing their job, they also applied this ability to moving around obstacles. Remember that Debra lost her job as manager of a large retail store and her first plan was to open a competing store in the same city. She had dreamed of doing something like this for the past five or six years. But when the lease negotiations for retail space fell through, she changed gears and started a consulting practice instead. I asked her how she was able to get her consulting practice up and running so quickly, and she stressed the importance of her professional network. She created a newsletter and sent out a press release, but these were effective because of her established network. Now when she reflects back on this shift she says:

> I used to think of change as being scary and hard. Now I realize that you can't really manage change but you can flow with it. I think of it like Chinese philosophy, like a river and that you can flow with a river, and you meet a rock . . . that's what I did when that lease negotiation fell through. Instead of going up against that rock I just flowed around it, and said "OK, what else? Let's dig deeper and find where I'm supposed to be." So the change has revealed new avenues, new ways of looking at things, and more about my potential than I ever imagined. I love the idea of change now, and had it not been for all that I went through—if I was still back in my old job—then it would be all about fear and bureaucracy and organizational change. Now it's more about market change and personal growth.

Lifton describes protean people as having this open, watery flow. The people I spoke with who weathered the transition best were fluid. Those who did not weather it as well seemed frozen when faced with change. Several years ago a colleague told me about a number of managers who were laid off from an aerospace company. For an interim period the managers were given the option of coming in to their offices. Most of them continued to come to their office day after day because they did not know where else to go or what else to do. This is what I mean by freezing in the face of change.

If we think about the properties of water, we are reminded that it possesses great power because it turns barriers or obstacles into channels. The strength of water is in its yielding movement. Shapeshifting is a dance with the environment that involves adaptation, but also will and creativity. It is not passive. Water yields but it also shapes the environment around it. Rather than continuously shaping ourselves to the environment, we also need to shape what is around us to the degree that we can. Each form our life takes then carries its own intention and meaning.

In the 1940s the social psychologist Kurt Lewin created a model for both individual and organizational change that is based on the properties of water. He described change as a three-phase process: unfreezing, moving, and refreezing. The change actually takes place during the moving phase, and then the person or group refreezes to maintain that change. This metaphor is still frequently used in organizations today but it is no longer as appropriate. In the 1940s change came more slowly so there were longer periods of stability. Today change is so fast and continuous that freezing no longer works.

Freezing is understandable, however. It is a defensive posture that is rooted in the flight-fight reaction. This is a reaction that both people and animals share when they are threatened. Freezing is actually the most passive fear reaction, but sometimes it is the best one to use—for instance, if you come across a grizzly bear. But often it is not the best response, as a deer might discover who freezes in the middle of a road, staring at the headlights of an oncoming car. We freeze to protect and defend ourselves. Yet ice is brittle, whereas water is not. This is the problem with freezing into one way of being or thinking. We tend to freeze our lives into a single cube of meaning.

This is a self-defended, and in many ways self-defeating, way to approach life. When we cut off the movement, the motion, that is inherent in life we end up feeling numb. Both joy and grief are suppressed so that our existence feels like a stable, but narrow, band of bland. Life becomes all means and no dreams. The dreams, hope, and courage we need to move beyond this frozen place rely on symbols to stir our imagination. Lifton's thesis about protean people is based on our symbolizing capability. Our capacity for creating and finding meaning in symbols is uniquely human. The word symbol comes from the Greek word *symballein,* which means to throw together or unify. However, this symbolizing capacity is a double-edged sword. It can lead us to our freedom and unity by allowing us to see beyond categories. Likewise, it can lead to divisiveness by locking us within mental constructs and images that serve as rigid, iron enclosures.

This frozen way of thinking is what Lifton calls the *fundamentalist self.* He describes the fundamentalist personality as "the closing off of the person and the constriction of self-process. It can take the form of widespread psychic numbing—diminishing capacity or inclination to feel—and a general sense of stasis and meaninglessness."[5] The fundamentalist person is rooted in the past and longs for the return of a glorified past. The fundamentalist personality seeks fixity, stasis, and certainty.

Just as we can freeze ourselves into one way of thinking, feeling, or acting, so can we become frozen in the eyes of others. Especially when we are with a family or even a work group over a long period of time, we can get frozen in time. This often happens between parents and adult children. In the eyes of the parents, their adult child may always be sixteen years old. A friend of mine who is forty-eight told me about visiting her mother's home. This friend now has her own children in college. But her childhood room has never been changed, even though she left home thirty years ago. She said that when she tries to sleep in her old bed she cannot breathe. The environment presses in on her, and presses her into an old form that no longer fits.

A shapeshifting approach does not mean cutting ourselves off from the past. We all need some continuity and as we move through change we need to bring along threads from our past that are important to us. Peter Marris calls this the *conservative impulse*.[6] The conservative impulse has to do with the very human tendency to want to be able to understand life and make predictions about the outcomes of our actions. We cannot function or even survive without having some sense of stability. This is why Marris believes that we must strike a balance between the conservative impulse and change or innovation.

Because of the accelerated rate of change in the workplace, however, it is self-defeating to cling too tightly to the way things used to be. As early as 1976, Douglas Hall, a professor at the School of Management at Boston University, wrote about the protean career: "The protean person's own personal career choices and search for self-fulfillment are the unifying or integrative elements of his or her life. The criterion of success is internal (psychological success), not external. In short, the protean career is shaped more by the individual than by the organization and may be redirected from time to time to meet the needs of the person."[7] Hall realized that increasingly people need to take responsibility for directing and shaping their own career and that they cannot rely on an organization to do this for them. He believes that we need to think of our career as being beyond the boundaries of a single organization, which means that it is pieced together from our experiences in a variety of organizations as well our experiences in other contexts such as home or school.[8] For the individual, a protean career is less compartmentalized. It means recognizing that both work and non-work roles overlap and shape our sense of who we are.

Money can also influence our sense of who we are. Many people become frozen in the face of job loss or career change because of fears about money. It is important to keep in mind, however, that money has this dramatic influence because it is such a potent symbol in our culture. Money symbolizes different things to different people—for some it is a measure of their self-worth or success, for others it is their freedom. In *Care of the Soul,* Thomas Moore reminds us that wealth is completely subjective and can't be measured by a bank account: "The problem lies not in having too much or too little, but in taking money too literally."[9] When we forget that money is merely a *symbol* of our self-esteem, freedom, security, love, or whatever, then it can rob us of our real sense of value and worth.

Certainly losing a job brings up many issues around money. Initially I thought that there would be a correlation between the amount of money people had when losing their job and their resilience. But this was not the case. Through the course of my research, I realized that resilience has more to do with our *relationship* to money than the amount of money we have in the bank. The people who experienced transformative change have a looser attachment to money and to concrete status symbols. Their self-worth and identity are not tied to money. Usually they live on less money than they make and have a long-term habit of saving. For instance, Cheryl had a very large financial cushion when she lost her job but this was partly because she had always saved. She lives more frugally now but it was not a difficult adjustment for her: "I try to tell people who lose their job that you don't need as much money as you've been spending to live. I mean, I clip coupons—I never did that before. I'm amazed at how much I can save . . . just buying groceries for myself I can save probably $35 or $40 a month. You can really find ways to economize without adjusting your lifestyle. You waste money when you have more than you need—you don't pay attention and you waste it." Cheryl acknowledged that it might have made it easier for her to save because she was single and did not have a family to support.

Jeff and Ron were each the sole support for their families and it was interesting to note the differences in their responses to job loss. Jeff is the former bank vice president who experienced a dark time. He drove up to my house in a Mercedes sports car. With his severance package, Jeff had close to a million dollars in assets when he lost his job and figured that he could go for two years without additional income. He said that even before losing his job he had suggested to his wife that they move into a smaller house and pay cash so that they could be debt-free, but "that went over like a lead balloon." I asked him why and he said that he thinks it is because his wife would view this as a "failure" and an "embarrassment." Jeff was still having a difficult time when I talked with him, and did not feel better off.

Ron is about the same age as Jeff. He, too, is the sole support of his wife and two children. But Ron experienced transformative change after losing his job and feels much better off than he was before. Ron is very friendly and outgoing and I got the impression that he feels comfortable with himself and with his world. He has had extensive experience with mergers and acquisitions and was in and out of organizations more than anyone else I spoke with. Since 1980, he joined and then left five different companies. Ron told me that "all of my involuntary departures resulted from divestiture of companies that I was associated with." Most of these were relatively small companies in the health care field.

Ron started his career on a very fast track. As a CPA, his first job out of college was with one of the Big Eight accounting firms. He left this firm in his late twenties and said, "I went into an industry where there was a lot of buying and selling." He explained that job loss has never been a major fear for him: "When I was thirty we sold our company and I had to go out looking. I didn't sit down and ponder it and say, 'Oh, here's a trend.' I simply said, 'Well, I was looking for a job when I found this one—I've got transferable skills, let's go on.'" By the age of thirty-one, Ron was the chief financial officer of a publicly traded company.

I asked Ron how his most recent involuntary departure came about. As with Jeff, it had occurred about six months before our interview. He said that the people who owned the company were actually two men whom he had known for many years. They asked him to join their company to help take it through a merger so it could go public. This failed, so then they decided to sell the company. Meanwhile, Ron said that the atmosphere at the company became "real protective, with a lot of paranoia." There was a lack of communication between the two partners and Ron often got caught in the middle, which put him in a very stressful situation. He said, "Every Sunday night I'd print out about five resignations." However, the precipitating event for his departure came from a family crisis:

> On Sunday night, October 2, I got a phone call from the emergency room in Chattanooga saying your daughter has been in a car wreck. So at 12:30 at night my wife and I jumped in the car and drove to Chattanooga. My daughter had totaled her car, but she was all right. We sat with her for a while—stayed up all night. At 6 A.M. we drove home and got back at 9. I called the office and told them what happened, and said I'd be in this afternoon. About 3:00 I got a phone call from the president saying, "Are you planning on coming in today?" I said I was planning to. I told him what had happened and he said, "Well we have a cash crisis. I think your priorities are out of whack and you need to be here."

Ron told me that when he left for the office that afternoon his wife said, "Whatever you do today is fine with me." He resigned.

Ron drew the vertical axis of his graph to represent his stress level such that high stress was high on the graph. I noticed that the graph peaked in 1991 and then there was a long and gradual reduction of stress until it peaked again during this last job. The earlier peak represented the time just before leaving his previous job. Between these two jobs he did consulting and project work. This was a two-year period. He said, "I'd always been able to find a job quickly but the economy wasn't cooperating." During this time he sold his house in an affluent neighborhood and moved his family into a smaller house: "We'd lived the corporate life where you get a new car every other year, and take vacations. We played the role in the eighties where you'd get a pay raise and you'd buy a new house that you couldn't afford this year but knew you'd be able with next year's raise. We finally said, 'Look, we've got to change all this.'"

Ron said that since 1991 his assets dropped from about $400,000 to almost zero. Given that, I was amazed that Ron's stress level dropped along with his net worth. He attributes this to strengthening his family life and his faith. He says, "My wife and I communicate better than we ever have." In terms of his spiritual faith he says, "I believe all of us on earth are miracles, we're all here for a purpose, we're gifts to each other, and that what we are is a direct result of what we've been associated with throughout our life."

Ron drove up to my house in his wife's old Toyota, which had 150,000 miles on it. He told me that he just bought an older BMW but wants his wife to drive it because it is more safe. You can see that Ron did sell his house and moved his family into a smaller one but evidently neither he nor his wife viewed this as a failure. He said that his kids probably had the hardest time with it. I asked Ron if he thought he would have experienced the personal changes he discussed, such as improving his relationship with his family and strengthening his faith, if he had not been through this experience and he said, "Maybe, but probably not. There would've been the financial stability so I would not have been forced to look at what was going on. I think we tend to think that as long as the checkbook is flush, why do I have to examine anything I'm doing?"

Interestingly, both Jeff and Ron come from working-class backgrounds and both did very well in terms of improving their socioeconomic status. They both said that growing up, they were "poor and didn't know it." However, you can see that Jeff's self-worth— or perhaps his wife's—is more tightly linked to the trappings of success than Ron's is. Job loss and financial strain caused Ron and his wife to look inward and toward each other. Ron ended up feeling better off because he realized that the love of his wife and family and his spiritual faith were more important to him than money.

I heard this sentiment echoed repeatedly among the people who felt better off after losing their job. Those who felt the best had less anxiety about money, more confidence that they would have enough, and little regard for status symbols. They also recognized the exchange between time and money and after losing their job they tended to place more value on time than on money. For instance, while working at the bank Cheryl served on the board of the YWCA for five years and said, "I was always racing to go to the board meetings or finance committee meetings, and now I have more time." So she became more hands-on by volunteering at a YWCA-sponsored residential house for teenage girls. She says,

"I try to think of other ways that I can give without writing a check. You get a lot back that way."

There is a grave danger in concretely attaching our self-worth to our money because money is so easily lost. The same danger exists when we attach our self-worth to a particular job or role. The people who experienced transformative change separated their sense of self from their work identity. For instance, many people I spoke with talked about dealing with the question of "What do you do?" after losing their job. This is what Jeff said: "The first couple of weeks, I remember being on a Boy Scout hiking trip. And someone asked me, 'What do you do?' and I didn't have the courage at the time to say, 'Well, I don't do anything now.' I just said I work for a bank, and left it at that. I mean technically it was still true, but also at the same time I realized, 'Gee, I just can't tell someone I'm unemployed or I'm not working.' For my psychological need, at least for me, there's a need to say I am something." You can see that Jeff was very forthright in his interview and expressed his feelings quite honestly. The psychological need he mentions is an understandable need because our society puts so much emphasis on our work identity. But it is interesting to note Cheryl's response to the same question:

> I went to a cooking class the other night and I didn't know any of the people there. People always first ask, "What's your name," and then the second thing they ask is, "What do you do?" That's just the way it is. So that is one thing you have to be prepared to answer and not feel bad about—people will say, "What do you do?" That's your identity in this society. So I said I work part-time as a financial consultant and I'm helping my little niece learn how to speak. I try not to make it sound like what I do has to be what I get paid for.

All the men and women I spoke with were professionals who had strong professional identities. Yet the ones who experienced transformative change had a clearer sense of themselves as distinct from their work. This gave them greater fluidity and the freedom to try different roles.

One way that we lose our shapeshifting ability is when we get frozen into our work role. We may develop a frozen image of ourselves that we carry with us after leaving or losing our job. Or perhaps while working, we feel the organization press in on us as my friend felt in her childhood bedroom. This makes me think of a Superman movie I saw many years ago, where Superman was in a cubical room and the walls were moving in. Superman, of course, could hold them apart to escape. But many of us can't. The tragic irony of Superman is that now the real-life icon, Christopher Reeve, is physically immobile. The triumph is that he is transcending his literally frozen form by accessing his spirit. Now he moves people with words and inspiration to a greater degree than when he could move. His mere presence is an inspiration. The root word of inspiration is *spirit,* which means "breath." Christopher Reeve now breathes with the help of a respirator. But he has accessed something much bigger than himself. Perhaps the most important aspect of shapeshifting is having this access to something that moves us and is bigger than us. This gives us the freedom to assume new shapes and the energy to move others.

Shapeshifting requires imagination. Imagination and creativity require a certain permeability of both thought and boundaries. Too much permeability, however, can lead to a shape*less* existence—and in its extreme form, to psychosis. We all need a protective layer that provides buffering and form. The people who weathered job loss best are capable of being simultaneously permeable and impermeable, porous and protective. They maintain the integrity of their personality and values while still exercising their imagination. Finally, they move beyond the past by finding meaning in the present and hope for the future.

*Chapter Thirteen*

# Faith, Hope, and Imagination

*The poet's eye, in a fine frenzy rolling,*
*Doth glance from heaven to earth, from earth to heaven;*
*And as imagination bodies forth*
*The forms of things unknown, the poet's pen*
*Turns them to shapes and gives to airy nothing*
*A local habitation and a name.*
—WILLIAM SHAKESPEARE

The people who experienced transformative change all talked about tapping into something bigger than themselves that helped them through their transition process and put their job loss in perspective. They interpreted their experience as part of a bigger plan or a bigger picture, and this provided solace because it laced the experience with meaning. These interpretations combine faith, hope, and imagination. Hope and imagination move us into the future, while faith allows us to relax into that movement.

The Greek myth about Pandora teaches us how hope came into the world. This story is one of several creation myths. Prometheus, a cousin of Zeus, is said to have created the first men by fashioning them out of potter's clay. The two gods became rivals when Prometheus tricked Zeus out of the best part of all animal sacrifices, so that from then on, men got to keep the good meat for themselves. This enraged Zeus, and as punishment he decided to keep fire from mortals. Yet once again Prometheus came to the aid of mankind by stealing sparks of fire from the sun and bringing them to earth. Now Zeus was really enraged and he swore revenge.

To get revenge, Zeus created the first woman, and each god and goddess endowed her with special gifts such as beauty, grace, and dexterity. They named the woman Pandora, which means "the gift of all." Zeus sent Pandora to Epimetheus, the brother of Prometheus. Prometheus had warned his brother never to accept any gifts from Zeus, but Epimetheus could not resist Pandora's beauty. When the gods sent Pandora to earth, they also gave her a box and forbade her to open it. The box contained many harmful things, but Pandora did not know this. One day her curiosity overcame her and she opened the lid of the box. Out flew all the evils of the world! In terror Pandora clapped the lid of the box shut and in doing so she trapped the one good thing that was left at the bottom: Hope. To this day, hope remains as "mankind's sole comfort in misfortune."[1]

Most of us forget—or perhaps never knew—that hope lay at the bottom of Pandora's box. Usually we just remember that all the troubles flew out. This story is important because it reminds us that even in the midst of these troubles, hope remains. Vaillant writes that, "Hope and faith are very simple words, but they encompass an essential facet of resilience. It is no accident that hope has long been seen, as in the myth of Pandora, as the psychic balm on which resilience depends. And hope and faith are inextricably bound to social supports."[2]

This issue of social support presents a paradox. On one hand, our relationships serve as a container that provides us with buffering so that we can learn and change. People who experienced transformative change had such protection. On the other hand, they also went inward and drew strength from personal, internal resources: "I felt such a strong spiritual growth happening because I felt like I was really relying on something inside." Spiritual growth is also paradoxical because it is not an entirely inward process. During important crossings we become like a vessel that has energy pouring into it. This is archetypal energy that is both within and beyond us.

As I mentioned earlier, the word *spirit* is rooted in images of breath, wind, or air in motion. The *Oxford English Dictionary* defines spirit as "the animating or vital principle in man and animals; the breath of life." Louise Erdrich provides this beautiful description: "In early spring I sit down on the old grass of winter and breathe

the newness rising from the earth. In the roots, life is gathering in shy waves of power. After a while, if I breathe deeply and slowly, drinking the watery, musical air, I feel a union with something larger, fuller, whole. Just for that moment, I move in harmony with one complex and dedicated design. I suppose that is spirit—the larger configuration—but so is each tough blade of grass my footsteps crush."[3]

Clearly spirit is not something we can grasp or see; it is something we can only intuit or feel. Sharon Parks, at the Harvard Divinity School, tells us that spirit combined with imagination is what forms our faith: "Faith is an act of the imagination and activity of Spirit."[4] These ideas are hard to separate because they are so intertwined.

Many of the people I spoke with said that their job loss had the effect of strengthening their spiritual faith and bringing it off the back burner. Some talked about this more in terms of a larger purpose or larger plan: "I got through this for a purpose, and the purpose is that sometime down the road I'm going to have to help somebody, and if I hadn't experienced this, then how could I do that with any credibility?" Thus their faith was not necessarily linked to religious beliefs or to a church. But in a very personal way, it was their belief in something more that helped them through dark times. For instance, Carol—who left the hotel corporation—said that her spirituality is what got her through dark times, but when I asked her how she accessed this she replied, "Solitude, meditation, friends, or thinking of a loving universe with creative solutions. I don't go to church."

Those who did access their faith through organized religion were open-minded and inclusive. Ron talked a great deal about how his spirituality came forward, without being at all dogmatic about it: "I don't know how to prove that spirituality works. I can tie things I encounter in business to the Bible; someone else might be able to tie them back to *Mad Magazine*. I just think it's very personal and individual. Just because I believe one way doesn't mean that someone else is wrong." The degree to which Ron felt supported by his spiritual faith strengthened while he was having trouble finding work. This is what helped him to lessen an attachment to money:

I think I just got spiritually based, more internal. I accepted that everything I have on this earth is borrowed from God. Since it's borrowed, the first guy I ought to give it back to is Him, I can't out-tithe him. Even when we were liquidating assets to make sure we were all right and our kids were taken care of, we increased our tithing over this time. We just said, we've got to do this. Also, I think we began to believe and live that whatever happens today, we'll just go forward. Things will work out. The analogy I give sometimes is that when a dentist drills a tooth he gets rid of all the decay but then he goes a little deeper and gets rid of some of the good, so that when he puts the filling in he knows it's anchored to something good. As I was getting rid of some of the garbage that we'd built up over twenty years of marriage and career, sometimes I'd say, when is this slide going to stop? And I just accepted that it would stop when we had a solid foundation that we could build on, and I didn't know when that would be.

Parks describes faith as a composing, relational activity that is basic to our human experience. It is how we organize the totality of our life and provides our most comprehensive frame of meaning: "Faith is the activity of seeking and composing meaning in the most comprehensive dimensions of our experience. Faith is a broad, generic human phenomenon. To be human is to dwell in faith, to dwell in one's meaning—one's conviction of the ultimate character of truth, of self, of world, of cosmos (whether that meaning is strong or fragile, expressed in religious terms or secular)."[5] She points out that the Hindu concept of faith is expressed through the word *sraddha*. This word comes from two words—*srad,* meaning "heart," and *dha,* meaning "to put." Therefore faith is seen as something that we trust as true—"the putting of one's heart upon."[6]

Faith, then, relates to trust and belief. Sharon Parks compares faith to the warp of a tapestry upon which the particular threads of our life find rest and order. It weaves the pieces of our lives into an ultimate holding container or net that carries us through difficult times. We must ask ourselves, where can I rest my heart? This is a deep resting place. Without it, it is hard to find peace. We can put our faith in our marriage, or family, or work. But we can also lose these things, and this is why betrayal feels like such a deep cut.

We can also place our faith in something larger and nonmaterial, such as the goodness of the world or a higher power: "I just always had the faith that things would work out. I knew if I sat in my chair they wouldn't work out, but if I worked things would work out. I just believe in the goodness of the world—it's all going to work out."

Faith is a holding together; we both hold and are held by faith. Sometimes we may not even be aware of it. Parks reminds us that, "For many, an awareness of the weavings that have ordered personal and corporate life emerges only in the suffering of the unraveling or rending of those weavings that held a personal value or public trust."[7] Losing a job and feeling that our trust is betrayed can bring about some unraveling. The beliefs that make up our faith are part of our assumptive world, and when this collapses we can lose faith. This can happen suddenly, or the meaning that has made a home for our soul can slowly erode. When we lose faith completely, it results in *nihilism.*

Nihilism is the opposite of faith. It is a bleak inability to find significance in our life or the world around us. It is the sense that the world has no order, meaning, or mutuality, and it results in deep feelings of alienation and estrangement. This is epitomized in the character of Meursault in *The Stranger,* a novel by Albert Camus. Meursault is a lonely and singular person who views life from a distance. Even when told of his mother's death he is unable to conjure up any feelings: "Maman died today. Or yesterday maybe, I don't know. I got a telegram from the home: 'Mother deceased. Funeral tomorrow. Faithfully yours.' That doesn't mean anything. Maybe it was yesterday."[8] James Anthony uses the term "Meursault phenomenon" to describe extremely invulnerable children and adults who insulate themselves from disturbing experiences through detachment and defensive distancing.[9] A related sociological concept is *anomie,* as described by the philosopher and sociologist Emile Durkheim. Anomie actually means "lawlessness" and it is a complete breakdown of binding social norms or ideals. It occurs when common values and common meanings are no longer understood or accepted, and new values and meanings have not yet emerged. The effect on individuals is called alienation. This is a sense of futility, emotional emptiness, and despair. It is a sense of being estranged from our community, work, the products of our work, and our self. Perhaps the greatest danger is self-estrangement. This is what Meursault suffered, the sense of being out of touch with everyone and everything—including himself. Sometimes this is revealed symbolically through our dreams, when we dream of trying to use the phone to call for help but the wires are cut. This is a clue that we have lost our connection to ourself.

By contrast, faith forms connections. It is a way of holding our life together that combines orientation, courage, meaning, and hope. How we compose our faith, or ultimate meaning, is a developmental process that involves ongoing forming and re-forming ways of experiencing the world. We do not passively receive our experience of the world; we actively compose it. You and I might experience the same event, yet end up with completely different versions of what happened. I have a childhood friend who likes to tell stories about experiences that she and I shared in high school and college. Based on her descriptions, I could swear I was never there.

The English poet and theologian Samuel Taylor Coleridge was the first to link our composing, imaginative abilities to faith. Coleridge described imagination as the highest power of the mind because it has "the power of shaping into one."[10] Through our imagination we are able to intuit life as a whole; to assemble the totality of our experience into a meaningful pattern. This reminds me of the idea of nesting, as in concentric circles or those Russian dolls where each doll contains a smaller one. We nest our story into larger stories and form a canopy of our own meaning. The ability to weave our experiences into a canopy that shields us or a net that holds us requires imagination. Yet a serious loss or tragedy can rip this canopy and throw everything we know into doubt.

When we lose faith, however, all is not lost. Sometimes when we create one pattern of meaning around a single cause or center—such as an institution, job, or person—it is not adequate or big enough to bring together the complexity, variety, and tragic elements of our experience. This is when our faith is very vulnerable to change and can collapse, for example, with the loss of a job or the loss of a child. Such a collapse brings forth feelings of chaos, fear, disorientation, and loss. Yet this is what moves us forward in our faith development. We create a new pattern to make sense of our experience and this new canopy of meaning is usually bigger and more inclusive than that which preceded it. Parks tells us that ultimately the question we must ask ourselves is whether "our pattern of meaning . . . can survive the defeat of its finite manifestations."[11]

I noticed that among the people I spoke with, their faith was *active* and *in the world*. Faith was not a set of religious beliefs they had, it was something that they did. In other words, they took responsibility for acting on their own behalf while also trusting in something larger: "I have a personal faith, too. I've always been a spiritual person I think—well I know. But I tend more now to—well, let me put it this way, I would pray and ask for help and love and courage but I would go ahead and take care of myself. I mean, I know I would be supported but I don't wait for something else to take care of me." Many also experienced their faith or spirituality as something that is quite present in their daily life:

> I guess I sort of think of my life as being my spiritual practice—how I want to be and that Godlike quality, seeing God in my life and trying to reflect that out in how I am in the world. It's how I am with everything. Part of it is about seeing God where I live and in what I do. It's how I look at my whole life—the hard, the easy, the good, the bad—all those things. It's important. It's what I try to reflect, what I try to practice, what I try to grow. A lot of the reading that I do is around the Tao. My newest phrase is, "Accept the ocean and float upon it."

This notion of acceptance brings up an interesting paradox about control. Many referred to a combination of simultaneously letting go and also taking control. The letting go related to faith: "There were times when I would visualize myself as in God's hands." The taking control related to a sense of personal responsibility: "I won't ever just place my total destiny in the hands of someone else." All the people who discussed their spiritual faith maintained this tension between letting go and taking control. They took action while simultaneously recognizing the limits of their control. The sense of having personal control over our environment and destiny is generally correlated with high motivation and achievement. An internal locus of control is the idea that the rewards we receive are contingent upon our own actions or attributes. However, these interviews suggest that our sense of control must be mediated by a recognition of things that are beyond are control.

Debra talked about reconciling her need for taking control through activity and letting go of control. During her dark time she said that she went to Mass every week and that her spiritual faith "was holding me together—but it was just holding me up, rather than an active thing. I was drained and I was doing my best to keep up with family and career." Since starting her consulting practice, she says, "Spirituality is more a part of my life than it was before." When she reflects back on her transition she says that she learned that at times you must ask for what you need: "Maybe that happens in a spiritual sense, and in a verbal sense too, with friends and family. You need to ask to have the floor for a while. And then you trust the Universe, or Spirit, or God—however you want to look at it—trust that you'll be taken care of so you can use your energy in more positive ways."

Faith is fundamentally relational. It is expressed in how we relate to people and things, and also how we relate to our ultimate environment which is framed by our largest canopy of meaning. Parks expresses the relational aspect of faith by talking about the need we all have for a "network of belonging." She explains that this network might consist mainly of a few nearby intimate relationships, or it may be geographically dispersed and include people who are not currently in our life. How we compose our meaning is determined in part by our relationship to this network: "Faith as a patterning, connective, relational activity is embodied, not in the individual alone, but in the social fabric of life."[12]

How do hope and imagination relate to faith? We would not have faith without imagination, and imagination fuels our hope. When our world is shrinking, it is hope and imagination that enlarge it and bring forth new possibilities. Sometimes I need to remind myself of this on gray, rainy winter days in Seattle. On days like this the clouds can make everything feel small and dark and oppressive. It is easy to forget that the clouds will lift and that the mountains and beauty and light have been there all along. Hope and imagination help us to see beyond the clouds and enlarge our world. In *Images of Hope,* William Lynch says, "We all hate people who go around transcending things. . . . But it is another matter to look at a fact and to create a context or a field for it with the help of realistic imagination. So that when a moment comes which is impossible we can at least wait for the emergence of a larger moment and a larger time."[13]

In a very concrete way, this is what happened for Elaine while she was returning from Guatemala. She explained that on the way home she started to feel depressed as all the thoughts about her job loss came flooding back to her. But this lifted when she stopped in Mexico and came across a big celebration: "On the plane as I was leaving Guatemala I was thinking, *what* am I going to do with my life? I still had that despair. But I got to Mexico right in time for the Feast of the Virgin of Guadalupe—I was at the cathedral on that day—the whole plaza was filled with dancers from different villages and the scene, the spectacle, the culture was all so exhilarating—so I felt better. I decided that life was going to be fine. It pulled me out of myself again." Elaine found her larger moment at the Feast of the Virgin of Guadalupe.

Hope is an interior quality. As in Pandora's story, it is an inward possession that can still be there when it feels like everything else is gone. Without hope we cannot move into the future. We literally cannot get out of bed in the morning if we have no hope. Hope lives in the imagination: "It is always imagining what is not yet seen, or a way out of difficulty, or a wider perspective for life or thought."[14] Lynch tells us that hope imagines *with*; it is fostered by help. Hope grows when we have a sense that there is an interaction between our call and response. Think of Sara. It was her mother who helped her to see a way out. Her mother's idea sparked her imagination and turned her despair back to hope.

Hope moves us into the future with a sense of the possible. Some things, however, are not possible. Not everyone can be a concert pianist, quarterback, or opera singer. Hope must be rooted in reality. Attaching our hopes to fantasy is actually a manifestation of hopelessness. It is a hidden despair over coping with reality. Lynch makes the point that for hope to exist, so must hopelessness—there are hopeless circumstances and times. He defines hopelessness as the "self-enclosure of despair."[15] It is the sense of being trapped in the present by a repetitious pattern from the past. It is like being in a prison with no windows. Hope's windows are the windows of our imagination, which provide images that we look through to see new possibilities. Hopelessness thwarts the freedom of our imagination and encloses our thoughts, feelings, and actions into a smaller and smaller range.

We can be very busy while remaining hopeless. The story of Sisyphus, also from Greek mythology, shows this. Sisyphus was a mortal who angered Zeus. So Zeus sent the spirit of Death (Thanatos) to put an end to this mortal, but Sisyphus was quite imaginative and outwitted Thanatos by chaining him up. Now no mortals could die, and Zeus was really mad. He intervened to free Thanatos. Of course once Death was free his first victim was Sisyphus, who was sent to the Underworld. To make sure that he would never conjure a way to escape, Sisyphus was given a task to completely occupy him. Sisyphus was condemned to roll an enormous boulder up a mountain for eternity. As soon as it reached the top, the boulder would roll back down and Sisyphus would start over again.[16]

Sometimes our jobs are the boulders in our life. They are so demanding that we do not have the time or energy to think of anything else. When our work is our boulder, we have the sense of working hard but never getting anywhere. In some cases, job loss can serve as a gift, removing the boulder and setting our imagination free to consider new possibilities. Imagination feeds our hope but it can atrophy from disuse.

Imagination requires space and freedom. We often associate imagination with creativity, but it is more fundamental. Creativity has to do with bringing things into being. Imagination precedes this. Imagination involves forming pictures of possibilities that are not part of our immediate, concrete world. Sometimes when these pictures come to our mind, we allow our heart to move ahead. Often we do not. We cut off the possibilities for any number of reasons, often because we think of them as impractical. We jump too readily to hopelessness. In doing so we may cut off our future.

The real trick is learning to live in the present while drawing from both the past and the future. Many of us drag our past around like Marley dragged his chains in Charles Dickens's tale of Scrooge. Our imagination is the active, creating part of our memory that goes beyond the past. Through images, we can also pull our future toward us and move into its current. We can feel it when this happens. It is as though we are lifted and carried along with greater ease. A friend of mine, who is an artist, recently told me that she felt as though something from her future hooked her heart and pulled her forward. When this happens, the best thing to do is to move with it.

Faith, hope, and imagination form a synergistic blend that is the basis of resilience. We are all given this capacity from birth. Many of the people I talked with are faith-full; they have created a personal canopy of meaning to make sense of their experience and to put it in a broader context. Their faith seems active in their daily life and it grows out of their relationships with others and through their own experience. Faith provides a deep resting place for our heart. Having faith in ourselves means resting in the confidence that we will know how to respond to whatever comes our way. We can do so with hope and imagination. If we cannot access this within ourselves, then we can access it through others. This blend of faith, hope, and imagination provides us with a more enduring source of security.

Involuntary job loss transformed the lives of some people I interviewed, but for a few it was little more than a blip in their journey that they wished could be erased. Those who changed basic assumptions about their work and themselves felt the best at the time that I interviewed them. These people combined both action and reflection, and they are the ones who shared a transformative response. What they have in common is a strong network of both personal and professional relationships, a shapeshifting ability, and a blend of faith, hope, and imagination. All of these qualities are intertwined and build upon each other. Of course, not everyone needs or wants to have a transformative response to job loss. It is largely a choice. The common ingredients that I found are something we can all access, if we want to.

Recently I attended a gathering for people who wanted to deepen their sense of spirituality. We were asked to introduce ourselves and explain why we came. One woman said, "I want to find a home" as tears rolled from her eyes. I look up home in the dictionary and it says, "an environment offering security and happiness." This is something we all yearn for. But it is an internal feeling; it is not a physical place. This woman who spoke lives in a house with her husband and children. How do we find our home? First we need to leave the home of our parents. We cannot return home until we have left. If we never leave home our life will lack any sense of mystery, spirit, or adventure. The journey home is in many ways a trail back to ourselves and to our soul. I use the hero's journey and references to mythology as a way of entering that meaning-filled dimension of kairos time. It helps us to see beyond our particular travails and realize that we may be partaking in something larger. It helps us to realize that we are not the first, nor the last, nor the only to run into obstacles, to feel lost, and perhaps to find a new way. Again, the greatest challenge in the hero's journey is returning home with new knowledge and sharing the lessons learned. Joseph Campbell tells us that the great paradox of the hero's journey is that we embark on the journey to save ourselves and not to save the world. But in doing that, we save the world.

# Part Four

# Lessons of Resilience

## Chapter Fourteen

# Befriending Change and Uncertainty

*Ten thousand flowers in spring, the moon in autumn,*
*a cool breeze in summer, snow in winter.*
*If your mind isn't clouded by unnecessary things,*
*this is the best season of your life.*
—WU-MEN

The lessons learned about job loss and resilience from people who speak out of their own experience cannot be described as techniques. These people do have skills for finding work in today's environment, such as résumé writing, interviewing, and networking. These skills are important and critical to learn. Without them it is extremely difficult to recover from job loss or navigate your career. Yet more profoundly, resilience rests on attitudes and ways of being in the world that go beyond skills and techniques. Many of these are lessons that go beyond a career. They are life lessons that will carry us into the future as we meet the 21st century.

It seems trite to say that we are in the midst of fast-moving, continuous change and that we must learn how to live with it. But we are, and we must. Over thirty years ago Alvin Toffler warned us of *future shock,* the stress and disorientation that people experience when they must absorb too much change too fast. Out of this stress we run the risk of increased physical, emotional, and spiritual disorders, such as ulcers, anger, depression, and alienation. Future shock has been with us for some time and will continue to be to the extent that we are overwhelmed by change. Perhaps the most essential lesson of resilience is learning to befriend change and uncertainty. I use the word *befriend,* rather than embrace, because the more resilient posture is to stand side by side with change—to consider it an ally, but not to grasp or cling. This perspective is expressed in William Blake's poem:

> He who binds to himself a joy
> Does the winged life destroy;
> But he who kisses the joy as it flies
> Lives in eternity's sunrise.

Actually all of us live suspended in uncertainty all the time. Sometimes I think about this when I am driving my car and hurtling down the highway. A distraction, a turn of my hand or head, could change everything in an instant. But we forget. Many of us forget the fragility of our circumstances because it is unsettling to think about. Some sense of predictability and constancy is crucial to our well-being and even our survival. Yet increasingly, our ability to respond to ever-changing conditions is just as crucial. How do we reconcile these two needs? Perhaps it relates to becoming more comfortable with not knowing.

An old Taoist story makes this point well. Once there was a man who owned a beautiful horse, and considered himself to be very lucky. Then one day the horse ran away. The man was distraught, so he went to a wise sage and told him how bad he felt that his horse was gone. The sage replied, "Who knows what's good and what's bad?" The next day the horse returned, bringing along an entire herd of beautiful wild horses. The man went back to the sage and told him how fortunate he was. Again the sage replied, "Who knows what's good and what's bad?" The next day the man's son was riding one of the wild horses and he fell and broke his leg. The man went to the sage in distress, only to hear, "Who knows what's good and what's bad?" The following day the military arrived at the man's house enlisting young men, but the son was exempt because of his broken leg. The man was overjoyed that his son was not going to war but the sage merely replied, "Who knows what's good and what's bad?"[1]

What this story teaches us is that we cannot place fixed judgments on a change of circumstance because the circumstance might change tomorrow. For most of the people I interviewed, job loss came as a shock and a blow. Given a choice, they probably would not have left. But over time, many ended up feeling better off than they were before they lost their job. Ironically, some talked about being envied by their former coworkers who did not lose their jobs. Who knows what's good and what's bad?

I think we may fear uncertainty even more than change. I have talked with many people who are not happy with their current work situation but do not want to leave because they lack clarity about where they'll end up. Many of the people I interviewed also did not know exactly where they would end up at the time they lost their job. To find out, they needed to travel into and through the dark. Fear of uncertainty is like a tar pit that keeps us stuck. We are afraid that we will end up in a worse place than where we are now. But the gift of ongoing change is knowing that there is no end point. It is not a matter of unfreezing, moving, and refreezing. Our life won't freeze. So even if we do end up feeling worse off than before, this may move us further along toward something better. It is easier to make a turn while moving than while standing still.

Sometimes it is just as well not to know too much. There have been several decisions in my life where had I really known what I was getting into, I never would have gone. But these have generally resulted in my biggest lessons. The difficulties may teach us new awareness and strengths that we carry into the future. They may prepare us for dealing with unforeseen situations that otherwise we could not have handled.

At some point, we must take a leap of faith. This is hard to do because it suggests a lack of control. Studies show that having a sense of control over parts of our life that we can control does decrease our stress and increase our happiness. Yet the problem with control is that there are simply a lot of things that we cannot control. Preoccupation with controlling the events in our lives makes us tense and compulsive. Often when too many events in my life are changing or converging and I feel as though I am losing control, I have a recurring dream. In this dream I am driving too fast and I cannot put on the breaks. I come to a curve that I cannot negotiate and spin off the road in my car. I am terrified—then I wake up.

I keep wishing that my dream mode of travel would be a sailboat rather than a car. Sailing seems like a better metaphor for travel in today's world. When sailing, you must be continuously responsive to shifts in wind and waves and to storms you may spot in the distance. Yet at the same time, it is possible to chart out a destination and get there. It is just that you cannot do it via a straight line, nor can you necessarily predict the exact route you will take in advance. The extent to which you control your journey is the extent to which you can dance with forces beyond your control.

Another way to think about this dance with change and uncertainty is improvisation. Improvisation is the ability to put things together in new ways. It is inventiveness. It is having a high level of response-ability. In her book *Composing a Life,* Mary Catherine Bateson talks about improvisation in her own life and the lives of four other women. Bateson observed the degree to which these women have improvised their journeys to create a unified whole between their achievements and their relationships. She introduces her book by saying that it is about "life as an improvisatory art," and then elaborates: "I believe that our aesthetic sense, whether in works of art or in lives, has overfocused on the stubborn struggle toward a single goal rather than on the fluid, the protean, the improvisatory. We see achievement as purposeful and monolithic, like the sculpting of a massive tree trunk . . . rather than something crafted from odds and ends, like a patchwork quilt, and lovingly used to warm different nights and bodies."[2]

In an interesting article about the Mann Gulch Disaster, Karl Weick also writes about the importance of improvisation. The Mann Gulch Disaster occurred in 1949 in Montana. A lightning storm began a fire in a dead tree, and because of the high temperature and dry conditions it quickly grew out of control. Sixteen smoke jumpers were dispatched to fight this fire, and only three of them came out alive. Weick examined the collapse of sense-making among this group and considered what might have shifted them from extreme vulnerability to resilience. One source of resilience that he identified is improvisation, or *bricolage.* Weick defined a bricoleur as someone who is able to create order out of whatever materials are at hand. He explained that, "Bricoleurs remain creative under pressure, precisely because they routinely act in chaotic conditions and pull order out of them."[3] An inability to improvise can result in paralysis or mindlessness, which in this case was disastrous for most of the men. Fifteen of the men instinctively tried to outrun the fire. One man turned and faced it by starting an escape fire then lying down in the ashes where the heat was less intense. He invented this tactic on the spot, and he was one of the few men who survived.

How many of us feel that we must routinely act in chaotic conditions? Recently the CEO of a young company told me: "It feels like I'm always on this boundary of total chaos, like it's all just about ready to fall apart, to become unglued—yet also sensing that it's about to come together. It's as if I'm out there hanging on the edge of it all. Maybe that's what a lot of organizations feel. As an individual I feel that way a lot. It's messy, and for people like me who don't like messes it's really hard to leave the messes there and live with all the unknowns and trust that things will work out."

What is interesting to me about this comment is the amount of scientific truth it holds. The relatively new science of complexity theory shows that life emerges at the edge of chaos. In physics this is the place between solids, where atoms are locked into place, and fluids, where atoms tumble around in chaos. The place where new life emerges is that space between chaos and order—the edge of chaos. This is where living systems can react to the world and are most spontaneous, adaptive, and alive. When we move too far on the side of order we become frozen and stagnant. When we move too far into chaos we become confused and disoriented. The edge of chaos strikes a balance between chaos and order. But it is not like walking on a razor's edge. It is actually quite vast, as vast as the surface of the ocean.

Unlike the Newtonian image of the universe as a clock, the science of complexity tells us "that we're part of an ever-changing, interlocking, nonlinear, kaleidoscopic world."[4] This world does not function in terms of linear cause and effect, but rather as emerging patterns that change and adapt. Today we know that the growth of a plant from a seed or the unfolding organization of an ant colony are more accurate metaphors for how life happens. These have less predictability and are less controllable than a clock or machine. It is amazing that back in 500 B.C. Heraclitus actually

had a more accurate depiction of the world than Descartes or Newton, one that is more aligned with our most recent scientific discoveries. Heraclitus described the world as being in a constant state
of flux, saying "nothing endures but change," and reminding us
that we can never step into the same river twice.

Knowing this, what is our response? As with sailing, we move
forward with intention and attention. We observe and pay attention to the events around us. We cannot do this unless we are fully
present. We notice patterns. We stay open-minded to new options
and opportunities because patterns emerge over time, and when
we jump too quickly to conclusions or closure we may lose sight of
the deeper order that is trying to reveal itself. We imagine new des-
tinations and are not afraid of committing to the stroke.

Several years ago I went on a canoe trip on Abiquiu Lake in
New Mexico. The guide reminded us that while canoeing, especially in turbulent waters, we must commit to the stroke. A weak or
half-hearted stroke has the same effect as the wrong stroke—neither will get us to where we want to go. Perhaps more fundamentally, we might ask ourselves why we are going there in the first
place.

The work of Mihaly Csikszentmihalyi, at the University of
Chicago, teaches us about approaching life as *flow*. Simply put, flow
is about how we find happiness. Yet happiness is actually a side
effect; it is not achieved when directly pursued. Flow is the psychology of optimal experience—those times when we forget about
the passage of time because we are so absorbed in what we are
doing. What may come to mind is the artist absorbed in creating a
sculpture or the athlete performing at his or her peak. It is the feeling a friend of mine described when she was in a rowing race. Prior
to the race she felt scared, but once her oar hit the water something took over and she was aware of a power and a relaxed yet
strong forward momentum as her team pulled their oars in uni-
son. Csikszentmihalyi was intrigued with this type of experience so
he and his colleagues interviewed thousands of people of many cultures, ages, and walks of life. What he found is that the more time
people spend in flow, the more happy they are. The flow experience contains three components: (1) clear goals or challenges that
we believe we can master, along with feedback about how we are
doing, (2) total involvement or immersion in the activity that

removes awareness of the worry and frustrations of everyday life, and (3) close attention and concentration on the activity without self-consciousness.[5]

People who spend more time in this state get more enjoyment out of life. It has very little to do with outer circumstances—even people in dire situations such as solitary confinement have reported flow experiences. It has everything to do, however, with intention and attention. Flow is not laissez-faire. It involves the channeling of energy toward goals and the refinement of skills. It also acknowledges that our greatest area of control is our attention. People who achieve flow focus their attention at will and can block out other distractions and unnecessary information.

Focusing our attention may be the most important and challenging task as we move into the information age. It is easy to get overwhelmed. We can surf the Net and find ourselves drowning in information. People who experience flow are able to concentrate on a goal. They are able to select information that is relevant and to screen out the millions of tidbits of information that are irrelevant. Yet again, this must be done with an attitude of open-mindedness and creativity. Becoming frozen into a single-minded approach toward a goal is not flow. It is what Langer calls mindlessness—an overreliance on rigid categories and distinctions and habits from the past.[6] When we are mindless, we screen out too much.

When we are in flow, time is distorted. We lose track of time. Most likely, this is when we are doing something that we find totally captivating, something that we love to do. It may be our biggest clue in terms of figuring out *what* to do, in terms of work. Our most natural inclinations are likely to converge with flow. In a sense, flow allows us to expand time. We stop thinking in terms of minutes and hours and live in what seems like one extended moment of time.

Flow is not the same as constant busyness. Many of us cram the hours of our days with doing as many different things as we possibly can. We try to do it all. We overcommit and compress time. I think we often do this because we fear free time. Busyness keeps uncomfortable feelings at bay. They are likely to show themselves when we take some time to pause or relax. If we get an inkling of this discomfort, we become more busy. But busyness keeps us preoccupied with *time,* rather than with the activity itself. It is a way of

losing our attention. It is also a way of feeling increasingly fragmented. Our life becomes ordered by the divisions of our calendar and often there is a disjunction between our schedule and who
we really are and what we really care about. We race through the
day as though we are on the Autobahn highway in Germany, where
you must drive at least ninety miles per hour whether you want to
or not. The only way to slow down is to pull off the road. This is
another potential gift of job loss. It may force us to slow down, to
pause, to think about the direction we really want to go.

Befriending change and uncertainty means living with some
doubt. Taoists express their comfort with uncertainty by saying,
"The sage steers by the torch of chaos and doubt." As much as we
might want to, we cannot know what lies before us. We can only
know what lies within us. Everything could change tomorrow. The
extent to which we can approach life as improvisation will ease our
ability to move with change. The extent to which we notice those
times when we experience flow will tell us more about who we are
and what we love to do. In terms of our career, improvising means
being clear about the skills and knowledge that we have and figuring out how to put them together and apply them in different
situations. It means being able to consider multiple options and
tracks and to shift gears when it seems appropriate. It means using
our imagination to create possibilities for our future. If we are comfortable with our ability to respond and to improvise, then we can
befriend change rather than resist it. In doing this, we may discover
more about our potential than we ever imagined.

## Lessons

*Before placing a fixed judgment on events or circumstances, wait until the
larger story unfolds.*

*Seek a middle ground between needing or taking control and letting go of
control; life is most fertile on the edge of chaos.*

*Move forward with a clarity of intention and attention; remember that these
two things are always within your realm of control.*

*Pay attention to the patterns that emerge from opportunities, events, peo-
ple, and experiences.*

*Think about how you might improvise to create new directions or opportunities; imagine what you can create out of the resources that you already have at hand.*

*Notice when you experience flow; what are you doing when you feel confident, focused, and so absorbed that you forget the passage of time?*

*Accept change, uncertainty, and doubt as part of the mystery of life, not as an obstacle or reason for taking no action.*

## Chapter Fifteen

# Transplanting Security

*What is our innocence,*
*what is our guilt? All are*
*naked, none is safe. And whence*
*is courage: the unanswered question,*
*the resolute doubt—*
*dumbly calling, deafly listening—that*
*in misfortune, even death,*
*encourages others*
*and in its defeat, stirs*
*the soul to be strong?*
—MARIANNE MOORE[1]

Over and over I have made the point that we can no longer think in terms of *job* security. Placing our sense of security in having a job with a particular organization is like building a house on sand. Our sense of security must be transplanted and rerooted in something that is more enduring, beyond an organization. This allows us to continue to work within organizations amid change and uncertainty.

Rather than thinking in terms of job security, we must think more in terms of *networked* security. In many ways, the people I interviewed found their network—both personal and professional—to be a more enduring source of security than their job. Like a net, the network provides an important holding function so that when we stumble it keeps us from falling too far.

In the future few of us will have a career that follows a linear path within a single organization. Organizations themselves need to have built-in flexibility so that they can weather sudden shifts and changes in the marketplace. Consequently work will increasingly be organized as assignments that last for a year or two, rather than as long-term jobs with titles. This shifts the burden of responsibility for defining a career path back to the individual. We will not find a lifelong path or track to success within a single organization. Most of us will have career paths that involve lots of curves and branches, and that will be built out of a network of organizations and affiliations (Figure 15.1). Our professional security rests in these linkages rather than in any single entity.

Our personal sense of security is another matter. Certainly it is augmented by knowing that we will be able to find work. But this may not be the deeper issue. The word security comes from the Latin word *cura,* which means care. Security means without anxiety or care. Security is linked to caring. We might ask ourselves: Who or what do I care about? Who cares about me? Who would care *for* me? How do I care for myself? The answers to these questions address deeper issues of security.

A story that poignantly illustrates this occurred in Oregon as a result of torrential rainfall and flooding in February, 1996. The rain came so fast that it caused the ground to soften, resulting in mudslides and floods. Tillamook County, an area where there are many dairy farms, was badly affected. Many of these farms have been on the land for fifty to seventy-five years. The original families homesteaded the land and then the farms were taken over by their children, their children's children, and so forth. On NPR, I heard an interview with a woman who was a flood victim. She and her husband had run their dairy farm for thirty-one years. As the rains continued to pour, they watched their house carried down a river of muddy water while they were rescued by a man on a big tractor and moved to higher ground. A few days later they returned to their farm and this is what the woman said:

> We were amazed to see that we still had animals because when we left our farm, the water was up to the cows' chins, and there was no way—it truly was a miracle, and if you don't want to even be religious, after something like this you will be. They were still alive, and they shouldn't have been because cows get cold, they get tired, they want to lay down, and when they lay down they're going to drown. . . . We had a newborn baby calf that was born on Monday.

## Figure 15.1.   Job Security Versus Networked Security.

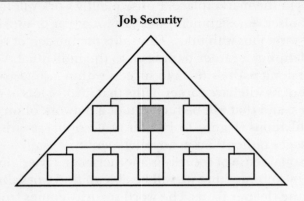

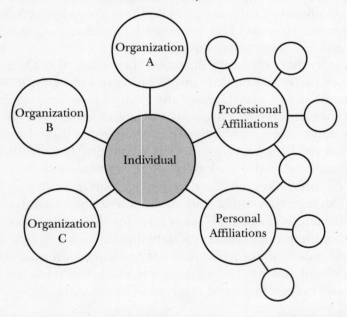

She had water clear over her back, and when my husband walked into the barn, he was still waist-high in water, and the calf was in a little bit of higher barn. As soon as she saw him, she started bellowing and so we've called her Miracle. We've named her, and we're going to keep her forever.[2]

The person interviewing this woman said that it must be awfully hard on you and your husband to try to carry on your work, while your farm is covered with mud and water. The woman replied, "It's difficult, but you know what is even more difficult is being able to accept all the help. It's been overwhelming. You know, a person can get through any disaster, really. I mean it's shocking and hard but there has been so much help from friends, neighbors, and people we don't even know."

While the flood waters nearly washed away this woman's livelihood, she focused on the support she and her husband received. She continued to talk about the strength of their community and the community spirit that exists in this small rural town. She also talked about their struggle to make a living as farmers and the realization that small farms will probably not survive economically. This story highlights in bold relief deeper sources of security. On one hand, this woman realizes that they have no "job security." On the other hand, her anxiety is assuaged because she is embedded in a network of support among friends, neighbors, and in this case, people she did not even know. This is a sense of security, a sense of being held, that cannot be washed away by a flood.

We must recognize, however, that we can lose people just as we can lose a job. The enduring aspect is the capacity to form and nourish relationships, the ability to bring people inside. Our resilience lies in our ability to remember lost loves and relationships with gratitude rather than bitterness, and to attract new people to our side. We may lose people, but we do not lose what we learned from them. This is what it means to take people inside. It means recognizing the connections that we have with people, past and present, nearby and far away. It means thinking of all our relations in a broader sense so that we experience a sense of relatedness and safety. It means having the sense that if we call for help there will be a response. This is what Sharon Parks referred to as a "network of belonging." It is a place that we carry inside ourselves that feels like home. It is a home that we will not lose despite the worst fire or flood.

We also can feel held by a system of meaning. A belief or faith in something larger creates a larger pattern or canopy of meaning. This puts the particular events of our lives into a different perspective and binds the pieces of our lives into a larger story. Yet even our canopy of meaning can tear or collapse when it is challenged by tragedy or disappointment that we cannot explain or understand. In fact, involuntary job loss can lead to such a collapse. It may bring into question basic assumptions that we rested our lives upon. What endures in this case is the capacity to reconstruct new meanings. It is the capacity to allow for some collapse and the faith that we can put the pieces back together again. It is our ability to reweave our canopy that endures and this reweaving is what leads to our growth. We weave our losses or disappointments into a larger canopy or net and once again create a coherent whole that holds us.

This is the basis of resilience. Resilience is often misunderstood as being invulnerable or unflappable. When we resist feeling bad or falling apart we often simply grow increasingly rigid. We begin to feel like barnacles clinging to the hull of a ship as waves crash around us. By contrast, resilience is acquiring skills and strengths so that we can move through periods of chaos and reintegration throughout our lives. The *inability* to do this is what leaves us crippled. From a spiritual or mythical level, we might think about these cycles of chaos and reintegration as being part of the life-death-life cycle. By opening ourselves to it, we realize that a metaphorical death heralds the beginning of something new. Failure to move through this cycle blocks renewal and transformative change, and impedes our learning.

Many of us are feeling insecure right now because we have incorrectly learned to equate security with job security. We do this because for most of us, our job is our source of money. In essence, we equate security with money. Many times I have talked with people who are losing or fear they might lose their job and asked about their source of security. Somehow they hear "money" rather than security, because they respond by saying something like "I have enough assets to live on for about a year." This tendency to equate money and security is actually increasing with new generations. Annual surveys by the American Council on Education show that the number of college students who believe that financial affluence is essential increased from 45 percent in 1967 to more than 70 percent in 1987. Meanwhile, those students who believe it is important to develop a meaningful philosophy of life fell from 84 percent to 40 percent in the same time period.[3] These students carry the false promise that they will find happiness and security somewhere on top of the economic ladder. Interestingly, however, research on lottery winners shows the error of this belief. Even people who win millions of dollars and are suddenly catapulted to the top of the ladder say that a year afterward, they feel no more happy or secure than they did before they won the money.[4]

Remember that security actually means being without anxiety. Today having a job is often just the opposite of this, especially if we live in fear of losing the job. One person I interviewed said, "I've got some friends who are still in a corporate environment and if somebody hiccups wrong they're afraid they'll lose their job that day." This is a terrible way to live. Rather than being free of anxiety, it is anxiety-ridden.

Money can have the same effect. I found no correlation between the way people felt after losing their job and the amount of money they had in the bank. In fact, one of the people I spoke with who felt the most anxiety about his job loss and about money had more money in the bank than nearly anyone else I interviewed. There is no question that in our society money is important because it is the only way that we can meet our basic needs. Abraham Maslow defined a hierarchy of needs and explained that in order to even think about higher-level needs, such as learning or growth, we need to meet basic physiologic needs such as food, clothing, and shelter. It is terribly frightening to have a sense that we may not be able to pay our rent or mortgage, or that we cannot afford to go to a doctor when we are ill. But once we are beyond the threshold of meeting basic needs, money doesn't help.

Money, alone, will never bring us real security. This is because money does not feed our spirit or soul. These are fed by nonmaterial things, such as meaning, love, imagination, and a connection to something larger than ourselves. But materialism dominates our society. This is the belief that the universe can be wholly explained by physical laws and that reality is only what we see or hear. We believe that the real world exists outside ourselves and emphasize objective reality as the highest reality. We become identified with things and tie our self-worth very literally to our net worth. This negates the mystery of life and our own mystery. It also negates much of who we are, and we end up turning ourselves into a commodity. The result of identifying only with the outer world at the expense of what lies within is that we end up feeling brittle, like an empty shell. We are in fact more brittle, because at some level we realize that our security is tied to something that is easily lost. This makes us feel insecure. This feeling is an indefinite, pervasive, objectless apprehension. We try to assuage it with concrete things but this doesn't work.

A common image that occurred in many texts from the Middle Ages is the wheel of fortune. Often in these drawings, there are lots of people grasping on to the rim of the wheel in various positions (Figure 15.2).[5] A material view of life keeps us on the revolving rim of this wheel, so that we always feel as though we are losing or gaining something. It is not too different from riding the stock market.

The only way to move toward a place of greater equanimity is to move toward the hub. This is a more balanced place. We do this by accessing the inner, nonmaterial world. We access this place by taking time to pause, to be quiet, and to listen. We realize that we cannot know or understand everything, and that this is the mystery of life. Sometimes we get fleeting glimpses of this mystery—often through images. These images come to us through our dreams and imagination and the images themselves are the language of our soul. Rather than discounting or ignoring these we need to hold them with tender curiosity and consider their meaning without making judgments. By moving inward toward the hub of the wheel of fortune we find an oasis of personal security that loosens our reactivity to the ups and downs of everyday life. Here we access a deeper well and find a more fertile and enduring source of nourishment.

At the same time we cannot cut ourselves off from the outer world. I am not suggesting withdrawing to a mountain cave to meditate. Nor am I saying that money is not important. I am suggesting, however, that focusing solely on the material world is what

**Figure 15.2.    Wheel of Fortune.**

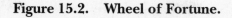

leaves us feeling empty. The people I spoke with who felt best after losing their job had access to both worlds. They were both active and reflective. They were also both imaginative and pragmatic. Several talked about budgeting the minimum amount of money they needed each month and then figuring out different ways of generating that amount.

The dominant metaphor when thinking about transplanting security is that of a network or canopy. It is the sense that we weave together the many threads of our lives—both the material and nonmaterial aspects—into something that will hold us or shield us. We can also apply this metaphor to our career. Howard Gruber, who studied the lives of creative people, uses the term "network of enterprise."[6] Gruber closely examined the lives of selected people such as Charles Darwin, and found that rather than having a predetermined goal, these people had a set of purposes that moved them in a particular direction. They had a scheme of activities that was broad enough to encompass a variety of goals, problems, and projects. These activities form the strands of the person's network of enterprise, and the strands relate to and support each other. Gruber found that over their lifetime creative people evolve strategies to move in a general direction and in doing so, they create a network of enterprise.

This is different from a fixed career goal. What stays the same is the general direction of movement, but the specific goals might vary. For instance, a person might decide that he or she has a gift for teaching, in the sense of helping others to learn. Perhaps this person starts off as a high school teacher, then becomes a corporate trainer, then becomes involved with designing training programs while volunteering to teach English as a second language, and so on. We may not even be clear about what our gift or general direction is, but usually a pattern emerges over time. This is similar to the notion in physics of a *strange attractor.* Scientists have found that as chaotic systems develop, they eventually assume a particular shape, which is dictated by the strange attractor. The strange attractor acts as a sort of magnet keeping the activity of the system within certain boundaries. The boundaries are determined by the pull of the strange attractor, and the shape emerges over time. Our strange attractors are made up of our prevailing values, interests, and talents. If we are true to them, over our lifetime our activities organize into a pattern. A network of enterprise is not a precise or predetermined path, but it is a pattern of purposeful activity that emerges over time.

I want to point out that this includes both work and nonwork activities. For instance, I know of an accomplished abstract painter who is clear that art is her gift and vocation. She believes that all the activities that nourish her spirit, such as making bread, taking a walk, or teaching an art class, contribute to her painting. Therefore when she takes the time to do these things, she does not believe that she is taking time away from her "real work." All these activities contribute to her network of enterprise.

The futurist Charles Handy advocates a similar notion, which he calls *work portfolios.* Handy believes that by the early 21st century, less than half the workforce in the industrial world will be in full-time jobs as we have known them.[7] Having a full-time job with one organization will be the exception, rather than the norm. Consequently Handy suggests that individuals need to develop a broader concept of work. He uses the work portfolio concept to suggest a way of organizing the different parts of our life into a balanced whole. The work portfolio would include these categories: fee work (what we get paid for), home work (activities relating to home and family), gift work (community service), and study work (learning).[8] Businesses often think in terms of their portfolios consisting of their products or clients. Similarly, most of us will need to think of ourselves as small business entities and consider multiple sources of money. But if we only think in terms of how we generate money and ignore all other aspects of our life, we will end up feeling dry and depleted. This is why Handy encourages us to think about work as encompassing the many activities of our life and how these fit together.

Transplanting security means that we stop thinking of a particular job as our source of security and cultivate various sources of security, both material and nonmaterial. We weave all of these into a network that provides us with some sense of safety and support. Relationships with others is the factor people mentioned most often when asked what helped them through their job loss and transition. Yet security also lies within the self. It is rooted in confidence and faith. Having an oasis of personal security gives us a place to return to when events are swirling around us. You can see that security has a lot to do with the linkages in our life—linkages with others, with our self, with something beyond our self, and with our activities. All of these linkages form a holding net that provides us with a more enduring source of security. Creating such a net means being able to unite the various parts of our life into a larger whole that provides meaning.

## Lessons

*Realize that from now on, professional security is more closely tied to a network of personal and professional relationships than to a job or organization.*

*Cultivate internal and enduring sources of support; consider who or what you care about most deeply, and who or what would care for you in need.*

*Intentionally create a network of belonging—connections with people who recognize and appreciate who you are and what you might become.*

*Distinguish between resilience and invulnerability; realize that deeper sources of security stem from the experience of both pain and joy, learning from these experiences, and weaving them into a larger personal philosophy or canopy of meaning.*

*Budget the amount of money you must have each month, and generate alternative ways to earn that minimum amount while you are working toward where you want to be.*

*Realize that balance is not just a matter of juggling tasks or roles, but also a balance between the external and internal, the material and nonmaterial, the visible and invisible aspects of life.*

*Think of the movement of your career as more of a pattern of activities—or a network of enterprise—rather than as a series of titles or positions.*

*Look for overarching themes that provide purposeful direction and link many of your activities and interests, such as teacher, manager, artist, or entrepreneur.*

## Chapter Sixteen

# Paradoxical Living

*Out beyond ideas of wrongdoing and rightdoing,*
*there is a field. I'll meet you there.*
*When the soul lies down in that grass,*
*the world is too full to talk about.*
*Ideas, language, even the phrase* each other
*doesn't make any sense.*
—RUMI

Can you answer this question: What creature is it that walks on four legs in the morning, two legs at noontime, and three legs in the evening? This is the riddle the Sphinx posed to all who tried to travel into the ancient city of Thebes. The Sphinx was a giant and imposing creature with the face and breasts of a beautiful woman, the body and claws of a lion, and the wings of an eagle. If voyagers could not answer the riddle, the Sphinx promptly devoured them. This blockade was as effective as any we have seen in modern times, so the people of Thebes were growing increasingly hungry and desperate. Finally Oedipus came along and gave the right answer: Man. We crawl on four legs as infants, two legs as adults, and lean on a cane in old age. The Sphinx was so dismayed to be outwitted that she leapt to her death over a precipice. The city of Thebes rejoiced, and crowned Oedipus as king.

The question of the Sphinx makes use of *paradox*. Paradox is a realization that a seemingly contradictory statement might be true. The word itself is linked to the word dogma, which means to believe. This is useful to know because dogma is associated with beliefs that we hold to be absolute. Paradox takes us beyond dogma by allowing us to see beyond the divisions of absolute truths.

Throughout my interviews with people who bounced back after losing their job, I noticed paradox. As I mentioned, these resilient people were both active and reflective. They were individualistic while embedded in a network of relationships, they took control while letting go of control, and they gained strength through vulnerability. They also combined imagination and creativity with pragmatism and realism. The idea of paradox is an intellectual concept; we did not discuss these issues as being paradoxical during the interviews. Yet I noticed that these people were able to bridge the tensions of their lives and bring them together into harmony. I call this paradoxical living.

As human beings we have been confronted with paradox throughout our history. Among the Greeks, it was the Pythagoreans who believed that reality is made up of pairs—light and dark, odd and even, better and worse, one and many, good and bad. The Pythagoreans strove to unite these pairs by figuring out how they could exist in harmony.

The Eastern philosophy of Taoism also sees life as containing opposites that must be reconciled. Taoism originated in China from the writings of Lao Tsu in the 6th century B.C. It is often associated with Yin and Yang, the symbol shown in Figure 16.1. Yin and Yang literally means the "dark and sunny side of the hill." Yin, the dark side, is associated with earth, night, female, receptivity, rest, and yielding. Yang, the light side, is associated with heaven, day, male, activity, movement, and penetrating. Life is seen as a rhythmic movement among and between opposites. The symbol shown in Figure 16.1 shows that Yin and Yang are intertwined and that they flow into each other. The small light and dark circles indicate that within any polarity is the seed of its opposite, just as each season contains the seed of the next.

Unfortunately, throughout history many belief systems have also emerged that split pairs of opposites. Just a few centuries after the Pythagoreans, the Gnostics could see no way of reconciling such concepts as "a world of splendor and of light without darkness," with "a world of darkness, utterly full of evil."[1] As I mentioned in Chapter One, serious splitting also occurred in the 17th

**Figure 16.1. Yin and Yang.**

century when Descartes separated the mind from the body, reason from emotion, and spirit from science.

We still live with this split thinking today. We hear it in phrases such as "keep your personal life at home while you are at work," or "be reasonable—not emotional," or "that's a man's type of work." Split thinking means that we put things into categories and believe that the categories are mutually exclusive, such as "this is good *or* bad, right *or* wrong." Paradoxical thinking moves beyond the categories and realizes that both might be true: "this is good *and* bad." Split thinking is characterized by either/or, whereas paradoxical thinking is characterized by both-and.

Paradoxical living is realizing that life cannot be put into compartments. It means realizing that everything we encounter—a person, an event, an organization, a job—carries the seeds of both good and bad, light and dark. It also means realizing that we carry these seeds within ourselves. The problem with split thinking is that it leads to a fragmented life. It is a life made up of rigid categories, judgments, and pronouncements, which leads to increasing divisiveness and rigidity. Right now this type of thinking is threatening the very unity of our country. When we split anything off from its opposite, the aspect that we embrace can become grossly distorted. In its tragic extreme we see 166 innocent people killed in the bombing of the federal building in Oklahoma City with the twisted logic that this is a proclamation for individual freedom over government.

On a personal level, the danger of split thinking is that we split parts of ourselves off from our own awareness. Jung calls this the *shadow*. Jung thought of the shadow as those aspects of our personality that we are not aware of and that we have essentially pushed underground: "The shadow personifies everything that the subject refuses to acknowledge about himself and yet is always thrusting itself upon him directly or indirectly—for instance, inferior traits of character and other incompatible tendencies."[2] These are often things that as children we were taught to believe were bad or unacceptable, such as feelings of anger, sadness, spontaneity, or sexuality. When we repress or disown these aspects of ourselves, it is like locking hungry dogs in the basement. The longer we ignore them, the hungrier and meaner they get and the louder they bark. Their energy does not disappear, it just gets distorted in the form of compulsions and projections. *Projections* are a type of defense in which we displace our shadow onto others. For instance, if we believe that it is not OK to feel anxiety, we lock that hungry dog in the basement and then blame our spouse or coworkers for their excessive anxiety.

The shadow itself is paradoxical. It is often associated with the dark side, with negative or undesirable traits or qualities. However, it also contains light. The shadow contains all those aspects of ourselves that we are not aware of and this includes positive qualities, as well. Our shadow may contain the germs of our potential and the seeds of our future.

The purpose of getting to know our shadow is not to make it disappear, but to become aware of it. This actually lessens its influence on our behavior. As Ken Wilber states, "We may wisely *be aware* of our opposites, or we will be forced to *beware* of them."[3] When the shadow is not acknowledged it is likely to force our attention by producing symptoms such as a physical illness or a pattern of difficulties that we bring upon ourselves. But when we have a relationship with our shadow it acts as a sort of psychic immune system. This is why Jung saw integrating the shadow as an "eminently practical problem." The goal is to place it in the proper relationship to our ego and Self. We do not need to *act* on our shadow, but we do need to be aware of it. We can only do so through self-knowledge, through a deepening and widening of our consciousness. In doing so we become more integrated, and typically improve our relationships with others and increase our creative energy.

Projection is the defense most commonly used to keep the shadow out of our awareness. Rather than seeing those things we don't like or accept in ourselves, we see them in other people—and react negatively. Vaillant considers projection to be an immature defense, in the sense that it can stultify our growth and create problems for ourselves and for people around us. But Vaillant also makes the point that we all need defenses. Defenses create a sort of psychological homeostasis; they help us to maintain an equilibrium as we adapt to situations over our lifetime. Through his studies of adults over their life span, Vaillant identified what he calls mature defenses. Mature defenses involve the synthesis, rather than denial, of conflicts that we experience either internally or externally. The five mature defenses include anticipation, altruism, suppression, sublimation, and humor.[4]

Vaillant also points out that each of these mature defenses contains an inherent paradox: "The capacity to produce paradox—to spin straw into gold, to find hopeful silver linings in storm clouds, and to find laughter in dispute—is part of the wisdom of the ego."[5] Anticipation involves the ability to experience the effects of future pain while in the relative safety of the present. This is why thinking through the worst thing that might happen from losing your job, before it happens, can soften the blow. Altruism is having the empathy to understand how other people feel and having the willingness to help while not losing touch with your own feelings. Many of the people I interviewed actually had an increased desire to "give back" after losing their job. Suppression is essentially following the advice of the serenity prayer familiar to people who have participated in 12–Step programs; it is having the courage to change the things we can change, the serenity to accept what we cannot change, and the wisdom to know the difference. Sublimation is channeling anxiety or frustration into energy for doing or creating something else. And we all know that laughter can be a balm for tension and distress.

Paradox goes hand in hand with creativity. Paradoxical living is a creative and improvisational approach to life. Remember the smoke jumper from the Mann Gulch Disaster, mentioned in Chapter Fourteen? Rather than running from the fire, he escaped it by starting a second fire, lying down in the ashes, and letting the other fire jump over him. This is paradoxical thinking! Paradox is associated with creativity because studies of highly creative people show that they are more easily able to reconcile seeming contradictions. Many creations come out of taking two disparate ideas or disciplines and creating a synthesis between them. For instance, Gutenberg invented the printing press after watching grapes being pressed at harvest and coins being minted by pouring metal into molds. He combined the pressing function from the vineyard and the minting of coins into the molding of movable type.[6] But we do not need to be famous inventors to be creative. We all have creative potential.

Vaillant finds correlations between resilience and creativity. He sees defenses as being *reactive* to life, while creativity is *proactive*.[7] For instance, Sara sublimated her anxieties when she wrote songs while in the midst of her depression after being dropped by the record company. Creativity is putting something into the world that was not there before. Childbirth is an ultimate form of creativity, but there are countless examples. We access our creativity by letting ourselves play, dream, and rest. Creative ideas often come when we take a break from concentrating or allow our thoughts to incubate. During this time our mind can sleep but our soul stays awake. This is one reason why taking a break, or retreat, was important for the people I spoke with. It gave them the time and space for different options and possibilities to emerge. Creativity comes from considering alternative points of view. What blocks creativity is single-minded concentration from a single frame of reference or prematurely judging ideas and locking them into categories or classifications.

Creativity is associated with generativity. The psychologist Erik Erikson used the term *generativity* to describe a developmental stage that we may reach in the second half of our life. It is the desire to care about the development of someone who is younger than we are, or to leave a legacy that will continue in future generations. Mentoring is a good example of generativity. Creativity is also associated with successful aging among both men and women. As they age, creative people are more likely to remain open to new ideas, approach life realistically and with a sense of humor, and accept their past.

Sometimes people associate creativity with emotional instability, but Vaillant has found no evidence of this. However, creative people are often more comfortable with disorder. They may deliberately allow parts of their life, or their art, to fall apart so that the parts will reassemble into something new. Chaos and creativity are archetypally linked, and this is seen in mythology throughout all cultures. This is why Sara found that in her darkest moments she created her most beautiful songs. It is the idea that out of chaos, disintegration, and darkness comes order, integration, and light. Most fundamentally, this is a reflection of the life-death-life cycle.

Joseph Campbell explains that the riddle of the Sphinx is the image of life through time, from childhood to maturity, to old age, to death. By standing up to the Sphinx, Oedipus faced death and in so doing showed that life is not contrary to death, but that life and death are aspects of each other: "Life in its becoming is always shedding death, and on the point of death. The conquest of fear yields the courage of life."[8] This is the most basic paradox that we all must come to terms with.

Much of the literature on job loss emphasizes the loss. The loss experience, and the grieving that goes with it (fear, denial, anger, depression) is one part of this cycle. But if we think of the loss as a type of death—the symbolic death of our identity, or role, or expectations—then we are reminded of the life-death-life cycle. Symbolically, death and chaos are a prerequisite for life and creativity. This might be graphically depicted as the sigmoid curve (Figure 16.2). The sigmoid curve is the wavelike S-shape that is seen in the earliest decorative art, such as the borders of Greek vases. This shape has fascinated artists, scientists, and engineers for centuries. Notice that it can be seen in the Yin and Yang symbol. It is also a basic pattern of nature. Jonas Salk used this curve to show the natural biological regulation of most species. It also might be used to depict the course of love and relationships, or the life cycle of a product or company.

We can use the sigmoid curve as a way to depict the cycle of life, death, and learning. For example, we might show the phases of life as described by the Sphinx on the arc of the curve that suggests a

**Figure 16.2.   Sigmoid Curve.**

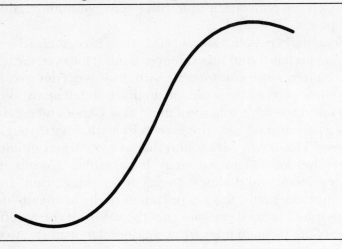

hill: childhood, maturity, and old age (Figure 16.3). Symbolically death takes us into the valley of chaos. We can think of the progression of our own life and learning as consisting of the symbolic deaths and rebirths that we experience throughout our life.

This can be shown by combining a series of sigmoid curves into a wavelike pattern depicting the full cycle of creation (birth), growth (childhood), integration (maturity), decline (old age), and death (chaos), which leads to back to creation, as shown in Figure 16.4. This wavelike pattern is the complete life-death-life cycle that reflects our deep learning experiences. Many of us hold the mistaken view that learning consists of a steady upward progression of improved performance continuing into perpetuity.

We think of the learning curve as an *upward* curve. But it is actually more like a valley or trough. It is when things fall apart, when they are blurred and indistinct, when chaos and turbulence are present, that there is greater plasticity and more potential for learning. Deep learning, such as that which might occur from job loss, takes place in the belly of the whale, in the valley of chaos. Deep learning occurs in that in-between time of liminality. It is a borderline place where we have greater access to our subconscious and to information from our spirit and soul. Taoists consider this to be a time of letting go and letting things happen and a place

**Figure 16.3.    Phases of Life.**

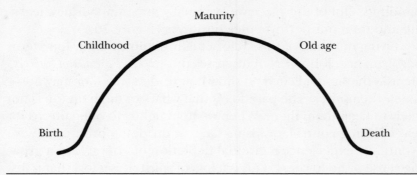

**Figure 16.4.    Life-Death-Life Cycle.**

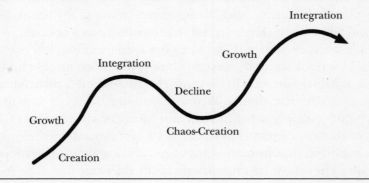

where we know before we know we know. This is our true creative center. From here we discover new insights, ideas, and understandings. Out of this place we eventually integrate our new learning and then our performance improves (Figure 16.5).

Living only half of this cycle actually diminishes our long-term performance. John O'Neil discusses this in *The Paradox of Success*.[9] He uses the sigmoid curve to show how leaders may—or may not—renew themselves. The paradox is that what got them on top is not likely to keep them there. When we hold tightly to old patterns for fear of losing control, or losing face, or dropping productivity, we eventually experience a gradual depletion of energy and a growing sense of hollowness. This is a loss of spirit. It is a loss that is just as serious as more concrete manifestations such as loss of a job or a relationship. Continuous learning and growth means that we move through cycles of chaos, creativity, and productivity and in doing so we renew our spirit.

Over twenty years ago Jonas Salk wrote a book called *The Survival of the Wisest*. Here he expressed the concern that we have created a split between what he called "ego values" such as intellect, reason, and objectivity, and "being values" such as intuition, feeling, and subjectivity. He believed that to survive as a species, we as a people must reconcile this split of opposing tendencies.

Salk used the sigmoid curve to show how nature unites and balances opposing forces. This is most clearly reflected through the balance of life and death. When any living thing or species is allowed to multiply without restraint, disaster strikes. We might think of the way cancer cells multiply until they destroy their host. Salk cautioned that human beings are running the same risk ecologically. Therefore he encourages us to shift our thinking from "survival of the fittest"—the notion of conquering and dominating—to "survival of that which fits best" in the evolutionary scheme of things. For the long-term survival of our species, Salk encourages us to cultivate our wisdom by bridging these dualities: intellect and intuition, reason and feeling, objectivity and subjectivity, competition and cooperation, power and influence. Salk stated that we have reached the point in our own evolution where we are in dire need of wise leaders who possess a "wisdom akin to that of Nature," who understand the natural processes of growth and development, and who see the whole process of which we are a part.[10]

## Figure 16.5.   Learning Curve.

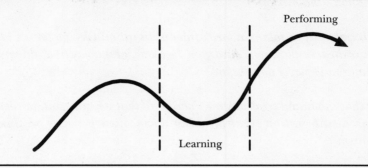

Performing

Learning

Paradoxical living is living life in its fullness. It means that we do not box in our thoughts or our lives, but instead consider multiple ideas and possibilities. The people I interviewed who were most resilient were able to imagine new ways of applying their skills in multiple arenas. But this was not mere fantasy. They used their creativity to imagine realistic possibilities. Paradoxical living means appreciating the mystery, beauty, and sacredness of life while also functioning at a practical level. It means recognizing the light and dark, and realizing that new learning and meaning can be mined from the valley of chaos. Paradoxical living is having the courage to fall through the deepest layers of ourselves to find new ground and the willingness to forge a path from that place. This is the place of our deepest learning and wisdom.

## Lessons

*Remember that everything contains the seed of its opposite.*

*Try to bridge what seem to be opposites; seeing these connections is often a key to self-understanding and understanding of others.*

*Seek to know your shadow; unwarranted or uncontrollable or extreme (either over or under) reactions may be a clue to a shadow aspect of yourself.*

*Cultivate the mature defenses of anticipation, altruism, suppression, sublimation, and humor.*

*Nourish creativity by taking a break from utilitarian tasks; go for a walk, notice dreams, play, rest, daydream, be alone, give away time, do something you've never done before.*

*Realize that chaos and creativity are linked and that new integration comes from disintegration, that breaking down often precedes breaking through.*

*Understand that life in its fullness is a cyclical pattern of loss, chaos, creativity, and productivity.*

## Chapter Seventeen

# Choosing Wisdom

*The world has need of them, those who stand upon the
bridge.
Who know the pain in the singing of a bird
And the beauty beyond a flower dying,
Who have heard the crystal harmony
Within the silence of a snow-peaked mountain—
For who but they can bring life's meaning
To the living dead?*
—JANE GOODALL[1]

Appreciating and living with paradox is a hallmark of wisdom. People who are wise see beyond apparent categories and link the disparate pieces of their lives into a meaningful story. Wisdom is the ability to integrate all that we know and the power to discern what is important. The risk we run in the information age is the exponential increase of information at the expense of wisdom. The paradox of the information age is that the more information we have available to us, the less valuable is each particular tidbit. How many of us have returned from work after a week's vacation only to find a hundred or more e-mail messages waiting? We then wade through all these messages and may stumble across one or two pieces of information that is relevant to us. As we move deeper into this time of exploding information we must ask ourselves, where is the knowledge we have lost in information, and where is the wisdom we have lost in knowledge?

I noticed that among the people I spoke with, their resilience was aided by their ability to bridge different aspects of their lives—their home and work, their realities and dreams, their past, present, and future. Many clarified their values as a result of their job loss and made choices more aligned with who they are and what they believe. Many also gained more direct access to their intuition, which several referred to as that small voice within. Perhaps most fundamentally, they learned from their experience. Recall that Matt said one of the major lessons he learned from losing his job was that he had not managed up as well as he managed down and in his next job he made a point of developing stronger relationships with the people above him. He reflected on the role that he played in his negative work situation and took responsibility for that, and consequently grew from the experience.

Learning from experience requires a bridging ability. It is an ongoing interaction between the external and internal, between action and insight, between the experiences we have in the world and reflecting upon those experiences. Kurt Lewin created a model of experiential learning that illustrates this ongoing back and forth interaction very clearly (Figure 17.1).[2] In this model, which was extended by David Kolb, learning is a back-and-forth interaction between ideas and experiences that are grounded in the external world, and internal reflections on those experiences and ideas. Kolb believes that learning is essentially the transformation of experience into new knowledge and meaning.

Because our cultural bias is toward the external and active, it is the internal and reflective piece that most often gets ignored. We busy ourselves with so many tasks that we do not stop to think about whether or why these tasks are important. We lose sight of what is important because we often spend so much time dealing with the tasks that seem immediate or urgent today. Or we operate on the basis of a set of assumptions and do not stop to think about whether or not the assumptions themselves are valid. The danger of *not* reflecting and *not* drawing lessons from our experience is that we will get caught in an endless cycle of repetition. For instance, we might jump as fast as we can from one job to another and then discover that we've merely gone from the frying pan into the fire. Or—like the former corporate vice president who sent out thirteen thousand résumés and got no response—we may just keep

## Figure 17.1.   Learning from Experience.

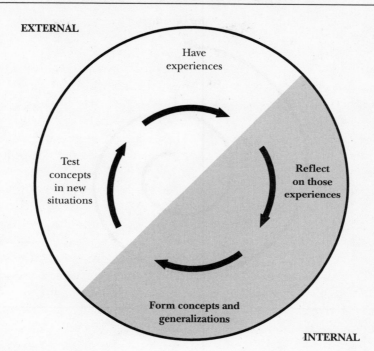

doing more and more of something that is clearly not working. Rather than learning, we may get stuck in a mindless rut and became bitter and cynical.

Learning is one of our most encompassing activities. It is what ties together our work, our education, and our growth throughout our lifetime (Figure 17.2).[3] When we think of learning, we are most apt to think of learning new facts or new skills. This is the process of acquiring and applying new information, and it is certainly important. Peter Drucker states that continuing education will soon be the fastest-growing industry in this country because things are changing so fast in every profession and occupation.[4]

This is why for all of us, no matter what our education or training, *learning how to learn* is a necessary skill that transcends any

## Figure 17.2.   Lifelong Learning.

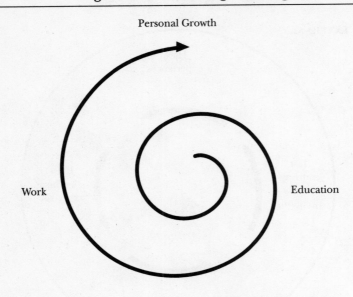

particular body of facts or skills that we presently have. Yet we must keep in mind that learning is also more than acquiring information, because it is only through learning that we derive our knowledge and wisdom.

What is the difference between information, knowledge, and wisdom? Of course they overlap, but drawing a distinction helps us to uncover the essential feature of each. *Information* is derived from analysis, which means taking things apart. In the liberal arts we receive praise for our ability to critically analyze concepts and in science we receive praise for our ability to dissect things. We gain information about a job by analyzing it and identifying the tasks that job comprises. Information usually yields data and facts. When uncovering facts we strive to make them objective and quantitative. The belief that permeates our culture is that if you can measure something, then it is true. Consequently we place a premium on the quantitative and on quantity. We believe that the more information we have, the more we know.

**Figure 17.3.   Information, Knowledge, and Wisdom.**

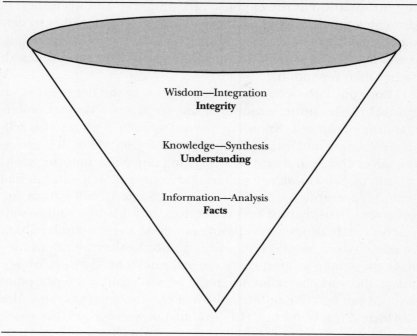

Wisdom—Integration
**Integrity**

Knowledge—Synthesis
**Understanding**

Information—Analysis
**Facts**

However, analysis does not explain the larger whole. It does not explain how the whole can be more than the sum of its parts, it does not explain the beauty of a flower. The tasks that make up a job do not explain its larger purpose or how it fits into the context of a particular organization or how that organization fits into society. *Knowledge* comes from synthesis, putting things back together. Synthesis gives us understanding because we can see how the parts relate to one another and we apprehend something more than the sum of the parts.

The ability to integrate all that we know yields *wisdom* (Figure 17.3). Integration means to make whole, to unify. It is related to integrity, the sense of being a complete and undivided self. Wisdom does not negate analysis; rather it *links* analysis and synthesis and puts them into context. Wisdom is both deep and broad. It is seeing both the forest *and* the trees and comprehending their interrelationship with the world.

The danger of the information age is focusing solely on acquiring information at the expense of knowledge and wisdom. It is through synthesizing that we create. We put things together in new ways and achieve new understandings. This is the basis for leading a creative life. It is the basis for ongoing discovery and renewal, rather than repetition.

Both our knowledge and wisdom grow to the degree that we gain a broader understanding of the world and a deeper understanding of our self. Knowledge about our self is what yields self-understanding and insight. Insight means seeing within. It is seeing ourselves clearly and also clearly seeing our impact on the world around us. Self-knowledge requires paying attention to our internal feelings, perceptions, motivations, and reactions. Self-knowledge involves introspection and reflection, but it is not simply self-referential. It also requires paying attention to cues and feedback in our environment. People who do not notice the effect they have on people around them are essentially narcissistic. We see this in the workplace a lot, when the person's only reference point is his or her ego. When the individual ego encompasses the entire worldview, it is blinding. The ego must move over to allow room for a larger vision, and an ability to see yourself in context.

People who are narcissistic do not see that much at all, which is why they often lack understanding and insight. A famous example from literature is Shakespeare's *King Lear*. In this play we see the tragic consequences of a king who can only see the world from his own narcissistic point of view. This creates such blindness that he is easy to fool—it only takes a few shallow and insincere strokes to his ego from his daughters Goneril and Regan. When his youngest daughter, Cordelia, who truly loves him, refuses to make exaggerated proclamations and promises, he becomes enraged and banishes her. Then he turns his kingdom over to his two hypocritical daughters, who mock him and cast him out of his own kingdom once they are in power. The result is that Lear's kingdom falls apart. He is humbled. He goes under. And only then does he achieve understanding. Only then can he see from a new perspective, and only then does he know what is true. His insight comes with a heavy price as his daughter Cordelia dies in his arms. How often do we see aspects of this Shakespearian drama played out in the workplace?

Losing your job can be humbling. But sometimes this helps the ego to move over so that we can see from a new perspective. Jack Mezirow calls this *perspective transformation*.[5] He believes that our most profound learning results from a disorienting dilemma, such as illness, divorce, death, or job loss, where we discover that our old responses no longer work. This is when we are more likely to engage in self-examination and to reflect on our beliefs, values, and assumptions. It is also when we are most likely to transform our knowledge into an entirely different perspective where we derive new meaning. Mezirow finds that when we engage in this type of ongoing learning and development our perspective becomes increasingly inclusive, differentiated, and open to other points of view.

Self-knowledge yields insight, and insight is often associated with wisdom. Wisdom involves accurate perceptions and clear-sightedness. It means looking directly at the world and seeing things as they really are. When we armor ourselves with psychological defenses, such as denial or projection, it is as though we are living in a fun house and seeing the world through distorting mirrors. The trouble is, this way of life is usually not much fun for ourselves or those around us.

In an interesting study of wisdom across the life span, Vivian Clayton and James Birren trace the historical roots of wisdom in both Eastern and Western traditions.[6] All traditions agree that wisdom is a way of knowing that involves a quest to understand the meaning and purpose of life and the ability to see things as they actually are. All agree that wisdom is reflected in behavior. Words that are associated with wisdom include *experienced, introspective, pragmatic, gentle, empathic, peaceful, humorous,* and *observant.* Wisdom is also frequently associated with life experience. But it is not simply the accumulation of years or experience because wisdom is not guaranteed with aging. Nor does wisdom equate to classroom learning or formal educational degrees. Instead it comes from the ability to learn from experience. It is the ability to pull the lessons out of both our accomplishments and mistakes. Wisdom is associated with insight, intuition, and integrity. It is knowing how to live. Wisdom is qualitative, not quantitative. It is experiencing life in its breadth and depths and its multiple layers of meaning.

Wisdom is frequently characterized by paradox. The story of Solomon's wisdom is a good example. When two women both claimed to be mother of the same child, Solomon resolved the dilemma in a seemingly irrational way by suggesting that they cut the child in half. Though this solution lacked logic, it reflected a depth of understanding about human nature. The biological mother's instinctual cry of alarm revealed the true mother. Wise people recognize that reality is largely nonlogical and paradoxical.

Wisdom combines thinking, feeling, and intuiting. It is the intuiting function that is most often associated with wisdom. Intuition comes from deep looking, from seeing beyond the obvious, from noticing and understanding the meaning of images and signals. Sometimes we experience this as that small voice within, or as a sudden flash of insight. Or we may simply have a gut-level hunch.

An important source of wisdom is the signals we receive from our body. When we armor ourselves continuously we become numb, and we lose this source. Or we may feel bodily signals but ignore them. We become split. Several of the people I interviewed referred to physical symptoms that they had prior to losing their job, such as high blood pressure or an upset stomach, and in their cases these symptoms went away after they lost their job. Of course this may not be the case for everybody. But in all cases, such bodily signals of distress are an important source of knowing. Our body also reveals excitement and joy, just as it reveals distress. It is equally important to notice what brings us joy so that we can find it more often.

Being "in touch" with the world means that we are sensate beings and access our senses. This also links us to our soul. In *Love and the Soul,* Robert Sardello writes: "When the interior life of the body is not a constant experience, there can be no experience of soul, neither the individual soul nor the soul of the world. The inner senses are at the same time a sensing of the soul."[7] Sardello also tells us that the heart is not simply a pump, as we typically think of it. Rather, the heart is also a sense organ that literally is moved by the circulation of blood. Thinking that the heart *pumps* the blood is similar to thinking that a thermometer controls the room temperature. The heart senses. People who have insight access what they know in their heart.

Angeles Arrien, an anthropologist, storyteller, and wise person herself, discusses this type of knowing based on her studies of indigenous cultures. She talks about our "four-chambered" heart in terms of our capacity to be full-hearted, half-hearted, closed-hearted, and weak-hearted.[8] Each of these can serve as a clue for our own understanding if we ask ourselves these questions and understand their implications:

*Where am I full-hearted?* This is the source of my creative spirit.

*Where am I half-hearted?* This is where I am experiencing soul loss and need to leave something behind.

*Where am I closed-hearted?* This is where I need healing and may need to forgive.

*Where am I weak-hearted?* This is where I lack the courage to be who I am.

The word courage derives from the French word *coeur,* which means "heart." Thus having courage means standing by our heart. It means listening to our heart and acting on our knowing.

When we are clear about our core values and beliefs, when we listen from both our head and our heart, and when we align what we know with how we act, then we live with integrity. Warren Bennis defines it like this: "Integrity. Integration. The integral personality. Such permutations are permissible plays on the word, which shares roots with integer, the untouchable (in and tanger) whole number which links the most abstract of endeavors, mathematics, to the human condition. . . . It's a merging of identities and resolves into a coherent and effective whole."[9]

Living with integrity means that we are both inner-directed and interconnected. It is creatively bridging the tension between our abstract ideals and values with our concrete practicalities and needs. It is holding the tension between the demands of today and our dreams for the future, between what is and what might be. All of this is put together into a coherent whole that holds meaning. Creating an alignment between our knowing, our action, and our context is an ongoing learning process. It is important to realize that integrity is not simply a set of traits. As Kolb points out:

> Integrity is a sophisticated, integrated process of learning, of knowing. It is not primarily a set of character traits such as honesty, consistency, or morality. These traits are only probable behavioral

derivations of the integrated judgments that flow from integrated learning. Honesty, consistency, and morality are usually, but not always, the result of integrated learning. One need only reflect on the "immoral" behavior of men like Copernicus and Galileo to realize that integrity is the learning process by which intellectual, moral, and ethical standards are *created,* not some evaluation based on current moral standards and world views.[10]

Wisdom gives us both a broader and deeper view. We see the linkage with our surroundings but also have the objectivity and courage to stand apart. Being both inner-directed and interconnected means that we can see what's going on and can choose not to follow. When we find ourselves in a work situation where the prevailing norms are unhealthy, we can choose to stand by our own values. This is hard to do when you're driven by fear of losing your job. Such a fear can create enormous dissonance between what we see, feel, and believe and how we act. If fear of losing your job feels as though a gun is being held to your head, then it makes going along with the crowd sound like a pretty good alternative. But among the people I spoke with who did lose their job, the worst had happened—and it had a freeing effect. Many became more clear about their values and more determined to stand by them in the future.

Weick believes that wisdom has as much to do with attitude as it has to do with knowing. It is the middle ground between extreme confidence and extreme caution: "In a fluid world, wise people know that they don't fully understand what is happening right now, because they have never seen precisely this event before."[11] Wisdom is the capacity to doubt and the ability to act in spite of and because of doubt. It is the knack for making sound decisions in the face of uncertainty. It is being able to respond to novel situations by drawing from past experience without being locked into that experience. It is making use of analogy and metaphor to see what is common between dissimilar events or situations.

Weick refers to a Naskapi Indian ritual to illustrate this capacity. The Naskapis use caribou shoulder bones to determine the direction of their hunt. They hold the bones over a fire until they crack and then hunt in the direction to which the cracks point. This ritual draws from past experience because only seasoned hunters read the cracks and can interject their own interpretations.

Yet for each hunt, a new set of cracks is formed. The interplay between the new map and the experience of the interpreter creates a highly adaptive approach to hunting.

This ability to creatively apply the lessons of experience to new situations is as important for success in the workplace as it is for the Naskapi Indians in their hunting. *The Lessons of Experience* is a compilation of research out of the Center for Creative Leadership on 191 successful executives. The authors found that no amount of experience can prepare executives for the countless novel situations they will encounter. This is true for all of us. However, the authors did find some common ground among their subjects: "What did seem to characterize the successful executives we studied was not their genetic endowment nor even their impressive array of life experience. Rather, as a group, they seemed ready to grab or create opportunities for growth, wise enough not to believe that there's nothing more to learn, and courageous enough to look inside themselves and grapple with their frailties. Not only did they do these things, they also seemed able to do them under the worst possible conditions."[12] The wisdom of these successful professionals is rooted in their willingness to take advantage of opportunities to learn, their search for meaning, and their self-understanding. As Weick suggests, this has more to do with attitude than with any amount of information or body of knowledge. Approaching life with such an attitude is our choice. The power of wisdom lies in making choices.

The fear of job loss can cause us to abdicate our power of choice. If we are afraid to say no to any request or assignment that comes our way, then we have lost our power of choice and its inherent wisdom. Paradoxically, the new psychological contract between organizations and employees empowers workers to a greater degree than before. It is a two-way contract but is often interpreted as being solely advantageous to organizations. The new contract assumes that workers will provide their skills to organizations so long as they are needed. When the organization no longer needs this set of skills, it has no particular obligation to continue to retain the worker. At the same time this contract assumes that workers will offer their talents to the marketplace at large. Workers have no particular obligation to work for an organization if they have better offers or can better meet their employment needs elsewhere.

This does not mean that organizations and workers must have an adversarial, nontrusting relationship. It offers the possibility for a win-win relationship in which both the organization's and worker's needs are being met.

*Empowerment* has become a popular buzzword in the past six or seven years. The notion is that organizations must empower employees by allowing them to make more autonomous decisions, work as self-directed teams, and so forth. I agree with these strategies but I do not agree that they necessarily empower people. Empowerment means power in, or power within. Ultimately we must empower ourselves and we do so through wisdom and courage. This includes the power of choice. For example, Carol (described in Chapter Seven) was placed in charge of a project that had such great odds against it she could see no way to pull it off. Not only did she think the project would fail, but she also knew that the process would be draining and negative for her. When her supervisor gathered everyone involved with the project and gave a rousing speech, saying that anyone who lacked the necessary energy or passion should get off the boat, Carol—as project manager—volunteered to do so. She was then given the choice of managing that project or leaving her job. She chose to leave her job. Carol could do so because she had a large professional network that she had built up over the years, and knew it would not take her long to get new work.

During the first three-quarters of this century, the type of power we saw most commonly in organizations was power *over*. This is a top-down management style where the boss tells the subordinate what to do. The subordinate follows orders. With the advent of the human relations movement in the 1970s, we began to shift our thinking toward power *with*. This is the idea that managers and their reports can jointly identify objectives and work toward them together. In the 21st century, we must again shift our thinking toward power *within*. This is really what empowerment is about. It means that we take responsibility for our choices and for identifying our own career goals and paths. It means continuous learning and learning how to learn. It means accessing our multiple ways of knowing and listening to what we know to be true. It means being able to say yes *and* no, and not being afraid to persevere or to walk away.

Power within combines wisdom and courage and vitalizes our resilience. In the information age, this type of personal power will be considerably more important to our career success than positional power. Personal power drawn from wisdom is an unlimited resource. Yet like energy itself, it must circulate. When power gets stuck in a closed system—that is, when it is walled off so there is no circulation with the larger world, entropy sets in. This is a gradual diminishing of power, of energy, so that there is no energy available for change. We access our power from within and we also must give it away. We access it by choosing to learn the lessons of our experience and by taking responsibility for the course of our life. We give it away by living with integrity to create coherence between ourselves and our context. In doing so we recognize that we have some responsibility for the world's future as well as our own, and that we have the power to shape both.

## Lessons

*Learn how to learn by moving back and forth between the external and internal, combining action with reflection to derive lessons from experience.*

*Continuously clarify what is most important for you and try to direct your activities toward this, rather than toward what is most demanding or urgent in the moment.*

*Try to bridge objective, fact-finding analysis with creative synthesis so that you are able to see both the forest and the trees simultaneously.*

*Seek self-knowledge by paying attention to your internal feelings, perceptions, motivations, and reactions while also noticing the feedback and cues that you get from the environment.*

*Foster intuition by noticing hunches or flashes of insight, as well as your physical sensations in relation to people, events, or decisions.*

*Live with integrity by creating alignment between your feelings, beliefs, values, and actions.*

*Recognize your power of choice and that having the courage to act on these choices is a source of freedom.*

## Chapter Eighteen

# Reclaiming Your Soul

*We are entering a time of total instability. Absolutely no
one will be unaffected by or protected from this worldwide
shifting that shall accelerate in the near future . . . the
primary task of the age is to face the world with soul.
Facing the world with soul does require the development of
the soul capacity to work toward individual soul
experience held in conjunction with world soul—to be
solitary, but not isolated.*
—ROBERT SARDELLO[1]

Our wisdom lies in our ability to make connections, to tell meaningful stories, and to link the particulars of our own story to the
larger cross-currents of life. Over time these stories weave together
into a larger story and a pattern appears. Our faith is in trusting
that such a pattern exists, and our task as we go through life is to
notice the pattern as it becomes revealed. The particular pattern
of our life is what points to our uniqueness and potentially to our
unique contribution. This is our gift. When we honor it, we reclaim
our soul.

In a one-act play called *Krapp's Last Tape,* Samuel Beckett por-
trays an alienated and pathetic old man named Krapp.[2] We find
Krapp sitting alone, disheveled and weary, reviewing his ledger of
audiotapes that he recorded throughout his life. The tapes are his
memories, and we realize that his pathos lies in his inability to find
the linkages that would tie these memories together and make
sense of his life. Krapp lacks a unifying story, and consequently he

lacks wisdom and his life lacks meaning. We realize that wisdom has a narrative structure: "The communicability of wisdom is tied to the communicability of a *life story*. In telling the tale, it is the storyteller who teaches us how to live."[3] Of course storytellers must put the pieces together before they can relay the story. Likewise, we must link the pieces of our lives into a narrative that makes sense and holds meaning for us.

In an interesting study of resilience, the researchers interviewed women between the ages of sixty-seven and ninety-two who had experienced a major loss within the last five years but who continued to be active and feel positive.[4] Clearly their experience of aging is opposite to that which Samuel Beckett portrayed in his play. Many of these women commented on the importance of humor and of putting things in perspective. These women also commented on the importance of believing that they lead a meaningful life. This is the sense that life has purpose and that they are making, and have made, a valuable contribution. The particulars are not so important as the interpretation; the ability to extract meaning out of experience. One widow talked about initiating a group to watch slides and movies that her husband had taken throughout his life. For her, this was a way of keeping the memory of her husband alive while also giving pleasure and entertainment to others.

Meaning and purpose are what create a central theme for our story. This is why resilience over the life span largely means that out of the weavings and renderings of our life, we are able to find a personal why. Without a personal why, information, skills, and accomplishments eventually mean less and less. When we fill our days with content and activity, but no context, we eventually begin to wonder why we are even getting out of bed. Using our wisdom to integrate, to create a larger context, is what gives us a sense of meaning and purpose. People who are most satisfied with their work make their living out of this place.

A person I know who has had much professional success but recently left her job told me that she feels as though her "pilot light has gone out." She asked me about theories of motivation, and said that all she can find are goal-oriented models that talk about how to get from point A to point B. She knows how to do this, but it no longer motivates her. It does not *move* her. This approach is too cognitive, too linear. She wants a sense of felt meaning and purpose, something that is fueled by her heart. Where do we find this? Sometimes it is harder to find when we have a successful persona. A lot becomes invested in the facade. This is fine, unless we begin to lose sight of the person underneath. *Persona* means mask; it is the mask we wear for the world. When we meet the world only through a mask, we are not meeting the world with soul.

Why are so many people talking or writing about soul these days? With his book *Care of the Soul,* Thomas Moore triggered an avalanche of public interest and books on the topic. On one hand soul seems elusive and impossible to nail down or define. On the other hand, soul seems everywhere or anywhere and pops up in our life and our language as soul music, soul food, soul dancing, and soul love. We all have soul. We do not lose our soul. However sometimes we do lose sight of it. Or we lose touch with it. This is when we have the feeling that our "pilot light has gone out." So perhaps all this talk about soul reflects a yearning to reclaim . . . what?

It is a yearning to reclaim our calling, in its deepest sense. It is a yearning to remember our life's purpose and to fulfill its promise. It is a yearning to reclaim the mystery of our life that is more than the roles we play and the tasks we accomplish. We understand this if we consider how soul is portrayed in myth. In *The Soul's Code,* James Hillman summarizes Plato's Myth of Er.[5]

According to Plato, after completing their time on earth, souls get together and mingle in a mythical world. Then each soul selects a *lot,* or a portion of fate, to fulfill in its next time on earth. This lot relates to its previous experiences. For instance, Atalanta had been a young woman runner and her soul chose the lot of an athlete, while the soul of Ajax, who had been a warrior, chose the lot of a lion. After choosing their lots, souls are given a "genius," or "daimon," to accompany them through their various passages back to and into the world. During their time on earth, the daimon acts as a protector of that soul's chosen lot. Before entering human life, souls pass through the plane of Lethe, which means oblivion or forgetting, so that once they are born they have forgotten their choices. Only the daimon remembers.

Hillman interprets the lot that each soul chooses to be a central image that embraces the whole of a life all at once. The image itself is the pattern of a life, a pattern that needs to be reselected and lived out. This process is the soul's task on earth. Keep in mind that a pattern is not the same as a path. A path implies that there is one way and that all the choices of life are predetermined. A pattern can be pieced together in many ways, but it does serve as a guiding image. Hillman points out that ancients located the soul in or around our heart. Most likely the image is held in our heart, so that when we hear our calling we feel its pull from our heart.

Similar mythology about the soul is echoed in Jewish spirituality. Eliezer Shore describes it like this:

> The soul begins in unity. Prior to entering this world it exists in a state of attachment to the Divine. It gazes in a light that shines across creation and learns a supernal wisdom. However, at the moment of birth, this original connection is lost. As the soul descends into the world, it becomes fragmented and broken, splintered into millions of pieces and scattered across creation. Like rain upon the fields, the soul seeps deeply into all things animate and inanimate. It is these drops of soul, embedded within the objects of this world, that give life and vitality to existence. . . . Because their life-source is derived from a particular individual, these things will, over time, re-enter his domain."[6]

The task over our lifetime is to gather up these soul fragments, to put them back together into the unified whole they once were. Soul, then, is a *process*. It is a process of piecing back together the whole. It is the process of rediscovering the purpose of our life. As we come across these soul fragments some of them shine brightly, while others remain elusive and hidden. Shore elaborates by saying that during the soul's initial descent to the world, the brightest soul fragments fall to the lowest levels, to the darker aspects of life or human nature.[7] Therefore if we are to reclaim these, we must enter into those dark places, those places of anger, depression, or despair, and in doing so we recover the brightest pieces. This is why confronting personal tragedy, despair, or hopelessness often leads us to higher levels of integration, compassion, and spiritual understanding.

For this same reason, it is when we are falling that we are likely to hear our calling. We reach into our depths and notice something we have not seen or heard before. Our calling is our vocation in the true sense of the word. This is not the same as a job.

Our calling may have nothing to do with how we earn a living. But it is our real work. Mystics say that it is "performing The Great Work."[8] Our life is our work, and reclaiming our soul is attending to the greatest promise we hold and heeding the purpose that is our unique contribution.

This does not have to be grandiose. Our soul's calling has more to do with *why* we do things, and with *how* we do things, than with what we do. Several years ago I was doing some consulting work with the Port of Seattle and asked various employees about the relationship between the organization's mission and their work. This is what one employee said:

> The way they write these missions is concise and specific with nice-sounding "in" words, but I bet 90 percent of the people wouldn't understand it. What means something to me is how I can work with the other people around me, and the customers, and get the job done. What's important to me is the guy down on the boat who needs a cleat—he's paying my wages. The public is important to me. The elderly man who walks through here every day who I say good morning to is important to me—I'm the only person he knows at the Port; I create his impression of the Port. I know every boat on the marina. When you can comment on the customer's boat, you've made that person happy.

This person was able to articulate her personal why. It is what draws her to work every day and why she finds satisfaction. Having some sense of why she gets up and goes to work every day, and how she lives that out throughout the day, is considerably more important to her than the corporate mission statement. Corporate mission statements are abstract and global and in themselves, they seldom motivate. On the other hand, a personal why is created out of the small things, the particulars, the everyday.

At the same time, our soul's calling connects us to something larger. In *Care of the Soul,* Thomas Moore paraphrases the 15th-century scholar, Marsilio Ficino: "The mind . . . tends to go off on its own so that it seems to have no relevance to the physical world. At the same time, the materialistic life can be so absorbing that we get caught in it and forget about spirituality. What we need . . . is soul, in the middle, holding together mind and body, ideas and life, spirituality and the world."[9] We might think of soul, then, as an interface between what we embody and what is beyond us, the junction between that which is time-bound and that which is eternal.

The soul does not call us toward a purpose that is completely self-absorbed or self-serving. It calls us toward something that connects us with the world. Bette Midler expresses this in a tongue-in-cheek way when she talks about the work she is doing for the environment as the first "Compost Queen" of Los Angeles: "My whole life had been spent waiting for an epiphany, a manifestation of God's presence, the kind of transcendent, magical experience that lets you see your place in the big picture. And that is what I had with my first (compost) heap . . . I love compost and believe in it with every fiber (so to speak) of my being."[10]

Though Midler jokes about her role as Compost Queen, she is in fact dedicating herself to a cause beyond herself. This idea is expressed in the book *Sound Mind, Sound Body* by Kenneth Pelletier. His research involved extensive interviews with fifty-three prominent people who represent prototypes of optimal health. He interviewed people from all walks of life, including David Rockefeller, a banker and philanthropist, Dennis Weaver, an actor, and Murray Gell-Mann, a Nobel Prize laureate in physics. One of Pelletier's key findings was that each individual he interviewed is driven by a "deep and abiding sense of purpose." He goes on to say: "This strong sense of purpose is like a guiding light that comes from within, from their innermost intuition. They feel they have a role to fulfill in the universe. This role is their life's true work, and there is no turning back. It is not their egos that motivate them but rather this personal mission is to serve a greater cause. Out of this pervasive sense of purpose they develop an unwavering commitment to their values."[11]

Although many of the people in Pelletier's study have achieved material success, he found that materialism and competition were not primary motivators. Rather, "Every participant consistently cited a deep sense of altruism as the primary motivation infusing his or her larger service to humankind."[12] Pelletier emphasizes that the people in his study do not merely talk about a philosophical or altruistic purpose—they *act* on it. Further, many of these people did not grow up with optimal childhood conditions; in fact, many suffered difficulties or trauma as children. Yet rather than focusing on the trauma itself, they transformed the trauma into a purpose:

"Through the transformed trauma of their childhood or adolescence, these individuals 'discovered' a sense of their 'true mission,' 'real vocation,' or 'destiny' usually in their mid-to late twenties. Often this discovery was accompanied by a sense of inevitability and a renewed, deeper commitment to the altruistic purpose they had sensed more vaguely as a child or young adult."[13]

Losing your job, or even feeling a sense of meaninglessness or aridity in your daily life, offers the possibility for getting in touch with your soul's calling. Many of the people I interviewed who lost their jobs increased the alignment between their core values and their work, and several gained insight about how this work fits into a bigger picture. Debra, the person who lost her job as manager of a large retail store and then became a self-employed consultant, expressed it like this: "The energy I spend is guided, directed by spirituality—my sense of who I am in this world, my sense of stewardship. This is what shapes what I choose to do with my work and how I choose to interact with my clients, or how I am in relationship with my friends and what I choose to talk about." When I asked Debra if she had an overriding purpose or guiding principle she said, "It would be about stewardship, rather than about money or a list of things that I could do. The spirit of my business is about helping people by developing their skills and awareness, and their sense of themselves in their own business. They're just like me— they're trying to figure out what they're in business for and who they are to serve—so the more I can clarify that and help them on the journey, then marketing is easy, and inventory is easy when you know who you are and what your passion is."

I've heard people say that they simply don't have time to think about such lofty things like their deeper purpose or soul's calling. How do we reclaim our soul when nothing in our life seems to support that? How do we reclaim our soul if we are spending most of the hours of our day attending to all the tasks and logistics that need to get done? We do so by making choices around our intention and attention. When all of our attention is focused on what is external, visible, and concrete we forget that there is more to life and more to who we are. Paying attention to the internal and invisible is not a matter of being an introvert or extrovert, it is a matter of being human. When all of our life is devoted to what we can see, measure, and touch, we starve our soul. This leads to feelings of emptiness, dryness, and brittleness. "Not having time" is a self-betrayal, it is a betrayal of tending to our soul. It is a betrayal of our soul's calling.

Remember that mythically the soul chooses a purpose before coming to earth, but then it forgets. The daimon, however, remembers. In Plato's myth the daimon acts as a sort of invisible guide or companion throughout our life to help us retrieve the pieces and put them back together again. So our life becomes a continuous process of trying to remember, an act of remembering the promise that was originally made. How do we do this? Sometimes our calling is thrust upon us all at once, as with Sarah and Jim Brady when a single bullet changed everything about their lives and directed their purpose toward gun control laws. Sometimes we just know from an early age. An interviewer once asked Geena Davis when she knew she wanted to become an actress and she replied, "When I was 3 years old."[14] But for most of us, remembering comes in small flashes or whispered hints. If we pay attention to these clues, then we may come across them more often and gradually remember more. We may realize that experiences we had years ago, that made no sense at the time, helped to prepare us for a future we are now living.

Reclaiming our soul begins with intention, and it is sustained by attention. If we pay attention to the whispers or occasional shouts of our soul's calling, over our lifetime we will align our life with our purpose. What are these clues? They are the times when we have an experience of flow, when we become completely engaged in what we are doing and lose a sense of time. They are times when tears spring to our eyes or our skin prickles because we have a flash of something that is deeper than words. They are times when we use our talents or skills and they seem like gifts, so that we experience an increase when we give them away and we feel filled, rather than depleted. Or they are times when ideas or images come to our mind and our heart says yes and feels pulled toward them.

Our soul speaks a symbolic language expressed largely through images rather than words. This is why we associate soul with artistic expression, with dancing or singing or poetry or painting. It is because those things that we know at a soul level are precognitive; they do not pass through the filter of our mind. Many of us experience a tug-of-war between what we know in our heart and what we think in our head. Bringing the two into alignment is usually a process that takes time.

Ron Medved, who was a professional football player and then worked with a consulting firm for twenty years, expressed this quite poignantly. Ron began to feel dissonance with his work around the time he was turning fifty, and he began to write poetry as a creative expression of his gnawing despair. He told me that he had a two-day period when he completely and clearly "bottomed out." On the first day he wrote this poem:

> Unarmed.
> when I could really use a weapon.
> Dangerous.
> to be this naked at this point in my life.
> I gather my confusion around me.
> and use what I can to keep warm.
> this summer afternoon.

On the second day, he wrote this poem:

> The day I died
> Really scared my wife
> She was mostly worried about my health
> Less so
> About changing careers
> Selling the house
> The day I died
> I went to the office anyway
> And for a change, everything clicked
> People materialized
> On the street outside the office
> On the carpet in the reception area
> The day I died
> I was brutally honest
> Concerning my future with the company
> I told the truth
> In my first unscheduled meeting
> In my second, I told it again
> The day I died

Was my happiest day in months
I was clear and hopeful
I connected
And was surrounded by ideas
Surrounded by angels

This poem that Ron wrote on the second day represents his realization, at a soul level, that something inside him had died. At the same time, something was born. He knew that he had to leave his job and that he needed to align his work more closely with his values and inner calling. However, about a year and a half passed before he actually took steps to leave the company and start his own business. The transition has not been easy, but it has been transformative. Ron now says, "My vocation has transformed, and now the work I am doing is perfectly suited to who I am."[15]

There is an old story about a man who went to a tailor to be fitted for a new suit. The man noticed that the jacket was uneven at the bottom but the tailor told him not to worry, just hold the shorter end with your left hand. The man also noticed that the lapel would not lie flat and the tailor said no problem—just hold it down with your chin. The hems of the pant legs were uneven, but the tailor told him to walk on his right toes and no one would notice. The man went for a walk in the park the next day in his new suit, following the tailor's advice with all the accompanying arm, chin, and leg "alterations." Two old men noticed him walk by. The first one said, "Look at that poor crippled man!" The second one thought for a moment and then said, "Yes, the crippling is too bad, but you know I wonder . . . where did he get such a nice suit?"[16]

This is what happens when we contort ourselves to fit a situation that does not really fit who we are. It can cripple us. Marion Woodman says that soul murder is when we are taught that it is not OK to be who we really are.[17] It is when we are taught to live as someone else's image of who we ought to be. Or it is when we are in a setting that does not allow us to be true to ourselves. This is when we become all persona, and lose the person underneath. But paradoxically, it is the hole inside that moves us toward wholeness.

Many of us do not hear our calling until the second half of our life. We reach a dead end or a crossing. Or like Ron, we may just bottom out. Ron was able to surrender to this and in doing so he heard a calling and heeded it. This infused him with new energy and motivation to move in a new direction. Symbolically, dying involves surrender. Deadening occurs when we contract in fear and continue to hold our breath and fortify ourselves. The more we fortify just a fragment of our being, the more deadened we begin to feel. At some level we know that we are acting out of a fragment of who we are or who we might become. Our soul wants us to move toward wholeness. Moving into this place may make us feel more vulnerable, but with this comes a greater openness to our creative source. We go into the well and touch the depths inside of us. This internal and eternal living core is the deepest source of our resilience. As we travel through the dark, we may find the guiding light of our soul. When we find and answer our calling, we finally move forward with greater ease as though carried by the wind.

This is a solitary process but we cannot do it in isolation. The people I interviewed who experienced a transformative change as a result of their job loss stressed the importance of their relationships. This includes all their relations—both intimate and professional—that together wove a net so that when these people lost their job they did not fall too far. Such a net is also constructed out of our assumptions, values, and beliefs so that ultimately we create a larger tapestry or canopy of meaning. This is a weaving of our own making but it is not woven alone. It is made up of our experiences in the world and how we interpret them. We nest our own story into larger stories to create a larger context. All of these are held together through our imagination.

Our imagination is our soul's language. It comes from inside of us. When we use our imagination to put something new into the world, we call it creativity. But the source is inside. It is forming pictures in our mind and deriving meaning from them. We use the images as windows through which we come to understand our experience. Images that come to us through dreams or daydreams or play or art or writing reveal our connection to something deeper and bigger than our own small self. We look *through* the images, not at them. When we use images as symbols to point beyond themselves, our world becomes more meaningful and we nourish our soul. The good thing about imagination is that it can never be taken away. I once read about a survivor from a concentration camp where he and the others were stripped of every aspect of their former life and dignity as human beings. Each day as he trudged with the other prisoners to a day of backbreaking labor he looked into the window of a house along the way. In that window, he imagined the family who lived there. This reminded him of the love of his own family, a love he carried inside. He was one of the few survivors of that death camp. His imagination kept him alive.

It is when our imagination dies, when our images lose their life, that we lose sight of our soul. Soul murder is when we are in situations where we cannot be who we really are or are not accepted as our authentic self. But soul suicide is when we allow our images to die. It is when we see all things as mere objects and evaluate our time, our things, and our relationships only in terms of their utilitarian or monetary value. It is turning everything, including ourselves, into commodities. When we concretize the world then our world becomes hardened, frozen, soulless, and we feel deadened.

Reclaiming our soul involves dying to parts of our life that no longer fit. This process can be likened to the hero's journey in the sense that it involves an initiation, departure, and return. The initiation is often precipitated by a loss, perhaps a job loss. The departure involves going down and within, and noticing things we have not noticed before. In doing so, we may begin to reclaim our soul. The soul is receptive and we touch it through our own receptivity. Perhaps we notice images or hear a small voice within, or both. If we pay attention and listen, we may discover a new wisdom and realize that we have a power and potential that we did not even know about. The completion of the hero's journey is the return. This means coming home, and sharing what we learned with the world at large.

Not everyone has a transformative change as a result of job loss but some people do. Why not pay attention to them? Why not use their stories as fodder and guidance as we move into the new world of the 21st century? These people felt much better off because of the way they responded to a personal crisis about which they had no choice. They allowed it to serve as a catalyst to reassess their life—their assumptions and values and priorities—and then acted to align their life with a greater sense of integrity. Many ended up feeling much better off than before they lost their job.

Perhaps the overarching lesson is having the courage to live the story of our life rather than simply playing a role. Roles are often prescribed for us. Our story is of our own making. When we live our story we may play many roles, but we tie them together so that they have meaning. We create a larger theme, and this theme becomes our life's purpose. A story has linkages, and the meaning is in the linkages. It is the pattern that connects. The anthropologist Gregory Bateson spent the last ten years of his life asking, "What is the pattern that connects?"[18] What is the pattern that connects our life despite and because of its discontinuities? What is the pattern that connects the helix of our DNA with the whorl of a grapevine and the spiral of the Milky Way?

Involuntary job loss offers the possibility of reclaiming our soul because it breaks us out of our usual habits and boundaries and brings forth new questions. We have to ask the questions before we can hear. But when we do ask, and listen, we may find that we connect with both old and new relationships in a deeper way and in so doing we create a larger pattern that gives our life new meaning. One way to imagine this is through a mythic image from India called the Net of Indra. This is a net held together by gems. In every place where one thread crosses another—at every crossing— is a gem that reflects all the other reflective gems. The Net of Indra shows us that everything is in relation to everything else, and the pattern is revealed through those relationships.

Perhaps this image suggests a new myth that will help to carry us into and through the 21st century. Our myth of job security as we've known it is dying, and culturally we are in need of a new myth. The Net of Indra—an old, old image—suggests a web, and now our most advanced technology is shaping itself around the Internet. We hear about the World Wide Web in our daily news and many of us are connected by it. Today companies are using intranets to link themselves internally. The web, or network, is replacing the machine as our dominant metaphor. The important point is the *metaphor,* not the technology. The metaphor is the guiding image. And unlike our old machine metaphor, this new metaphor is relational. Martin Luther King beautifully expressed the implications of this:

All life is interrelated. We are all caught in an inescapable network of mutuality, tied into a single garment of destiny. Whatever affects one directly, affects all indirectly. . . . Did you ever stop to think that you can't leave for your job in the morning without being dependent on most of the world? You get up in the morning and go to the bathroom and reach over for the sponge, and that's handed to you by a Pacific islander. You reach for a bar of soap, and that's given to you at the hands of a Frenchman. And then you go into the kitchen to drink your coffee for the morning, and that's poured into your cup by a South American. And maybe you want tea: that's poured into your cup by a Chinese. . . . And before you finish eating breakfast in the morning, you've depended on more than half of the world. This is the way our universe is structured, this is its interrelated quality. We aren't going to have peace on earth until we recognize this basic fact of the interrelated structure of all reality.[19]

Reclaiming our soul involves finding and fulfilling our life's purpose. This means realizing our values and aligning them with our talents and gifts. It is our unique contribution. Yet at the same time the soul connects us to a larger whole. We must see ourselves in a dynamic relationship with the world, and take responsibility for shaping our context. Our life's journey, our soul's journey, involves paying attention. And when we do hear our soul's calling, it means having the courage to act.

## Lesson

*Reclaim your soul by remembering your life's purpose and fulfilling its promise.*

# Notes

**Introduction**
1. Uchitelle, L., and Kleinfield, N. R. "On the Battlefields of Business, Millions of Casualties." *New York Times,* Mar. 3, 1996, p. 15.
2. Sanger, D. E., and Lohr, S. "A Search for Answers to Avoid the Layoffs." *New York Times,* Mar. 9, 1996, p. 11.
3. Uchitelle, L. "The Humbling of the Harvard Man." *New York Times,* Mar. 6, 1994, p. 1 (Sec. 3).
4. Vaillant, G. E. *The Wisdom of the Ego.* Cambridge, Mass.: Harvard University Press, 1993, p. 299.
5. Estés, C. P. *Women Who Run With the Wolves: Myths and Stories of the Wild Woman Archetype.* New York: Ballantine Books, 1992, p. 20.
6. Schank, R. C. *Tell Me A Story: Narrative and Intelligence.* Evanston, Ill.: Northwestern University Press.
7. Pritchett, P. *New Work Habits for a Radically Changing World: 13 Ground Rules for Job Success in the Information Age.* Dallas, Tex.: Pritchett & Associates, 1994, p. 24.
8. Houston, J. "A Mythic Life." Program presented at the Elliott Bay Book Company, Seattle, Wash., Jan. 27, 1996.
9. Carse, J. *Breakfast at the Victory.* San Francisco: Harper San Francisco, 1994, p. 33.

**Chapter One**
1. Gardner, J. W. *Self-Renewal: The Individual and the Innovative Society.* New York: Norton, 1981, p. 54.
2. Toffler, A. *The Third Wave.* New York: Bantam Books, 1980.
3. Uchitelle and Kleinfield, 1996, p. 1.
4. Caminiti, S. "What Happens to Laid-Off Managers." *Fortune,* June 13, 1994, p. 69.
5. Bridges, W. *JobShift: How to Prosper in a Workplace Without Jobs.* Reading, Mass.: Addison-Wesley, 1994.

6. Laurie, B. *Artisans into Workers: Labor in 19th-Century America.* New York: Hill & Wang, 1989, p. 15.
7. Laurie, 1989, p. 87.
8. Hammer, M., and Champy, J. *Reengineering the Corporation: A Manifesto for Business Revolution.* New York: HarperCollins, 1993.
9. Smith, A. *The Wealth of Nations.* New York: Penguin, 1970, p. 171. (Originally published 1776.)
10. Bolman, L. G., and Deal, T. E. *Leading With Soul: An Uncommon Journey of Spirit.* San Francisco: Jossey-Bass, 1995, p. 146.
11. Solomon, J. "The Fall of the Dinosaurs." *Newsweek,* Feb. 8, 1993, p. 42.
12. Pritchett, 1994, pp. 44, 49.

## Chapter Two

1. "Living Arrangements of Children Under 18 Years Old, by Selected Characteristic of Parent: 1994." *Statistical Abstract of the United States 1995.* Table 78, p. 65. Washington, D.C.: U.S. Bureau of the Census.
2. *Washington Spectator,* May 1, 1991, p. 3.
3. Bond, S. D. *Living Myth.* Boston: Shambhala, 1993, p. 26.
4. Hyde, L. *The Gift: Imagination and the Erotic Life of Property.* New York: Vintage Books, 1983.
5. Hyde, 1983, p. 4.
6. Mauss, M. *The Gift: Forms and Functions of Exchange in Archaic Societies.* (I. Cunnison, trans.). New York: Norton, 1967, p. 19.
7. Hyde, 1983, pp. 3–4.
8. Eliot, T. S. *The Waste Land and Other Poems.* Orlando, Fla.: Harcourt Brace, 1934, pp. 29–30.

## Chapter Three

1. Hickman, S. *Necessary Angels.* Compact Disc Recording No. 77010. Santa Monica, Calif.: Discovery Records, 1994.
2. "'Necessary Angels' Help Singing Artist." National Public Radio, *Morning Edition,* Dec. 20, 1994.
3. "'Necessary Angels' Help Singing Artist."

## Chapter Four

1. Rousseau, D. M. "Psychological and Implied Contracts in Organizations." *Employee Responsibilities and Rights Journal,* 1989, 2 (2), 121–139.
2. Noer, D. M. *Healing the Wounds: Overcoming the Trauma of Layoff and Revitalizing Downsized Organizations.* San Francisco: Jossey-Bass, pp. 45–47.

## Chapter Five

1. Rilke, R. M. *Selected Poems of Rainer Maria Rilke*. (R. Bly, trans.) New York: HarperCollins, 1981, p. 13.
2. Dauten, D. A. *Quitting: Knowing When to Leave*. New York: Walker, 1980, p. 7.
3. Dauten, p. 132.

## Chapter Six

1. Quoted in W. Bridges, *Managing Transitions: Making the Most of Change*. Reading, Mass.: Addison-Wesley, 1991, p. 35.
2. Campbell, J. *The Power of Myth*. New York: Doubleday, 1988, p. 147.
3. Campbell, 1988, p. 115.
4. Halifax, J. *Shaman: The Wounded Healer*. New York: Thames and Hudson, 1982, p. 14.

## Chapter Seven

1. Quoted in Kolb, D. A. *Experiential Learning: Experience as the Source of Learning and Development*. Englewood Cliffs, N.J.: Prentice Hall, 1984, p. 52.
2. Jung, C. G. *Memories, Dreams, Reflections*. (Recorded and edited by A. Jaffé; R. Winston and C. Winston, trans.). New York: Vintage Books, 1965, p. 225.
3. Jaffe, A. (ed.). *C. G. Jung: Word and Image*. Bollingen Series XCVII:2. Princeton, N.J.: Princeton University Press, 1979, p. 68.
4. Jaffe, 1979, p. 189.
5. Hollis, J. *The Middle Passage: From Misery to Meaning in Midlife*. Toronto: Inner City Books, 1993, p. 94.
6. Estés, 1992, p. 293.

## Chapter Eight

1. Schmidt, W. *Organizational Frontiers and Human Values*. Belmont, Calif.: Wadsworth, 1970, p. 3.
2. Sardello, R. *Love and the Soul: Creating a Future for Earth*. New York: HarperCollins, 1995, p. 46.
3. Langer, E. J. *Mindfulness*. Reading, Mass.: Addison-Wesley, 1989, pp. 62–63.
4. Kabat-Zinn, J. *Full Catastrophe Living: Using the Wisdom of Your Body and Mind to Face Stress, Pain, and Illness*. New York: Dell, 1990, pp. 264–273.

5. Partridge, E. *Origins: A Short Etymological Dictionary of Modern English.* Old Tappan, N.J.: Macmillan, 1959.

**Chapter Nine**
1. Eliot, T. S. *Little Gidding.* Orlando, Fla.: Harcourt Brace, 1942.
2. Boorstin, D. J. *The Discoverers.* New York: Random House, 1983.
3. Figure from C. Hampden-Turner, *Maps of the Mind: Charts and Concepts of the Mind and Its Labyrinths.* Old Tappan, N.J.: Macmillan, 1981, p. 9.
4. Anthony, E. J. "Risk, Vulnerability, and Resilience: An Overview." In E. J. Anthony and B. J. Cohler (eds.), *The Invulnerable Child.* New York: Guilford Press, 1987, p. 10.

**Chapter Ten**
1. Campbell, J. *The Hero With a Thousand Faces.* Princeton: Princeton University Press, 1968, p. 16.
2. Kübler-Ross, E. *On Death and Dying.* New York: Collier Books, 1969.
3. Parks, M. "Psycho-Social Transitions: A Field for Study." *Social Science and Medicine,* 1971, *5,* 101–115.
4. Fowler, J. W. "Faith and the Structuring of Meaning." In J. W. Fowler and A. Vergote (eds.), *Toward Moral and Religious Maturity.* Morristown, N.J.: Silver, Burdett & Ginn, 1980, p. 53.
5. Weick, K. E. "The Collapse of Sensemaking in Organizations: The Mann Gulch Disaster." *Administrative Science Quarterly,* 1993, *38* (4), 628–652.
6. Marris, P. *Loss and Change.* New York: Routledge, 1986.
7. Marris, 1986, p. 34.
8. Campbell, 1988, p. 22.
9. Campbell, 1988, p. 163.
10. Hamilton, E. *Mythology: Timeless Tales of Gods and Heroes.* New York: Mentor Books, 1942, p. 54.
11. Orlock, C. *The Goddess Letters: The Myth of Demeter and Persephone Retold.* New York: St. Martin's Press, 1987, p. 12.
12. Campbell, 1968, p. 51.
13. Hillman, J. *A Blue Fire.* New York: HarperPerennial, 1989, p. 107.
14. Campbell, 1968, p. 59.
15. Stein, M. *In Midlife: A Jungian Perspective.* Dallas, Tex.: Spring, 1983, p. 22.
16. Campbell, 1988, p. 156.

## Chapter Eleven

1. Rilke, R. M. *Letters to a Young Poet.* (M. D. Herter, trans.). New York: Norton, 1962, p. 69.
2. Moon, B. (ed.). *An Encyclopedia of Archetypal Symbolism.* Boston: Shambhala, 1991, pp. 171–173.
3. Josselson, R. *The Space Between Us: Exploring the Dimensions of Human Relationships.* San Francisco: Jossey-Bass, 1992, p. 29.
4. Higgins, G. O. *Resilient Adults: Overcoming a Cruel Past.* San Francisco: Jossey-Bass, 1994, p. 89.
5. Vaillant, 1993, p. 196.
6. Stack, C. *All Our Kin.* New York: HarperCollins, 1983, pp. 9, 90.

## Chapter Twelve

1. Quoted in W. Bridges, *Managing Transitions: Making the Most of Change.* Reading, Mass.: Addison-Wesley, 1991, p. 44.
2. Grimal, P. *The Dictionary of Classical Mythology.* New York: Blackwell, 1986, pp. 395–396.
3. Lifton, R. J. *The Protean Self: Human Resilience in an Age of Fragmentation.* New York: Basic Books, 1993, p. 10.
4. Levitt, T. "Marketing Myopia." *Harvard Business Review,* 1975, *53* (5), 26–48.
5. Lifton, 1993, p. 10.
6. Marris, 1986, p. 4.
7. Hall, D. *Careers in Organizations.* Glenview, Ill.: Scott, Foresman, 1976, p. 201.
8. Mirvis, P. H., and Hall, D. T. "Psychological Success and the Boundaryless Career." *Journal of Organizational Behavior,* 1994, *15,* 365–380.
9. Moore, T. *Care of the Soul: A Guide for Cultivating Depth and Sacredness in Everyday Life.* New York: HarperCollins, 1992, p. 191.

## Chapter Thirteen

1. Hamilton, 1942, p. 72.
2. Vaillant, 1993, p. 314.
3. Erdrich, L. "Spirit." *Self,* July 1994, p. 134.
4. Parks, S. "Imagination and Spirit in Faith Development: A Way Past the Structure-Content Dichotomy." In S. Parks and C. Dykstra (eds.), *Faith Development and Fowler.* Birmingham, Ala.: Religious Education Press, 1986, p. 149.
5. Parks, 1986, "Imagination and Spirit in Faith Development," p. xv.
6. Parks, S. "Faith Development and Imagination in the Context of Higher Education." Unpublished doctoral dissertation, Harvard University, 1980, p. 38.

7. Parks, 1986, "Imagination and Spirit in Faith Development," p. 22.
8. Camus, A. *The Stranger.* New York: Vintage Books, 1989, p. 3. (Originally published 1942.)
9. Anthony, 1987, pp. 5–6.
10. Parks, "Imagination and Spirit in Faith Development," 1986, pp. 137–156.
11. Parks, S. *The Critical Years: The Young Adult Search for a Faith to Live By.* San Francisco: Harper San Francisco, 1986, p. 18.
12. Parks, *The Critical Years,* 1986, p. 61.
13. Lynch, W. F. *Images of Hope: Imagination as Healer of the Hopeless.* Notre Dame, Ind.: University of Notre Dame Press, 1974, p. 37.
14. Lynch, 1974, p. 23.
15. Lynch, 1974, p. 27.
16. Grimal, 1986, pp. 422–423.

## Chapter Fourteen

1. Smith, H. *The Religions of Man.* New York: HarperCollins, 1958, p. 212.
2. Bateson, M. C. *Composing a Life.* New York: Penguin Books, 1990, p. 4.
3. Weick, 1993, p. 639.
4. Waldrop, M. M. *Complexity: The Emerging Science at the Edge of Order and Chaos.* New York: Simon & Schuster, 1992, p. 333.
5. Csikszentmihalyi, M. *Flow: The Psychology of Optimal Experience.* New York: HarperPerennial, 1990.
6. Langer, 1989, p. 11.

## Chapter Fifteen

1. Moore, M. *Complete Poems.* Old Tappan, N.J.: Macmillan, 1967, p. 95.
2. "Oregon Dairy Farmer Questions Future After Flood." National Public Radio, *All Things Considered,* Feb. 13, 1996.
3. Coontz, S. *The Way We Never Were: American Families and the Nostalgia Trap.* New York: Basic Books, 1992, p. 93.
4. Adler, J. "The Happiness Meter." *Newsweek,* July 29, 1996, p. 78.
5. Figure from Ouspensky, P. D. "Trapped on a Wheel." *Parabola: The Magazine of Myth and Tradition,* 1988, *XIII* (2), 62.
6. Gruber, H. E. "The Emergence of a Sense of Purpose: A Cognitive Study of Young Darwin." In M. Commons, F. Richards, and C. Armond (eds.), *Beyond Formal Operations: Late Adolescent and Adult Cognitive Development.* New York: Praeger, 1984, pp. 3–33.
7. Handy, C. *The Age of Unreason.* Boston: Harvard Business School Press, 1990, p. 31.
8. Handy, 1990, p. 184.

## Chapter Sixteen

1. Lynch, 1974, p. 232.
2. Jung, C. G. *The Collected Works of C. G. Jung: The Archetypes and the Collective Unconscious,* Bollingen Series, vol. 9i (R.F.C. Hull, trans.). Princeton, N.J.: Princeton University Press, 1934–1955, p. 513.
3. Wilber, K. "Taking Responsibility for Your Shadow." In C. Zweig and J. Abrams (eds.), *Meeting the Shadow.* Los Angeles: Tarcher, 1991, p. 276.
4. Vaillant, 1993, p. 36.
5. Vaillant, 1993, p. 228.
6. Hampden-Turner, C. *Maps of the Mind: Charts and Concepts of the Mind and Its Labyrinths.* Old Tappan, N.J.: Macmillan, 1981, p. 102.
7. Vaillant, 1993, p. 226.
8. Campbell, 1988, p. 152.
9. O'Neil, J. R. *The Paradox of Success: When Winning at Work Means Losing at Life.* New York: Putnam, 1993.
10. Salk, J. *The Survival of the Wisest.* New York: HarperCollins, 1973, p. 72.

## Chapter Seventeen

1. Quoted in P. L. Berman (ed.), *The Courage of Conviction.* New York: Ballantine, 1986, p. 102.
2. Figure adapted from D. A. Kolb, *Experiential Learning: Experience as the Source of Learning and Development.* Englewood Cliffs, N.J.: Prentice Hall, 1984, p. 21.
3. Figure adapted from Kolb, 1984, p. 4.
4. Galagan, P., and Wulf, K. "Signs of the Times." *Training & Development,* Feb. 1996, p. 34.
5. Mezirow, J. *Transformative Dimensions of Adult Learning.* San Francisco: Jossey-Bass, 1991.
6. Clayton, V. P., and Birren, J. E. "The Development of Wisdom across the Life Span: A Reexamination of an Ancient Topic." In P. B. Baltes and O. G. Brim (eds.), *Life-Span Development and Behavior,* Vol. 3. New York: Academic Press, 1980, pp. 103–135.
7. Sardello, 1995, p. 137.
8. Arrien, A. "The Four-Fold Way Training." Workshop presented at Chinook Learning Center, Whidbey Island, Wash., Mar. 2–3, 1991.
9. Bennis, W. G. "A Goal for the Eighties: Organizational Integrity." *New Jersey Bell Journal,* Winter 1981–1982, *4* (4), 1–8.
10. Kolb, 1984, p. 225.
11. Weick, 1993, p. 641.
12. McCall, M. W., Lombardo, M. M., and Morrison, A. M. *The Lessons of*

*Experience: How Successful Executives Develop on the Job.* San Francisco: New Lexington Press, 1988, p. 122.

## Chapter Eighteen

1. Sardello, R. *Facing the World with Soul: The Reimagination of Modern Life.* Hudson, N.Y.: Lindisfarne Press, 1992, p. 179.
2. Beckett, S. *Krapp's Last Tape and Other Dramatic Pieces.* New York: Grove Press, 1960, pp. 9–28.
3. Moody, H. "Late Life Learning in the Information Society." In D. Peterson, J. Thurnton, and J. Birren (eds.), *Education and Aging.* Englewood Cliffs, N.J.: Prentice Hall, 1986, p. 136.
4. Wagnild, G., and Young, H. M. "Resilience Among Older Women." *Image: Journal of Nursing Scholarship,* 1990, *22* (4), 252–255.
5. Hillman, J. *The Soul's Code: In Search of Character and Calling.* New York: Random House, 1996, pp. 44–46.
6. Shore, E. "Through a Dark Passage." *Parabola: Myth, Tradition, and the Search for Meaning,* 1996, *XXI* (2), 54.
7. Shore, 1996, p. 56.
8. Ellis, N. "Ba and Khu." *Parabola: Myth, Tradition, and the Search for Meaning,* 1996, *XXI* (2), p. 23.
9. T. Moore, 1992, pp. xiii–xiv.
10. "Newsmakers." *Seattle Times,* May 8, 1996, p. 2.
11. Pelletier, K. R. *Sound Mind, Sound Body: A New Model for Lifelong Health.* New York: Fireside, 1994, p. 109.
12. Pelletier, 1994, p. 27.
13. Pelletier, 1994, pp. 221–222.
14. Rader, D. "I Created My Own Life." *Parade Magazine,* Sep. 15, 1996, p. 4.
15. Ron Medved, personal communication, 1996.
16. Estés, 1992, p. 275.
17. Woodman, M. *Chaos or Creativity?* Pacific Grove, Calif.: Oral Tradition Archives, 1990.
18. Fox, M. *The Coming of the Cosmic Christ.* San Francisco: Harper San Francisco, 1988, p. 133.
19. King, M. L., Jr., *The Trumpet of Conscience.* New York: HarperCollins, 1967, pp. 69–70.

# Index